The Inaugural Addresses and Ascension Speeches of Nigerian Elected and Non-Elected Presidents and Prime Minister, 1960–2010

Edited with an Introduction by
Solomon Williams Obotetukudo

UNIVERSITY PRESS OF AMERICA, ® INC.
Lanham • Boulder • New York • Toronto • Plymouth, UK

Copyright © 2011 by
University Press of America,® Inc.
4501 Forbes Boulevard
Suite 200
Lanham, Maryland 20706
UPA Acquisitions Department (301) 459-3366

Estover Road
Plymouth PL6 7PY
United Kingdom

Library of Congress Control Number: 2010930636
ISBN: 978-0-7618-5274-2 (paperback : alk. paper)
eISBN: 978-0-7618-5275-9

I am dedicating this book to my entire family—the Obotetukudos and the Orukpes, but most particularly to my late parents, Chief William Akpanessien Obotetukudoessien and Madam Nkomarie William Akpanessien Oboetuku-doessien; and to my late parents-in-law, Mr. Emmanuel Orukpe and Mrs. Cecilia Orukpe, all of whom passed away during the years I was studying in the United States.

Symbols, developed and used to make common values richer by the diversity of approaches to them and to make differences compatible by common courses of action that solve common problems even when the problems are differently conceived, provide the one practicable alternative to the imposition by force of a single set of symbols in the form of a single set of institutions interpreted by a single philosophy.

—Richard McKeon
Symbols, Myths, and Arguments

. . . Any form of government other than democracy is evil because its motive forces are greed and utter disregard for the rights, welfare, and happiness of the people. Unless it is exceedingly benevolent (which is rare), or the masses of people concerned are primitive, ignorant, and disease-ridden, an oligarchical, autocratic, and tyrannical regime can only be sustained by fraud, intimidation, or violence. At the same time—and this is the incontrovertible verdict of history—it is more often than not changed by soul-less intrigue, satanic terror, or extreme violence . . . In its common form, oligarchy, autocracy, or tyranny in any State automatically generates its own antithesis which, through dialectic processes, produces change which may be evolutionary or revolutionary, bloodless or bloody. In contrast, however, since a democratic Government is installed by the free consent of the majority of the people, it is equally alterable by similar consent—sans intrigue, sans terror, sans violence.

—Obafemi Awolowo
The People's Republic

Our problem revolves around consciousness and epistemology—especially around relevant and functional epistemology. It is a damning evidence, for instance, that in all the constitutional conferences and bureaux we have set up to help us fashion a political system, no one has recognized the need to pursue the idea that there can be for Nigeria viable alternatives to the Anglo-Saxon version of democracy, and that one of those alternatives could come from Nigeria. Similarly no one has recognized that we can begin the process of domesticating that which we borrowed by *naming* it in our own local languages.

—Adiele E. Afigbo
Nigeria and the Myths of Modern Democracy

Contents

Appendixes: Coup Announcements 1966–1990

Illustrations

FIGURES

PHOTOGRAPHS

Foreword

Nigeria gained its independence from Britain in 1960. In the fifty years since independence it has been torn apart by ethnic, tribal, and religious strife, endured a civil war, experienced several coups d'etat, and produced fragile fledgling democratic governments. Rich in natural resources, and blessed with an important strategic location, the nation has struggled to produce a government capable of meeting the needs and aspirations of its citizens. As in many other developing nations, graft, corruption, and inefficiencies have diminished the effectiveness and undermined the stability of successive governmental administrations. Add to these problems the legacy of slavery and colonial exploitation and the pain and suffering of poverty. As recently as a decade ago the majority of the population lived on less than US $1.25 per day. Recently, however, the nation has experienced significant economic growth and has enjoyed political stability and the return to democratic rule. Today Nigeria boasts the second largest economy in Africa, and is one of the fastest growing economies in the world. Although Nigeria has long played an important role in Africa, however, scholars in the United States and Europe have paid greater attention to the constitutional and structural deficiencies in the young nation than they have to the attempts to move the nation forward. This book examines the discourse of nation building, focusing specifically on the rhetoric developed by Nigeria's leaders as they have sought to articulate the dreams, goals, and policy proposals that the nation should pursue to spark and sustain its development. This volume promises to become the most comprehensive and extensive compilation and examination of Nigerian national leadership political communication yet undertaken.

Solomon Obotetukudo, a native Nigerian who earned a doctorate in communication in the United States, has in this volume compiled all of the inaugural addresses presented during the fifty years of Nigerian independence.

Readers will discover in these unique rhetorical texts a nation that is struggling to be born as it seeks to overcome its differences and troubled history
and create a new national identity that will simultaneously develop and nurture the collective imagination of Nigerians.

The volume is especially interesting in that Obotetukudo is challenged
to identify and account for the unique differences between the inaugural
addresses given by leaders who achieve power through elections and the
speeches given by those who have achieved power via the barrel of a gun.
Clearly the rhetorical exigencies faced in these speeches share some of the
same characteristics but differ in important respects. Both must try to unify
the public in order to win public compliance if not active support for their
policy choices. Elected leaders, however, can appeal to the rituals and electoral processes that gave them power in order to legitimate their authority to
govern. Nonelected leaders, on the other hand, must justify their use of force
and argue for their legitimacy based upon a wholly different set of criteria.
Typically this kind of discourse emphasizes that the nation faced a state of
crisis that required immediate action by the force of will of a strong and decisive actor.

Inaugural speeches are especially important in the political life of a nation
because they shape the national culture and help to define the values that
come to guide political choice. Scholars interested in African history, and
especially in the history of Nigeria, will find these speeches and Obotetukudo's introductory discussions of the speakers and the historical moment in
which the speeches were delivered especially interesting. Scholars interested
in political communication or presidential rhetoric will wish to attend to these
speeches in a search for the insights that they will provide into the genre of
inaugural discourses as they cross cultures and political boundaries.

Communication scholars have long understood the important role that rhetorical discourse plays in the construction of a democratic political identity.
In the United States, for example, presidential inaugural addresses are understood to be important speeches that shape the public values and emotions of
citizens in their own time and that also contribute to public narratives that
are in a sense timeless. These addresses have become historical resources
that other speakers, citizens, political reporters, and scholars can turn to in
attempts to gain insights into the enduring and changing political values and
conditions that shape history. Certainly these addresses have played a similar role in Nigeria. During the past decade, Nigeria has enjoyed its longest
sustained period of democratic governance. Perhaps the lessons contained in
these speeches can provide insights that can guide thinking in other African
nations who are trying to establish their own paths to sustainable democratic
governments.

This volume should especially appeal to those who teach courses in political communication or public address, scholars engaged in the study of public address, and political candidates, consultants, and even elected officials.

Thomas A. Hollihan
Annenberg School for Communication
University of Southern California

Preface

I am a child of Nigerian independence, born on the eve of Nigeria's struggle for the attainment of self-rule from Great Britain. I remember as a child in primary school participating with other children in the Independence Day parade on October 1, 1960. It was a tradition then for students all around the country to attend the parades, lining the streets and walking the distance from our schools to the community parks to welcome the local, county, and regional representatives who were visiting to share the joys of independence. Today, looking back on October 1, 1960, I also remember that we were given the flag of Nigeria and plastic cups with the inscription "Unity and Faith" proudly embossed on each.

Fifty years have passed since that day and time. It is nostalgic to think of the time and age of innocence, when a young mind dreamed of possibilities and hoped they would come true. But the memory of the celebration, and the excitement and the jubilation of the day, come back to me as I study, live, work, and reflect on Nigeria and the other democracies where I have lived and actively voted as a citizen. I notice the differences in interpretations and practices of *democracy*—the word and the system.

When I did my doctoral work on presidential communication, I saw and felt the connections even more. My love of language and interest in history and politics converged. These studies and my professors rekindled the enthusiasm for politics, history, philosophy of language, and rhetorical studies. However, when Nigeria underwent an economic crisis in the 1990s just as I was entering the professional world, I bowed to new realities. Nevertheless, the flame burned inside me. My academic research, publications, and professional consultancies have pivoted around campaigns communications, political communications, speech writing, and leadership communications in general. Now as a professor, I teach speech communication and related subjects.

Nations, like people, evolve and mature. At fifty years of age, Nigeria as a nation has indeed evolved and is still maturing. Yet nations, like individuals, face challenges that detract, distract, and sometimes stall their growth. This book is a personal reminder of the dream that started for me on October 1, 1960 to celebrate the freedom to do, to become, and to march with the beats of independence. That dream is now a page in Nigeria's history. And as I reflect on that dream, I hope that the pages of Nigeria's history will reveal a path toward a stronger, more mature, more united, and more prosperous nation, reminiscent of its old motto: «Unity and Faith, Strength and Progress.»

This work is the first known attempt to put in one volume all the elected leaders' inaugural addresses, and the military dictators' speeches of ascension to power in Nigeria since it attained self-rule. This edited volume is most appropriate as it coincides with Nigeria's fiftieth anniversary of independence. From this vantage point, this collection of public addresses and speeches to the Nigerian people presents a collage of rhetorical artifacts that have helped to shape Nigerian history and its public philosophy over the first fifty years of independence from colonial rule. This is also a book on the political and public discourses on Nigeria. It is my hope that these addresses and speeches will demonstrate to lay readers and observers how Nigerian political leaders speak about Nigeria as a nation and Nigerians. I hope it will show the reader how Nigerians initiate and engage one another in conversations about public affairs.

I have divided this book into fourteen chapters, each corresponding to the elected and military speaker on the Nigerian political scene at the time. At the end of the introduction, I have references for those who would like to reexamine in detail the earlier situations that led to the creation and development of Nigeria. A portrait of the speaker and short biographical notes precede each full text of speeches and addresses.

This collection includes two major speeches by President Obasanjo to a joint session of the National Assembly because these two speeches added context, relevance and vitality to the historical significance of the moments in Nigeria's democratic experiments.

I also have added military coup announcements in the appendix to this book, for these speeches serve as historical and political footnotes to the growing pains and trials of postindependence Nigeria.

These speeches also invite the reader into the life and times of Nigeria's military and elected leaders over the past fifty years—their minds, thoughts, and aspirations, as articulated in their first public pronouncements. Their words may help to reveal and uncover reasons or assumptions about why Nigeria after fifty years as an independent country is still seeking a sense of nationhood.

Also, their words may help readers find support for and against the emergence of truly Nigerian democratic experiences. I hope that reading these speeches will increase opportunities and give readers the confidence to ask the right questions about why democracy does not speak the same language across national boundaries, dialects, peoples, cultures, languages, and societies.

Solomon W. Obotetukudo
Clarion, Pennsylvania
January, 2010

Acknowledgments

This book is a by-product of my dissertation under the direction of Professor Walter R. Fisher of the Annenberg School for Communications and Journalism at the University of Southern California, Los Angeles. Walt Fisher's patience, acumen, and intellectual support planted the seeds of this project and kept the thought brewing in me all these years. I greatly benefited from the encouragement of Professors Everett M. Rogers, Margaret (Peggy) L. McLaughlin, and Thomas A. Hollihan, all of whom shared their intellectual, personal, and emotional resources at critical moments during my graduate studies at the University of Southern California, Los Angeles. In particular, I owe this career and these research interests to Walt Fisher who pointed me to presidential rhetoric, political leadership communication, public address, and rhetorical studies; and to Dr. Everett Rogers who enthusiastically linked my interests to international communications and development.

Over the years, new colleagues too many to list here have added fresh insights to my vocations in communications consulting, speech writing, and as communications professor at California State University, Dominguez Hills-Carson, California; The College of Wooster, Ohio; and Clarion University of Pennsylvania, Clarion, Pennsylvania. As a keen observer of the political landscapes in the United States, on the African continent, and of Nigeria specifically, I have gained wider perspectives and deeper thoughts on the directions and functions of political language, presidential leadership communication, and the role of language, signs, symbols, and codes in democratic governance in advanced and emerging democracies. My students in all of the courses I have taught over the years deserve a special gratitude for allowing me to enter into their thinking spaces to share and challenge them as they critically reexamine the role of language, signs, and symbols in their worlds. Of particular relevance here is the course, Language and

Symbols in Human Communication, that I designed and taught at Clarion University. The students whom I have had the opportunity to reach in this course have given me new ways to meaning making in the age of new telecommunication technologies. I have them to thank for the opportunities to share our experiences through human symbolic action given the varied and interdisciplinary nature and functions of language, signs, and symbols. And finally, I extend my gratitude to my professional colleagues at Clarion University of Pennsylvania, especially Dr. Myrna Kuehn and Dr. Brenda Dede, for their unwavering support that has sustained my research and scholarship over the years.

Through casual and heated conversations on Nigerian and African politics, other friends have added spice and new critical turns to my thinking. They have convinced me that although individuals write books, it is through engagement with readers in and through the writing process, that makes for the extraordinary intellectual symbiosis necessary to creating a community of thinkers, scholars, and writers. My appreciation goes to all those who have, in one way or another, shaped my ideas and thinking in this project.

I also want to extend my heartfelt appreciation to the officers and staff at the Permanent Mission of Nigeria to the United Nations in New York, Mr. Kio S. Amieyeofori, Mr. Joseph Menyaga, and Mrs. Joy Gold; the staff and administrative officers and consular personnel at the Embassy of Nigeria in Washington , D.C., and those at the Ministry of Information, Communication and Culture in Abuja and Lagos, who over the years have rendered tremendous assistance toward this project.

I am indebted to the librarians at Clarion University's Carlson Library: Ms. Kathy Bell in circulation, Ms. Ginger Griffin in Illiad, and Ms. Judy Bowser, of interlibrary loan and circulations. Also, my deepest appreciation goes to the librarians at the Rebecca M. Arthurs Memorial Library in Brookville, Pennsylvania, Director Rosalee Pituch and Library Assistant Patricia Conway. And finally, my copy editor, Ms. Patty Zion, and my editors at the University Press of America for shepherding this work through to publication: Ms. Brooke Basccieto, Associate Acquisitions Editor, and Mr. Brian DeRocco, Manager of Editorial Administration.

My family deserves a special space and the highest praise, especially my wife, Agnes Williams, for always being there; and my children who do not always see their dad, as they would love to do. And my elder brother, Pastor Akpan Williams Akpanessien and his family deserve a page to themselves in the journey of all that I have become.

The photograph of Shehu Shagari is used with permission of Heinemann Educational Books, Ltd. (now HEBN Publishers, Plc.).

Abbreviations

ADC	Aide-de-Camp
AFRC	Armed Forces Ruling Council
CMS	Church Missionary Society
ECOMOG	ECOWAS Monitoring Group (Peacekeeping Force)
ECOWAS	Economic Community of West African States
ESIALA	Eastern States Interim Assets and Liabilities Agency
GOC	General Officer Commanding
ICSA	Interim Common Services Agency
IITA	International Institute of Tropical Agriculture
IMF	International Monetary Fund
INEC	Independent National Electoral Commission
ING	Interim National Government
NCNC	National Council of Nigeria and the Cameroons
NEPA	National Electric Power Authority
NEPAD	New Economic Partnership for African Development
NET	Nigerian External Telecommunications
NLC	Nigerian Labour Congress
NITEL	Nigerian Telecommunications Limited
NNPC	Nigerian National Petroleum Corporation
NPC	Northern Peoples Congress
NN	Nigerian Navy
OAU	Organization of African Unity
OPEC	Organization of Petroleum Exporting Countries
PRC	Provisional Ruling Council
SMC	Supreme Military Council

UAC	United African Company
UN	United Nations
UNESCO	United Nations Educational Scientific and Cultural Organization
WHO	World Health Organization

Introduction

Nigeria as a country was born on January 1, 1914 with the amalgamation of the Northern and Southern Protectorates by the British Colonial Government.[1] The unity brought together disparate ethnic, linguistic, religious, and cultural groupings, for the administrative convenience of colonial Britain. This tenuous glue held the unit together as separate entities in spite of the unification, until independence from Great Britain on October 1, 1960. Between 1914 and 1960, several developments had occurred that necessitated the final withdrawal of Britain from direct administration of Nigeria.

Foremost among the forces that accelerated the exit of Britain from colonial Nigeria was the start and ending of the Second World War, 1939–1945. In many ways, the colonial Nigeria assisted the war effort of Britain by the aggressive production of palm oil, cotton, rubber, cocoa, and other essential raw materials Britain needed to sustain its economy and preserve its entrance into the war. By the war's end, most of these products were no longer in high demand as there were alternatives following the boom in industrialization and the inventions and discoveries of new modes of production. Secondly, the British Colonial Office thought it expedient at the end of the Second World War to initiate a gradual withdrawal from its former colonies, as a strategic initiative to accommodate outcries at home by anticolonialists who now saw colonies as imperialistic. Thirdly, colonies were no longer as profitable and prestigious in the wake of industrial breakthrough with the invention of better products to replace many of the raw materials previously obtained from the colonies. Fourthly, the most crucial factor in the colonial disengagement was that at the end of the Second World War, 1939–1945, in which many Nigerians were conscripted to fight on the side of Britain as British subjects in North and East Africa, these Nigerians came to witness, feel, and understand firsthand the inequities, discriminations, and injustices

1

of colonialism. Lastly, cries for independence from Britain and from all other colonial powers in Africa gathered momentum from there on.[2]

These Nigerians who had direct contacts with the Europeans on their return, and some who remained in Europe and elsewhere, formed political parties at home and abroad.[3] Other Nigerians were encouraged by the repatriated ex-slaves, who were now resident in Lagos and neighboring West African territories of Ghana, Liberia, and Sierra Leone.[4] West Indian nationalists were readily available to render spiritual and emotional, as well as intellectual support to Nigerians, nay, West African early nationalists.[5] Many student and labor movement groups and cultural associations began to form, to confront the issues of colonialism in Africa, and especially in the West African subregion.[6]

These groups were the precursors to the political parties that energized the independence movement in Nigeria. Several parties come to mind. Most prominent were, the Action Group led by Chief Obafemi Awolowo;[7] the National Council of Nigerian Citizens and Cameroons, cofounded by Herbert Macaulay and Dr. Nnamdi Azikiwe, who later became its leader;[8] and the Northern People's Congress of Sir Sardauna of Sokoto.[9] When independence arrived, it was the Northern People's Congress, in alliance with the Nigerian Council of Nigerian Citizens and Cameroon, that formed the first independence government for and by Nigerians. Alhaji Tafawa Balewa, a Northern Nigerian of Fulani ethnic extraction, was the prime minister under the British-styled parliamentary system of democratic governance. Dr. Nnamdi Azikiwe, an Eastern Nigerian of the Igbo ethnic group, emerged as the first and only parliamentary-styled (ceremonial) president of Nigeria.

Thus, Nigerians' first taste of democracy was a national government of compromises and functional coalitions of many and diverse peoples, policies, ethnicities, religions, and regions. These peoples hardly knew or even heard of each other. The time was too short to get to know each other between 1914 British amalgamation of the Northern and Southern peoples and the 1960 independence. The Constitutional and Legislative Council conferences between these periods were orchestrated, convened, and micromanaged by the Colonial Office in London. The few hand-picked Nigerians who represented some portions or sections of the country were unknown by the ordinary citizen whom they purported to represent.[10]

Thus, the birth of a Nigerian democratic experiment necessarily implanted certain inescapable exigencies that later constituted the guiding metaphors for leadership communication[11] and political rhetoric[12] in Nigeria's errand into nation building. The communication of Nigerian national identity and history by these early Nigerian leaders became wrapped around the communicative imperatives of creating a plural society, constituted by diverse ethnicities,

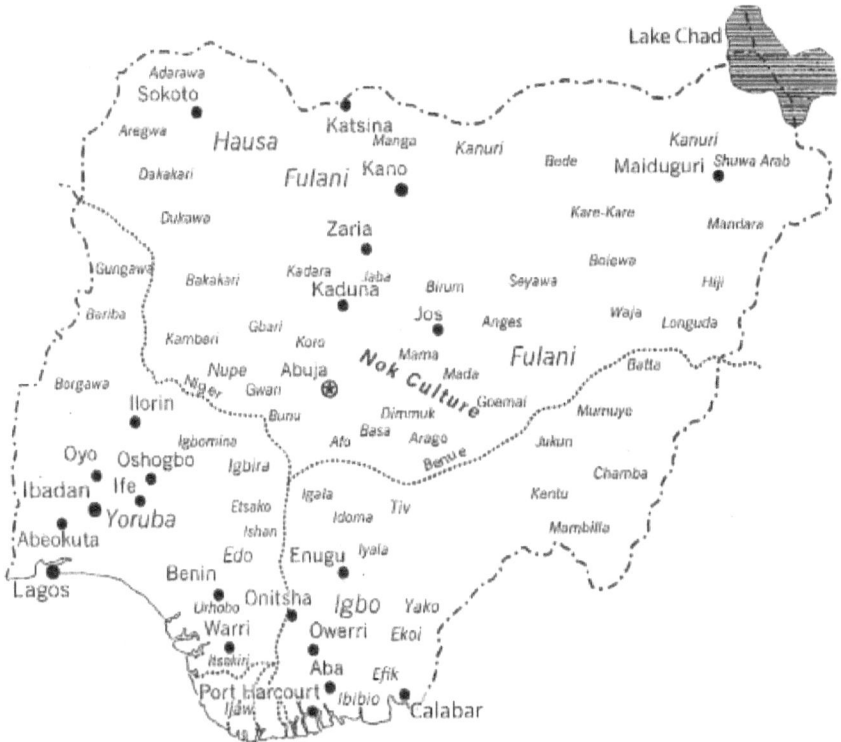

Figure I.1.   The ethnic composition of Nigeria. Source: Created by the author.

languages, cultures, customs, religions, disproportionate education standards, traditionalism, communalism, conservativism, feudalism, monarchism—all of these made worse by different perceptions of colonial experiences by these native political elites.[13] These defects at Nigeria's creation constituted the political markers, and later would dictate the rhetorical outlines for negotiating Nigerian governance and nation building.

These imperfections have haunted or sometimes goaded, and I may even add, hamstrung the emergent Nigerian political elites since independence. There can be no better starting point to examine as well as document the evolution of the Nigerian state, than from the words, signs, and symbols of governance by these native leaders before, during, and after independence from Great Britain. The impetus to demand self-rule, and the language they created and used as they sought to create, nurture, sustain, and transition from anti-colonialism combative rhetoric,[14] to the communication of and for a plural democracy and nation-statism, through national integration and effective political governance, is vital in the emergence, understanding,

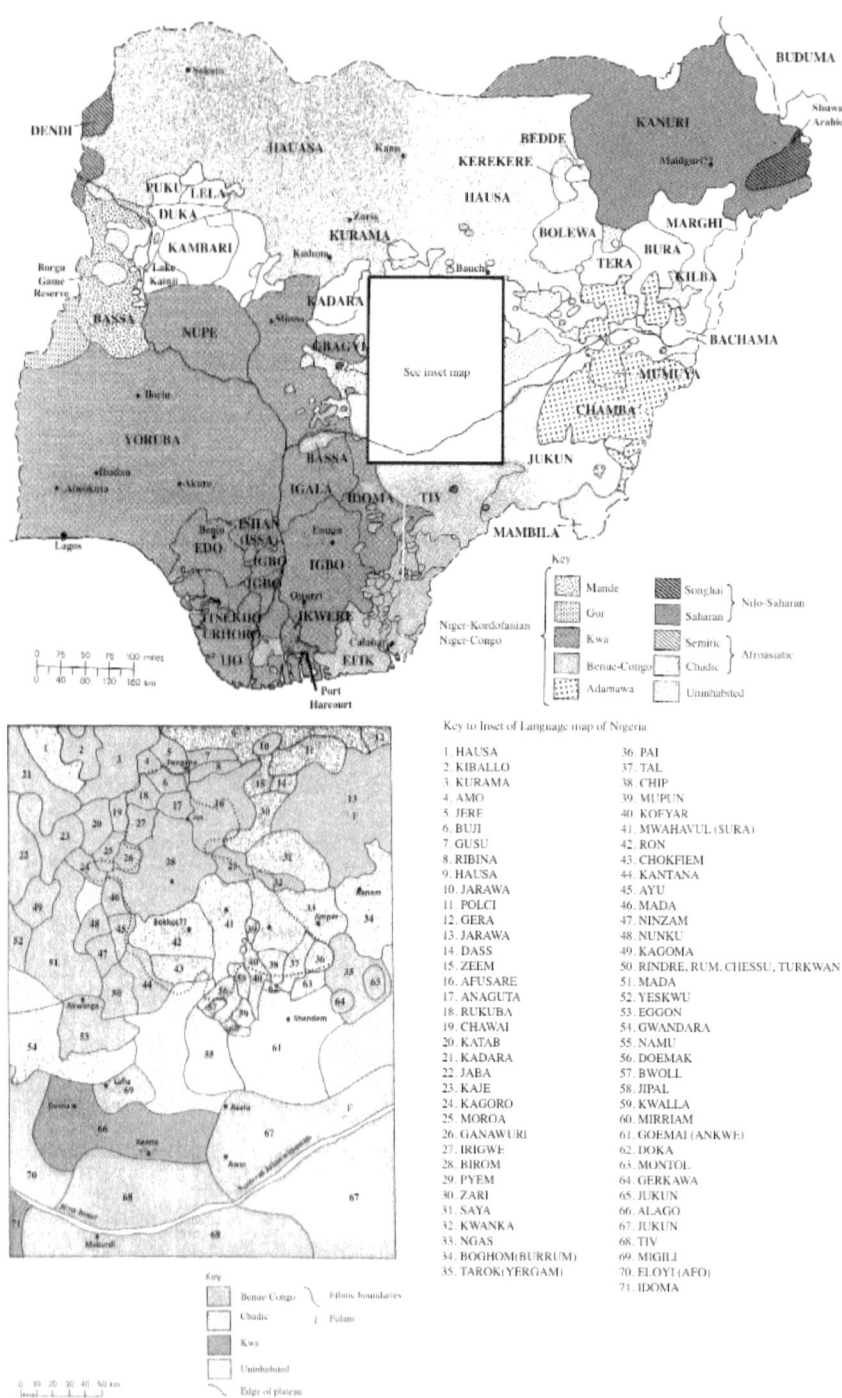

Figure I.2.   The Linguistic Makeup of Nigeria. Source: Elizabeth Isichei—*A History of Nigeria*, p. xvi–xix.

articulation and investigation of political leadership communication of Nigeria.

The maiden speeches of political ascension by the nonelected, and political inauguration of the elected Nigerian leaders, subsequently, present a repertoire of a people's desires, dreams, fears, victories, and failures. Even speeches of social and cultural rulers inadvertently align with those of political leaders to constitute the nation. Speechmaking is, consequently, not only instrumental and terminal, but also indispensable in the life of any nation.[15] The leader uses speeches to connect with the people, announce policies, cultivate desired values, explicate national philosophies, and endear the leadership to the citizenry. Above all, it is through speech that leaders galvanize the support of the people in times of national crises.

This project is only concerned with political speeches of ascension and inauguration addresses. In this exercise, the first public speeches by elected leaders are called inaugural addresses, while those given by the military dictators are called ascension speeches. I have endeavored to make this conceptual distinction because of the contextual constraints and orientation, as well as philosophical differences between military and civilian governments and their leaders, which many times compel specific or certain kinds of communicative responses due to particular exigencies in Nigeria.[16]

NATURE OF INAUGURAL AND ASCENSION SPEECHES

The maiden speeches of Nigeria's military rulers are included in this anthology because such constitute the first public pronouncements of the ascending ruler. I have dubbed these speeches ascendancy speeches, to distinguish them from those speeches given by elected leaders. Military rulers rise to power by fiat. Ascendancy denotes a putsch—a forced elevation or forced entrance. By their own admission in many of their maiden speeches, the military rulers come into the corridors of politics as corrective regimes. Thus, most military governments are perceived, and want to be tolerated as an aberration; a temporary surgical type government, that would retire to their assigned roles in the barracks as the protectors of the territorial integrity and sovereignty of the nation-state. Moreover, because these forced entrances start new governmental administrations, they constitute new beginnings. Such speeches by these newly ascended military rulers become parts of the communication of the beginning of a new administration, howbeit nonelected.

Military dictatorial speech is hortatorical. That is, it is prescriptive, proscriptive, and full of warnings, and is sometimes apocalyptic. This speech style intentionally communicates urgency of the situation that needs attention and is, therefore, action ridden, and more likely to cry fire in the crowded theatre. A dictator's ascension speech usually seeks immediate outcome or reaction from the listeners, and is oftentimes highly dramatic. To a despot, language is a vocal missile aimed at the weak and decadent citizens who must be set straight and on the right path as determined by the speaker.[17]

A civilian political address, on the other hand, has the nuance of a conversation, in contradistinction to the hortatory style of a military dictator's speech. Democratic speeches are inherently deliberative, laudatory, conciliatory, consultative, co-orientational, and demonstrative. By its very representativeness, the language and the communication style of democratic governance and its elected leadership is sensitive, cautious, reflective, compromising, consensual, engaging, and thus deliberative in word choices toward policy options. The speakers in this tradition tend to praise more than blame; they are sensitive to the emotions of the audiences, and thus are more ritualistic in tone, diction, and delivery.[18]

While my distinction here may not be watertight, it however remains a fact that all leadership styles rely on language, signs and symbols to gain and maintain power. Moreover, following in the Aristotelian classification of rhetoric in ancient Greece into three distinct categories of deliberative (persuasion), forensic (judicial, law-making/legislative), and epideictic (ceremonial),[19] ascension speeches in my judgment, and inaugural addresses, would come under the epideictic genre.

Communication, language, and rhetorical scholars regard speeches that praise and blame; that celebrate or denigrate the moment, place, person, and thing or object; and those that affirm and reaffirm long-held traditions and values of any given community as constitutive of the epideictic genre of discourse.[20] These are speeches given in special moments that call forth such deliveries. Similarly, the beginning of any new administration, whether elected or nonelected, presents one such pivotal moment for a speech of investiture and reconstitution of the people and their values, as well as the ideals and aspirations of the nation.

From the words of both the Nigerian elected and nonelected leaders, it has become clearer that all leaders of all forms of government—totalitarianism, authoritarianism, communism, socialism, monarchism, dictatorship, and democracy—rely on language, signs, and symbols of ingratiation, legitimation, identification, stability and continuity, development or progress, unification, patriotism, nationalism, internationalism, law and order, deference, and transcendence, among many other themes, at inauguration and ascension occasions, and much more so during governance.[21] The communication strategies created and utilized, and sometimes abused, by these leaders remain crucial to leadership emergence, institutionalization, and legitimacy.

FUNCTIONS OF INAUGURAL AND ASCENSION SPEECHES

Inaugural and ascension speeches chronicle the courses of a nation's history. The speeches celebrate the dreams and fears, triumphs and tragedies, facts and fantasies, and the points of convergences and divergences in a nation. Some of the speeches have challenged, while others rebuked. Still, many inspired, while others instructed the citizens to reflect on the contours of the nation's history. These speeches call forth a profound sense of responsibility to and from the people and the nation.

Furthermore, these speeches evoke a high apprehension of the spirit that attends any leader who respects and accepts the imposition of the will of the people on such an individual, and the office. Obedience to the peoples' call to lead demands a cautious, faithful, and diligent service in the discharge of national duties, to the best of one's ability. That obedience imposes a heavy responsibility on the self and to the nation-state during each inauguration and ascension. It is therefore not an exaggeration that most inaugural addresses call forth enduring and time-honored values of humility, service, devotion, commitment, pride in the self and the collective, deference to tradition, reflectivity, anticipation, hope, faith, and courage in both the speaker and the audience. From the readings of the ascension speeches compiled here, it would seem that there is not much difference from the inaugurals, other than that the military speakers tend to indemnify honor, integrity, stability, law and order as their God-terms. In both types of deliveries, one sees the history of the nation and its peoples recounted and rehearsed in the words of these leaders.

According to Obotetukudo in his 1992 study, "Inaugural and ascension addresses must not only be seen and understood as announcing the beginning of a new administration; they must be accepted as special moments in the life of a nation when the leaders invite audiences to participate in affirming their values as a community and as a nation." Obotetukudo argues for the expansion of this epideictic genre of speechmaking to serve more than mere commemorative functions. He asserts, "The addresses must be seen heuristically to incorporate the past and the future; praise the institution of the leadership and those values and forms or structures of the government that are already in place. The leaders need to go beyond a mere rehearsal of traditional values, to enunciate the public philosophy and political philosophy that will inform the incoming administration."[22] Therefore, inaugurals, and ascension speeches straddle the genres delineated by Aristotle; they may persuade, celebrate, praise, blame, as well as inform—but never legislate. These speeches serve to convene the people, and thus remind them of their roles, and responsibilities as citizens.

Generally, inaugural and ascension speeches function to reconstitute an audience, remind the citizens of shared communal values, point to the governing political principles that would guide the incoming administration, demonstrate the limitations of leadership roles and functions, urge a collective imagination of the possibilities and realities, (inauguration) and action (ascension), praise the institution of the presidency (inaugural) and blame the deposed regime (ascension), and finally, strive to establish a permanent covenant between the ruler-leader-speaker and the people. Therefore, any student of presidential and political leadership communication would find inaugural and ascension speeches as ready resources for constructive and insightful analyses as well as comparative studies across epochs, personalities, leadership types, and ideologies. These speeches give clues to the political philosophies of the incoming administration. For the elected leaders, remarkable promises made during the campaigns are restated, howbeit with nonbinding specificities. For the military speakers, the ascension is a moment of performatory rhetoric,[23] where action words replace oath taking with its binding rituals and sacredness.[24]

For the Nigerian prime minister, Alhaji Tafawa Balewa, the inaugural speech on Nigeria's Independence Day was both momentous and historic. It was a moment for writing and rewriting the history of Africa's most populous country. Besides, his inauguration symbolized the emancipation of the African from colonial tutelage and domination. Given the fact that the content of every inaugural and ascension speech traditionally and rhetorically mirrors the contexts of delivery, these speeches, like all other speeches, serve as strategic responses to situations that needed such responses. Thus, the meanings in inaugural and ascension speeches would only be meaningful if the audience is able to relate the content of the speeches to the Nigerian situations at each turn on the road to nation building, and particularly, at the specific moments that the speeches were delivered. And inaugurals and ascensions are such pivotal and memorable moments in the life of any nation.

The president, Dr. Nnamdi Azikiwe, gave his presidential inaugural address on November 16, 1960. Nnamdi Azikiwe assumed the post of the former British governor-general on Independence Day, and technically, he became the ceremonial president under the parliamentary system of government. The meaning he sought to create was a function of both the time and the space he was assigned in the Nigerian political scene, as the ceremonial parliamentary president. His speech was conditioned by the ideology of the moment. That ideology was codified in sets of beliefs and values the president held, being an erudite American-trained libertarian.[25] He set out to create his own social and political realities as foundational to the Nigeria he wished to see after the departure of British colonialists. Furthermore, in Azikiwe's speech one notices a contest and competition for the creation and control of meaning, by the Nigerian political and cultural elites, a meaning that towers over that of the British rule. But this manifest and latent contest between these newly minted Nigerian elites, symbolized in the prime minister's and the president's inaugural speeches, confirmed the inherent conflict and contradictions over the dethronement of one cultural code—which was British, foreign, and colonial—to be replaced by one that was indigenous, nativizing, and African. Both Balewa and Azikiwe created and used their inaugural speeches to establish identification and separation simultaneously,[26] with complex Nigerian political and cultural scenes, as well as with the departing British colonialists, to whom they still owed allegiance until the attainment of the republic status on October 1, 1963.[27]

As rituals for identification, transition, initiation, investiture, and affirmation, inaugural addresses and ascension speeches present the nation with a shining moment for the leader or the speaker to bond with the audience, using those commonly shared verbal and nonverbal communication acts. Maiden speeches of political and nonpolitical leaders guide the audience into the minds of the speakers, their motivations, their perceptions of the Nigerian reality, and their projections onto that reality.[28] Thus, the act of Investing one with the responsibility of the head of state, prime minister, and/or president evokes new knowledge from both the leaders and the followers. That knowledge, collaboratively created in the case of elected leaders, for example, mandates reciprocity in understanding the audience and their speakers. When these leaders speak, their words are expected to echo the voices of the peoples constitutive of the nation and the community they represent.

As political communication, inaugural and ascension speechmaking seck to fulfill the unique functions of persuading or winning assent, legitimizing authority, constituting and reconstituting a people, and institutionalizing a new era, while simultaneously providing a retrospective policy assessment of the passing era, and at the same time projecting into the future of the country. It is consequently very important to note the epochal linking, legitimizing and persuasive functions of the maiden speeches contained in this volume. For example, Tafawa Balewa and Nnamdi Azikiwe, the Nigerian prime minister and the president respectively, on the eve of Britain's colonial and direct political disengagement from Nigeria, could not avoid establishing and maintaining the historical and political links to the departing colonialists. Nevertheless, as nationalists, they needed independence from that colonial past, to begin to cultivate a sense of dignity, self-worth, and freedom to do for themselves as they desired. Implied here is the freedom and the independence of thought and actions, both prerequisites and foundational to the evolution and maturation of the newly independent country. Thus, these early speeches were paradoxical.

These earlier first speeches by Nigeria's political leaders present as well as represent the paradox of the Nigerian political, social, cultural, and psycho-emotional independence. While these early leaders persuaded their new citizens to accept their newly won authorities as legitimate Nigerian leaders, the speakers also felt constrained by the hovering presence of the British imperial power. In short, as much as independence portends freedom to do and become as one desires and chooses, the Nigerian independence was fundamentally a converse of this idealism: it tied Nigeria and Nigerians to its former colonial masters at the hip and in perpetuity, as events in later years affirmed. In fact, that a military coup overthrew the civilian government to which the colonialists handed over power was a stark reality to the unfinished business of national self-discovery and self-assessment. From the language and symbols in that first coup announcement, one discerns the contradictions, paradoxes, and conflicts embedded in Nigeria's independence from the beginning. See Appendix A.

Nevertheless, in the immediate postcolonial rhetoric of inauguration, these newly installed Nigerian political elites had to rhetorically capture, create, and nurture the new realities of an independent nation. Their first public utterances provide the starting point with which to note and record the points of convergences and divergences in the rhetoric of new identities and political leadership. The speeches contained in this volume consequently provide the readers with a profile of values in the Nigerian society, as evident in the repetition of similar issues across inaugurals and ascensions from independence in 1960 through the fourth attempt at democratically elected governance in 2007.

The speeches compiled here serve or could be viewed as contracts entered into between senders and receivers. As a result, they constitute invaluable rhetorical artifacts providing both the rhetorical turning points as well as rhetorical markers for future policy makers and analysts. As contracts, they are mutually binding. As markers, they are socially, politically, and culturally differentiating, yet unifying. That is, these leaders, in spite of being Nigerians, confronted governing realities in an autonomous nation with a cultural, linguistic, and religious heterogeneity that make governance by the natives after political independence almost impossible. But their continuous emphasis on unity, continuity, progress, development, law and order, and freedom, among other democratic ideals, was a testimony to a commitment to belong and remain constituted as plural communities of democrats.

SPEECHMAKING IN THE MAKING OF NIGERIA

To their credit the early Nigerian leaders did not resort to force in order to settle competing claims to legitimacy and authority. Instead, they invented symbols of compromise and tolerance, to acquire, retain, and distribute both the natural and non-natural resources in the Nigerian political estate, even though they felt incapacitated from the beginning. That said, the contracts between the ruled and the rulers, negotiated and entered as gleaned from the speeches here, have oftentimes been broken, reneged upon, and sometimes discountenanced outright, by the leaders and rulers in the past fifty-year period of self-rule. A good read through these pages would alert a curious mind to those instances of betrayals and failed promises in words and deeds. But above all, the exercise in engaging the words of these leaders would demonstrate the indispensable role language and symbols play in crafting, negotiating, communicating and maintaining the social and cultural as well as political contracts needed for democratic governance in a plural society like Nigeria.

The extent that these pioneering Nigerian leaders and their successors rely on language, speech, signs, and symbols of legitimacy and authority to assist them in shaping and reshaping the history and political culture of a plural Nigeria is indisputable. Nevertheless, this so far has been insufficient to mesh and meld the peoples together toward a national purpose, because a contract between peoples and entities on levels of status disequilibrium poses problems of enforcement. In Nigeria, no single community regards, or wants to accept itself as a subordinate unit to any other. The reasoning is that all the constitutive peoples of Nigeria were brought together on the same day on the same understanding, to constitute the Nigerian state. But the colonialist machinations and manipulations made for expressed disproportionate power relations between the three regions (see Figure I.1) at inception, thereby privileging one section of the country over the others, and implanting ethnic suspicion and resentment between and within the diverse ethnic groupings in each of these regions (see Figures I.1 and I.2). Indeed, the departing British officials sanctioned these imperfections and inequities in the various constitutions they drafted and handed over to Nigerian elites.[29]

Grounded and goaded by the governing document of the departing colonial power, alongside the constitutive authorities of the native rulers, these early Nigerian political leaders remained politically, structurally, administratively, as well as constitutionally overwhelmed. The speeches contained here lay bare the tensions between words and deeds, good intentions, good governance, good people who mean well; between good policies and poor performances; and how these leaders have remained constrained by the exigencies in the context of doing, being, and becoming what they always wanted. The words and symbols contained in this compendium would help curious observers of the Nigerian political and rhetorical situation to understand the politics and rhetoric of social contract that has become a quest for consensus and compromise; tolerance and mutual respect; trust and sensibilities in this gradually evolving plural Nigerian democracy.

In view of the tensions and contradictions inherent in plural Nigerian democratic experiments, speechmaking becomes increasingly indispensable. Persons deprived of the ability to speak, either by law or through physical-biological ailments, have heightened appreciation for the near-magical power of speech. Take the example of a stutterer, who struggles desperately to utter a word during a conversation many of us take for granted. The cancer patient whose larynx has been removed understands the difficulties of expressing his/her thoughts. In some ancient cultures, humans were punished by the removal of their tongues so that they could not be critical with words, of the misdeeds of the ruling authorities. It is through speaking that articulate and able-bodied men and women initiate, interact, engage, relate, and make sense of their worlds, negotiate contracts and other business, personal, and private deals, and consequently learn to live, work, and love together.

Democratic governance is impossible without talk. And in a society of multiple languages with competing and oftentimes conflicting interests and aspirations, the ability to speak with, and to, each other becomes a scarce resource to be sought after and acquired. Speaking reveals as well as closes those worlds near and far from the audiences because language has the capacity to express or not express ideas and opinions. From the speeches by Nigerian rulers and leaders collected here, it would become increasingly evident that it is not the volume of speech and the lexical dexterity of the speaker that make for the sharing of meanings and experiences. Instead, it is the experiences speakers share with their audience members that make for what Kenneth Burke calls *consubstantiality*.[30] The Nigerian democratic experiments will benefit the citizenry when they realize the power of sharing meanings, and relating with one another, with the expressed intent to get to know and understand one another as valuing and substantive individuals and peoples.

As much as talk is essential for political governance, language and speech in general have their limitations in exciting the imaginations and expectations of a unified nationhood. However, it is in their symbolic essences that humans relate, transact, and sustain, even though language and speech cannot always render the true and complete account of human experiences. Simply put, meanings cannot always be shared as much as humans try, because all those who speak do not always share or communicate experiences.

From the collection of speeches here, the reader would come to understand that governance in a plural democratic society is dependent on language, signs, and symbols of both the rulers and the ruled; and that democratic meanings must be negotiated and consummated through symbolic action. Inaugural addresses and ascension speeches present moments to create and bring together a national audience to try to share a common national experience and rituals of communion and commonality. From antiquity, commonly shared experiences often move humans, whether through threats, words of powerful exhortations, or through emotional excitements by populist orators.[31] And in fact, humans have sometimes been readily aroused to evil deeds by ideologues who manipulated all sorts of signs, symbols, and words to advance selfish causes.[32]

Nigerian political speaking in the twentieth century, however, has not experienced excesses or tyranny of words in action reminiscent of the hate and vitriol of the ethnic cleansing type that Eastern Europe and parts of Africa witnessed in recent memory. However, the new Nigerian nation of the twenty-first century desperately needs its speakers to be humans who care to share Nigerian experiences among themselves. Nigerian experiences are scarce. The inaugural addresses and ascension speeches have so far presented such experiences where most Nigerians have similar topics to talk about, thereby generating similar Nigerian communicative interactions as desirable for the Nigerian collective experiences.

Many Nigerians habitually greet every military coup with euphoria and nostalgia,[33] while others tend to be lukewarm toward civilian governments.[34] For example, the inaugural speeches of the prime minister and the president were historical, social, and cultural, as well as political events with which to define, frame, and share the winning mythology of the Nigerian state in the 1960s. As one would expect, the victor was Nigeria, whose independence the speeches were celebrating. Nigerians were overjoyed that finally they had the freedom to run their own affairs. Earlier on, I mentioned that inaugural speaking moments are not merely ceremonial events, but also are deliberative, ceremonial, and informational communicative moments. As significant as each occasion of inaugural and ascension moment is, it presents the Nigerian leaders the opportunity and space to define the path upon which the ship of the nation-state would travel starting in the succeeding years after 1960. In fact, the words from these 1960s inaugural speeches were to be the cardinal truths for national sustenance, survival, renewal, and revival in the following years.

Above all, the speeches were intended to reflect and celebrate the values and beliefs of the Nigerian society on Independence Day, and from then forward. The myth of the Nigerian State[35] on Independence Day needed to be wrapped in apparent truthfulness and transmitted along a national grid to every nook and cranny of the country. One such truth was that Nigerians were now leaders in their homeland. The prevalent thinking was that Nigerians could do for themselves what they wanted in order to liberate themselves from colonialism. The myth of the Nigerian State as I conceptualize it here derives from pre-independence stories Nigerians believed that energized their fight against colonialism. Yet, in the process of attaining independence, the myth of the state took over, and the true stories of Nigeria and Nigerians—especially those concerned with layers of competing and even more compelling myths—were twisted and trampled upon.

The colonialists, so the thinking of Nigerian nationalists went, were wrong to have marginalized the Nigerian peoples and their free spirits for all those years. Nigerian nationalists were right to have demanded, communicatively argued, and finally won independence on the platter of gold, without any bloodshed. It was unimaginable that the euphoria of independence, freedom, self-respect, human dignity—nay, African dignity—unity, and respect for authority, could be easily and suddenly halted by such a dramatic and disastrous event as the January 15, 1966 bloody coup.

Inaugural addresses and ascension speeches are traditionally suffused with patriotic symbols, as speakers invoke the values of nationhood and love of country and other ideals the collective hold dear. For Nigeria, these events have usually presented one of the few opportune moments, in which the leaders have the ears, heads, and eyes of the whole nation. I am hesitant to include the leaders' capacity to capture the minds of Nigerians at these events, because there is still more to be done to glue the more than one hundred ethnic groups together into an indivisible entity. Yet, there have been rare instances of the emotional connection between the leaders and the people. A clear example of that bonding fire of patriotism was evident when General Murtala Mohammad took over the reins of power in a 1975 bloodless coup. On the contrary, despondency set in with the abrupt and inconsequential termination of the Second Republic, when General Muhammadu Buhari overthrew the duly elected civilian government of President Shehu Shagari on December 31, 1983. Nigeria was similarly shamed and humiliated to the status of a pariah nation when Ibrahim Babangida annulled the June 12, 1993 presidential elections, where Moshood Kehinde Abiola was widely regarded as the winner.

Nevertheless, even General Buhari endeavored to capture the patriotic sentiment when he reminded Nigerians that there was no other home for them in these words, "This generation of Nigerians, and indeed future generations, has no other country than Nigeria. We shall remain here and salvage it together." Thus, inaugurations and ascensions avail the audience and the leadership the occasion to reignite the fires of civic responsibility and a civic culture a people wish to preserve. One can surmise that the key ingredient to a speech of inauguration and ascension is the preservation of the valued traditions of the polity. From these traditions emerge the public philosophy which I have elsewhere labeled *governing myths* of a nation.[36] These myths glue disparate groups together, as in a team, with a common purpose. When strategically orchestrated and evoked by an effective leader, governing myths can bind and bond toward a national and collective purpose that has eluded Nigeria in fifty years of independence.[37]

Besides celebrating victory at the electoral polls or shooting one's way to the center of power in a coup, both the inauguration and the ascension aim at the fundamental essence of humans—power and survivability. The aspiration to preserve the Nigerian nation for posterity and for individual production and reproduction echoes in each speech collated in this volume. To each leader, the task of holding together this tenuous entity called Nigeria becomes an onerous one. There can be no other symbolic and rhetorical act of unification and self-preservation to better exemplify this desire, frustration, and sometimes fear, than the first, and latterly, other public utterances of a Nigerian leader. Therefore, speech becomes a potent and pervasive instrument in the making and reshaping of the Nigerian nation.

Robert T. Oliver captured the nature and function of a national rhetoric best when he ventured into the humanistic and personality indexes of speakers who made a difference in the evolutions and development of older democracies such as Great Britain. He writes:

"Articulate leaders whether in politics, in religion, in the law or in general public affairs—are often a special breed of individuals who devote themselves to reaching out to cement their relationships with their chosen publics. Their personalities tend to be extraverted and self-consciously assertive. They believe in causes and they accept responsibility, often at great cost to themselves, for promoting them. What they believe intellectually, they also feel emotionally. The interest in their speaking derives from their superior verbal skills and partly from their sensitive relation with the needs and aspirations of their listeners. Their importance lies in the positions they assume concerning crucial decisions that have to be made. They are assessed as shapers of attitudes and supporters of policies. Their speeches illuminate the kinds of choices that have been made and the reasons for making them. Their speaking indicates why some courses have proved more appealing, or perhaps merely expedient, than others. And had they not spoke as they did, different alternatives might have prevailed, with some trends hastened, others delayed, or different courses pursued. In short, they are "makers of history" as such need to be assessed.[38]"

An inaugural and ascension speaker is therefore not an ordinary speaker, but one with a mission and the desire to connect and communicate the essences of the individual and the collective selves constitutive of the nation-state. Speakers who make history not only lean backward to recapture and recreate a past, but they also reinvent that past, so that it mimics the present. Inaugural and ascension speakers have to engage and relate to the audiences to make them see and live their pasts in their present existence as citizens, so much so that such a moment in time and place motivates them to live for the future from there onward. The inaugural speaker is a history maker, an idea inventor, a role model, a cultural custodian, and a political negotiator. Such a speaker communicates hope and affirms what the people believe and desire. The Nigerian speaker needs to make the case for Nigeria's preservation and continuity and possible greatness, and consequently must shoulder the responsibility to actualize the expectations or communicate their possibilities. Thus, at critical junctures in the life of man, woman, child, servant, master, leader, or follower, words make a difference; words, signs, and symbols do matter, and can stir, move, and influence humans to actions that can change the course of history.

In a traditional society such as Nigeria, speech permits the negotiation of social and cultural relations. Absent the vocal interactivity in the exchanges between the leaders and their followers, power and interactions become distant, cold, and insensitive. Nigeria's modern-day political leaders rely on written and formal deliveries at the expense of the much-needed interaction and relationships with the audience to excite a sense of national community and common will. In the end, much distance is created, and less sharing of meaning and experiences. Such orientation to speechmaking and governance exacerbates feelings of alienation between the ruled and the rulers, given the high rate of non-English-language-speaking citizens.

In Nigeria, with a comparatively high level of non-English-language-speaking and English-language-writing citizens, speech remains the main mode of expression given its tradition as an oral culture. In addition, this observation raises the question beyond access, to concerns with comprehensibility, and the effectiveness of political communication that is written and delivered in the official English language of governance and business. Nevertheless, the publication of these maiden speeches is critical for communication and rhetorical scholarship to the extent that it would invite oral communication enthusiasts to begin to analyze and pay closer attention to the spoken styles and verbal styles of Nigerian leaders, and seek to assess the impact of words in leadership and political performance in an emergent plural democracy in Africa and other developing parts of the world.

The words of newly elected leaders and nonelected military rulers provide a window into their minds, thinking, and values as leaders. Speeches at the beginning of every political administration are markers, as they make available to listeners and readers, the emotional and political makeup and maturity of the speaker and by implication the new government. Because words have power, the inaugural speeches have soothing, inspirational, and aspirational qualities. Inaugural and ascension speeches seek to evoke confidence and communicate optimism. Thus, inaugural and ascension speeches motivate and excite; they renew and rekindle interests in the nation as well as the speaker. Inaugural speeches have the capacity to reignite the flame of patriotism and nationalism. It is not surprising that inaugural addresses serve to rally the peoples' sentiments of regard, pride, and appreciation for their nations whenever a new leader ascends to power or is elected and inaugurated. Inaugural speeches therefore are rituals of contemplation, embodiment, empowerment, affirmation, identification, and reconstitution in the annals of nation building and national self-renewal.

An examination of the content of the speeches contained here allows the reader to participate, at least vicariously, in the logical, ethical, emotional, and mythical swings in the moods and thoughts of the speaker as they struggle through the making of Nigeria from independence to the present time. One sees and reads the passionate and patriotic and near patriarchal oratory of President Nnamdi Azikiwe, contrasted with the subdued, conciliatory, and introspective language and style of Prime Minister Tafawa Balewa. The enthusiasm and the euphoria of an independent Nigeria were quickly dimmed by the sobering ascension speech of General Aguiyi-Ironsi, which was quickly replaced with the consolatory and reflective language of ascension in Lieutenant Colonel Yakubu Gowon. Brigadier Murtalla Mohammed's ascension provides an example of a military dictator's rhetorical style—confident, combative, brisk, brash, direct, action-driven, patriotic, confrontational, and hortatory. His immediate demise was supplanted by rhetoric of comforting, consolation, reconstitution, and humility given by Brigadier Olusegun Obasanjo who succeeded Murtala Mohammed.

The tone of the presidential and leadership communication shifted dramatically with the inauguration of Nigeria's Second Republic with President Shehu Usman Shagari at the helm of the second experiment with democratic governance. As soon as Nigerians heralded a new era of democratic communication style, the pendulum swung in an opposite direction toward the powerful exhortatory rhetorical style of General Muhammadu Buhari, a moral crusader, socio-cultural reformist, ultra nationalist and patriot with authoritarian proclivities, who spoke with fervor of the need for "this generation of Nigerians, and indeed future generations of Nigerians" to "stay in Nigeria to salvage the country together" because it was the "only country they can call their own." General Ibrahim Babangida, who stepped in after Buhari was overthrown, relished a refined military rhetoric to move Nigeria away from the isolationism, anachronism, and feudalism of his predecessor. Babangida's speech tended toward a conversational and deliberative style, a tone reminiscent of an elected leader. He ruled that way for eight years as a military rhetor, yet his draconianism manifested in atrocious acts of violence against the Nigerian press, its peoples, intellectuals, and the general freedom of the citizenry that culminated in the annulment of the June 12, 1993 presidential elections after eight years of steady and nondisruptive transitional program.[39]

Because speech can both expose the pulse and provide the sense of direction of the speaker and the context he/she is addressing, the rhythm of the Nigerian nation was drastically changed when Babangida annulled the June 12, 1993 presidential election. In its stead, Babangida installed an Interim National Government, headed by Ernest Shonekan. In his maiden speech, Mr. Shonekan attempted a revitalization of the Nigerian spirit and a renewal of hope and courage to become what Nigerians always wanted. He spoke as an attorney and a veteran executive of a foremost multinational conglomerate in Nigeria. His style came through as a consensus seeker, a bridge builder and an introspective nationalist who knew much was at stake at that junction in the country's journey. However, that sun was not to shine for too long, because another military dictator, General Sani Abacha, toppled Shonekan, only eighty-two days in office.

The ascension of General Sanni Abacha portends the failure in military discipline, and its lack of will to stand aside while the elected officials engage the democratic experience through talk. Uncovering the failure of the Nigerian military leaders to recognize that democracy is not a government of bullets but of ballots is yet another contribution that this compilation can make in the comparative rhetoric of military and elected rulers across different geopolitical locations as well as ideological dispensations and orientations. When Abacha died of a sudden heart attack, the onus felled again on another military ruler, General Abdusalami Abubakar, a professional soldier. His sole responsibility was to engage in the process of military disengagement from the Nigerian political scene. His language was crisp but fortuitous and focused on democratization. Moreover, when the democratically elected Olusegun Obasanjo returned for the second time to lead Nigeria, this time as a civilian president to begin Nigeria's Fourth Republic on May 29, 1999, the language in his inauguration was emboldening, ennobling, enabling, encouraging, and hopeful.

On May 29, 2003, Olusegun Obasanjo was inaugurated as Nigeria's second (the first being President Shagari, 1979–1984) two-term executive president. His inaugural speech was an example of reaffirmation and an appeal for the legitimation of the process, the person, and the place called Nigeria. For the first time since independence in 1960, Nigeria succeeded in inaugurating a civilian-to-civilian president in the first inaugural address of President Umaru Usman Yar'Adua on May 29, 2007. President Yar'Adua's speech is a celebration of the Nigerian self and the reflection of the mood of victory—the ability, capability, resolve, pride, and joy of doing what Nigerians always wanted. He effused, "This is historic day for our nation, for it marks an important milestone in our march towards a maturing democracy. For the first time since we cast off the shackles of colonialism almost half a century ago, we have at last managed an orderly transition from one elected government to another." Yar'Adua's inauguration was an inferiority complex destroyer for most Nigerians who had come to see themselves as incapable and unsophisticated enough to lead themselves by choosing whom they want as their leaders. Yar'Adua's inauguration was both liberating and a fulfillment of nostalgia for many Nigerians.[40]

Before I conclude this section, let me mention here that five decades of Nigeria as an independent country is not long enough, nor is it too short to begin to measure the pulse and aspirations of greatness. This collection is thus an inroad into the study of making a great nation, by studying its words and signs and symbols of leadership at the top. The words here expose the recurrent themes of justice, equality and freedom, unity, progress, development, faith, courage, and hope in the preservation of the unity of the diverse democracy. Besides that, the successive pronouncements by succeeding rulers and leaders offer a barometer to measure the successes and failures of each administration through their words of praise, hope, unity, progress, blame, appreciations, thankfulness and excoriations or otherwise. Through these speeches, one would begin to relive the contours of Nigeria's history, and to measure the moods of the country at each turn on its journey toward unity, development, progress, and democratization, as well as its desire to forge a collective purpose.

PURPOSE OF THIS COMPILATION

This work's availability for use in educational centers, civic organizations, religious associations, cultural and community centers, as well as in diverse other interest groups would add to their beliefs in the role of communication in institutionalizing democracy. In traditional Nigerian societies, words of elders are regarded as words of wisdom. While these elected political leaders and the military rulers do not qualify as cultural leaders in the strict sense, they nevertheless serve as opinion makers and idea manufacturers due to the sheer positions of power and authority they occupy. Thus, their speeches constitute influential words that mirror and create social and political order, thereby staging legitimacy and power through words that have ineluctably shaped Nigerian culture and society before, as well as since, independence. In the end, this compendium can excite inquisitive Nigerians to pay closer attention to words by their leaders as constituting useful communicative artifacts to gauge the performances of their rulers and leaders in and out of office.

Specifically, this compilation intends to serve multiple purposes. First, the compendium would serve as a reference source for students and researchers, politicians, public relations and image management consultants, members of the diplomatic corps, policy makers, and think tankers particularly interested in attributive references on the leadership communications of Nigeria as an emergent African plural democracy.

Second, a book on the inaugural and ascension speeches of Nigerian leaders serves as a guide to the study of leadership communication in a multiethnic, multilingual, multireligious society. A one-stop reference guide to comparing inaugural and ascension themes, the times, challenges, perils and triumphs of democratization, development, nationalism, and cultural identity in advanced and emerging plural societies, is critical to the understanding of written and nonwritten communications in self-affirmation and self-discovery, and hence identity and nation-building politics and the stigma of failed states as magnates for terroristic tendencies.

Third, this project would, through comparison and contrasting, aid in understanding the democratic and nondemocratic leadership styles in an emergent African country, and all other developing countries struggling with nation building. The emphasis on the power of words and symbols presents those interested in speech communication, linguistics, history, political science, humanities, and mass media communication study, a ready access to compare and contrast the first words and symbols of Nigerian political and military rulers, as these leaders and rulers attempt to negotiate leadership and political legitimacy through spoken words.

Fourth, because most of the developing countries emerged from the pangs of colonialism, a one-stop resource on the language and symbols of reconstituting an indigenous elite at the exit of colonial masters, becomes a most welcome exercise in intellectual history and political oratory in postcolonial and postindependence euphoria. But more than that, this work exposes the inherent conflict and contradictions in the power of words in oral society and the written words of their leaders who now believe in the permanency of their words and thoughts in contradiction, and I can add, in competition and conflict with the ephemerality of the spoken words in most of the traditional societies including Nigeria and their rulers in antiquity.

Fifth, this collection is influenced by symbolic interactionism and related rhetorical and communication theoretical studies where the use of language, signs, symbols, and the pragmatics of human communication are crucial to human development. In relying on these approaches to my understanding of Nigerian political communications, I have concluded that communication is critical in a pluralistic independent African nation-state, like Nigeria, where realism and idealism complicate human political existence, leadership management, and legitimacy. Thus, this compilation is informed by my belief that political leadership is a symbolic act and thus nondeterministic and nonlinear, but constantly being negotiated; and that leaders must strategically invent and use symbols with intent to acquire and maintain political resources to effect changes in the lives of their peoples in time and place.

Sixth, this edition provides ready-made material for the study of emerging democracies and the attendant problems of negotiating the self in an increasingly complex international political terrain, where trade, commerce, technology, industry, and capital/financial fluidity drive political decisions and relations. From the contents of these speeches, the critical reader would come to see that every Nigerian leader constantly appealed to the international community for support and advice, even though Nigeria is an independent nation. From these pages, it would become consistently evident that political independence is a negotiated reality between competing and conflicting claims, wherein compromises and consensus would always emerge as the better options in all plural societies, where all interests are intertwined and oftentimes collide, compete, fuse, diffuse, diverge, and converge regardless of political and ideological persuasions.

Seventh, this book is crucial to the study of history, politics, communication, and nationalism. It reaffirms the interconnectivity of these academic disciplines with political practices in any nation. History as a study of events and peoples that make nations and the world go round necessarily depends on symbols, signs and words—spoken and nonspoken—to make sense of that world. Similarly, politics as both an academic and practical art and science of governance is engaged on devising and harnessing symbolic as well as nonsymbolic tactics and strategies to acquiring, distributing, and controlling natural and human resources. Lastly, language and communication remain the two most crucial instruments in initiating and maintaining human relations toward resource acquisition, goal attainment, and meaning-making. This book, therefore, provides an intellectual resource for comparative and interdisciplinary engagements in the history, politics, and communication of and about Nigerian leaders and their peoples, as they seek to create and use or even misuse language, signs, and symbols to institutionalize power and governance toward resource acquisition, control, and distribution.

Lastly, this anthology of Nigeria's premier political speeches of elected and nonelected rulers is a journey into the past as well as a peep into the future, for elementary, secondary school, and university students of history, language, politics, philosophy, communications, mass media studies, linguistics, psychology of language and communications, secondary and elementary education teachers, among many others. To university undergraduates and graduates, researchers, and policy makers alike, this source book becomes an indispensable guide to the life and times of Nigeria and its peoples, and the life and times of the respective leaders and rulers catalogued here. Therefore, I hope the book serves as a ready resource for teachers to invite class discussions and debates on word choices (semantics), word arrangements (syntax) and the use of words to affect desired outcomes (pragmatics), with specific references or nonreferences to issues of relevance to the citizenry. In the first public pronouncements by the presidents, prime minister and military heads of state to the different ethnic groupings in the country, attempts to build a strong and united country become most evident. In the words of these leaders, students would come to realize, appreciate, and criticize the challenges of identifying and relating to the different cultural and linguistic codes that inform the Nigerian citizenry. Where, for example, one leader tries to suppress the differences, another may strive to highlight them as impetuses to sharing in the mosaic of meanings that bind the disparate constitutive units in Nigeria together. I conclude here that both routes are initiated and negotiated in words and symbols.

Words of our leaders become signs of, and for, our times. Words become symbols of both our individuality and our collectivity. As signs, they point to something in and about us as individuals and as a collective. Words are laden with meanings. As symbols, they represent and connote the multiple meanings we all carry and sometimes attempt to share with others. Because they stand for many things Nigerians want, need, aspire to, and cherish, every word by every Nigerian ruler and leader is pregnant with meanings. It is hoped that this initial effort would begin to expose the real and hidden meanings behind the words of Nigerian elected and nonelected leaders, through the critical analyses and examinations of their styles, word choices, and content relevance to the aspirations of the collective.

Through the reading of the words by Nigerian leaders, every citizen would begin to "see," "hear," and "figure out" what the words mean. Such an approach would call for interpretive skills. Nigerians are best suited for that. Nigeria boasts and practices the freest press in Africa. The culture is one where rituals of self and acculturation are made real in speeches punctuated with straightforward ambiguities[41] of the proverbial lore. The individual learns to make sense of his/her world right from the earliest age by cracking open the meaning-laden admonitions of the elders' proverbs and other witticisms. The extent to which political leaders adhere to, or distance themselves from, the styles of delivery that are reminiscent of the traditionally oral Nigerian societies would become known in the compilation and examination of their public addresses, contained here or elsewhere.

AUTHENTICATING THE SPEECHES

In the process of compiling these speeches, I have spent many hours in the libraries of Columbia University, The University of Southern California, The Pennsylvania State University, The Honnold library of The Claremont Colleges, and The University of California, Los Angeles. I have also consulted private collections of many Nigerians and foreign experts on, and travelers to, Nigeria. The Nigerian embassies in many parts of the world have been very helpful along the way. The Nigerian Ministry of Information also aided in verifying the contents of the speeches contained in this book. I have also crosschecked the reliability with published editions in Nigerian newspapers, as well as foreign-based publications, such as *West Africa* magazine. It may be necessary in the future to verify the vocal or broadcast contents as delivered, by scrutinizing and vetting the audio and video recordings where such are available. That was beyond the scope of the present project.

In attempts to establish verbal validity and reliability, I have seen variations in word choices and word orders in published texts of the same speeches from different sources. I had to choose to go with one or the other, knowing that many of the variations were due to pronunciations resulting from variations in dialects given Nigeria's diverse ethnic and linguistic compositions. In fact, there could have been technical glitches in recording devices, or transcribers' errors. Other scholars would need to verify textual reliability with the speechwriters and those living speakers in subsequent projects. For me here, the concern is to record why they spoke as they did, and to which audiences, and what lasting impacts these words had on the general, specific, and particular audiences.

There is no compendium of Nigerian speeches by elected, cultural, religious, political, or military leaders at the time of this writing. Because no recorded volumes of these speeches exist, this initial compilation had to take longer to assemble and to vet for content reliability. In order to authenticate the speeches here, I had to read the speeches from the original texts as submitted to the Nigeria embassies in London, New York, and Washington, D.C, and elsewhere where I could assess the document through personal contacts. I also accessed the speeches from the Federal Ministry of Information, Culture, and Communications, when such was possible. I also cross-checked textual contents with other documented publications in libraries in many universities.

ORGANIZING THE SPEECHES

I have organized this volume chronologically, starting from the first inaugural speech by Nigeria's prime minister, Sir Alhaji Abubakar Tafawa Balewa in 1960, followed by the November 16, 1960 inaugural address by the first Nigerian parliamentary president, Dr. Nnamdi Azikiwe. The last entry in this anthology is the inaugural address by Umaru Musa Yar'Adua, the fourth Nigerian elected civilian president since independence. The importance of Yar'Adua's inauguration cannot be overemphasized in its relevance and importance to the Nigerian democratic experiment because it heralds the first civilian-to-civilian democratic transition in Nigeria's fifty-year history as an independent country.

The timelessness of inaugurals makes the sequential organization in this book most appropriate as each speech transcends its moment of delivery while it articulates and affirms the traditions in the country, rehearses the past, and reaffirms the guiding values and principles in the political estate, thereby forming, or at best attempting to form, a union between the ruled and their rulers.

Preceding each address, I have included a portrait of each speaker, and accompanied such with annotated biographical notes. I have also briefly pointed to the circumstances that necessitated the rise to power of each ruler or the election to the presidency.

I have included in the appendix all the military coup announcements, in order to add depth and width as well as to provide the rhetorical and contextual imperatives that have influenced the evolution of Nigerian society since independence. Above all, coup announcers were forerunners who rhetorically paved the way for the ascent of the military heads of state, and their words matter in contextualizing, interpreting and understanding the exigencies of the times and place.

CONTRIBUTION OF THE COMPILATION

The beginnings of any political administration inevitably draw the attention of the custodians of the political estate as well as the citizens of such nations. It must be noted that every new political administration attracts many detractors as equally as many sympathizers or even as many noncommittants, who generally remain skeptics and sometimes outright cynics. All said, there is always a kind of euphoria that follows every newly elected or nonelected administration. In the case of developing nations, especially in those newly independent countries, the resumption of any new political administrations, presents insights, challenges and prospects for prospective rulers or leaders. And the examination of their languages of authority, legitimacy, and governance become critical to the students of politics and governance.

This compilation in one single volume would provide a medium for a renewed and continuous immersion of Nigerians in the words of their leaders, even though from a distance, and in the isolation of their reading and listening spaces. Access reduces suspicion. In fact, access to, and knowledge of these words by elected and nonelected leaders may stimulate participation and citizenship curiosity, toward asking questions of the promises made at each inauguration of elected, and resumption of powers by the military rulers. This collection therefore provides a potent source for revealing social, cultural, and political meanings in the administration, constitution, reconstitution, reconciliation, and legitimation of Nigeria since independence, and that in itself is engaging the leadership.

This is an unabridged compendium of the maiden speeches of Nigeria's politically elected and military rulers, from independence in 1960 through 2010. It is my belief that putting these words together in one place would encourage critical analyses of their persuasive, informative, celebratory, and linguistic styles and functions in good governance, administrative rhetoric, and political communication. In addition, it is believed that this availability in one volume would invite and excite scholars of language, signs, and symbols to begin to evaluate word choices as indices of a leader's political philosophy, style, governing ability, political performance, decision-making capabilities, and motives, as well as their identification with their audiences.

The overriding motivation for this project therefore, is to make permanent and accessible in one volume, the words of Nigerian leaders for public consumption and scrutiny. It is through, and by, their words that we can begin to know them, and hold them accountable for their deeds and nondeeds or misdeeds. Words have lives of their own. The study of words with which leaders administer, govern, goad, cajole, chastise, endear, manage, direct, and lead is important to the assessment of the leadership policies, performances, styles, and characters. For example, when Major Chukwuemeka Nzeogwu announced Nigeria's first military coup on January 15, 1966, his words changed the course of Nigerian history forever. Similarly, in the words of Sir Tafawa Balewa in the chambers of the Nigerian Senate, heralding his resumption of office as the first and only prime minister of Nigeria, Nigerians have come to understand the inner workings of his mind, and the model of personality he harbored, and the political imperatives of the time. President Nnamdi Azikiwe's inaugural speech becomes a mantra for Nigerian leadership in Africa. In addition, when each speech is juxtaposed against all other speeches by Nigerian leaders from independence to the present day, one sees a mythical thread that runs through all these speeches.

In sum, I believe this book will become an important resource for readers and anyone interested in the political and current issues that concern newly independent African states. It may even serve to energize the discussions over the electronic web pages on democracy and its feasibility in nonwestern societies. The ultimate goal of such dialogues—or "chat rooms" and "blogs" as we have come to call them—would be to enter, participate, and influence discussions and decisions in public spaces. Participation in informed discussions, I believe, would help accelerate the rate of democratic adoption or rejection in the African continent. Moreover, what better ways to do so, than to make available to every educated, and not-so-well-educated citizen, the language, signs and symbols of leadership used by these rulers and leaders.

This work is an intellectual as well as a documentary historical sourcebook on Nigeria and the Nigerian identity, as well as the legitimacy struggles of Nigerian political leadership. The role of language, signs, and symbols in the processes of constituting a plural society is implicated here. In the end, I hope this premier assemblage would instigate further studies into the Nigerian presidency, political leadership communication styles, and presidential character in keeping promises, and evaluating presidential performances as constitutive of the signs and symbols of legitimacy, democratic institutionalization, and nation building in Africa and other developing and emergent democracies everywhere. Words of our elected or military leaders in government should derive from our experiences, expectations, ideas, visions, aspirations, and our myths of existence. When leaders talk of governance, it is believed that they refer to how the citizenry choose to govern themselves through those practices and systems they forge from their own lives and realities. As citizens struggle and negotiate relational, transactional, and interactional existence with each other, in order to acquire, sustain, preserve and conserve the human and natural resources necessary for continuous association and participation as members in our plural communities, the creation and deliberate invention and use of effective communication become indispensable toward a collective national purpose.

NOTES

1. I. F. Nicolson, *The Administration of Nigeria 1900–1960: Men, Methods, and Myth* (Oxford: Clarendon Press, 1969).This work makes wide and useful

contribution to the processes and persons involved in lumping disparate cultural, political, religious entities into one unit, but failed to highlight the persistent, and sustained British impact on Nigerians, and the responses of Nigerians to such policies, especially the Indirect Rule systems administered separately in the North and Southern Protectorates before the 1914 amalgamation. See also A.H.M. Kirk-Greene, *Lugard and the Amalgamation of Nigeria: A Documentary Record* (London: Frank Cass, 1968). For a more Nigerian and widely representative views by Nigerians, see I.M.Okonjo, *British Administration in Nigeria, 1900–1950: A Nigerian View* (New York: NOK Publishers); and Michael Crowder, *The Story of Nigeria* (London: Faber & Faber, 1966).

2. G.O. Olusanya, *The Second World War and Politics in Nigeria, 1939–1953* (Ibadan: Evans Brothers Publishers, 1973); Jacob F. Ade-Ajayi, *Milestones in Nigerian History* (Ibadan: University of Ibadan Press, 1962); Obafemi Awolowo, *Path to Nigerian Freedom,* (London: Faber & Faber, 1947); Frederick A.D.Schwarz, *Nigeria: The Tribes, The Nation or the Race: The Politics of Independence* (Cambridge, MA: M.I.T. Press, 1965); See also C.S. Whitaker, Jr. *The Politics of Tradition: Continuity and Change in Northern Nigeria, 1946–1966* (Princeton, NJ: Princeton University Press, 1970), where Whitaker argues for a gradualist approach to political independence in Nigeria, basing his reasons on the less confrontational approach of the Northern Nigerian political elites. For a general review of the continental developments precipitated by the Second World War in what Davidson describes as the forerunner toward liberation and nationalism, see Basil Davidson, *Africa in History: Themes and Outlines, Revised and Expanded Edition* (London: Phoenix Press, 2001), especially Chapter 8, 325–371.

3. E.E.G. Iweriebor, *Radical Politics in Nigeria, 1945–1950: The Significance of Zikist Movement* (Zaria: Ahmadu Bello University Press, 1966); Onigu Otite, ed., *Themes in African Social and Political Thought* (Enugu: Fourth Dimension Publishers, 1978); James. S. Coleman, *Nigeria Background to Nationalism* (Berkeley, CA: University of California, Press, 1958). See also Richard Sklar, *Nigerian Political Parties: Power in an Emergent African Nation* (Princeton: Princeton University Press, 1963); Nnamdi Azikiwe, *The Development of Political Parties in Nigeria* (London: Office of the Commissioner in the United Kingdom for the Eastern Region of Nigeria, 1957); also, his, *Political Blueprint for Nigeria* (Lagos: African Book Company, 1945); Obafemi Awolowo, *Awo: The Autobiography of Chief Obafemi Awolowo* (Cambridge: Cambridge University Press, 1960). And B.J. Dudley, *Parties and Politics in Northern Nigeria* (London: Frank Cass and Co. Ltd., 1968).

4. Elizabeth Isichei, *A History of Nigeria* (New York: Longman, 1983), 339–342. See also E.A. Ayandele, *A Visionary of the African Church, Mojola Agbebi, 1860–1917* (Nairobi: East African Publishing House, 1971). I owe this source to the excellent work of Professor E. G. Iweriebor, in note 6 below. Also, see Hollis R. Lynch, *Edward Blyden: Pan Negro Patriot, 1832–1912* (London: Oxford University Press, 1967), and Hollis R. Lynch, *Black Spokesman: Selected Published Writings of Edward Wilmot Blyden* (New York: Humanities Press, 1971). In, Richard Sklar, "The Colonial Imprint on African Political Thought," in Gwendolyn M. Carter and Patrick O'Meara, eds., *African Independence: The First Twenty-Five Years*, (Bloomington: Indiana University Press, 1985), 1–30, the professor sees the imprint of colonialism

in post-independence Africa, including Nigeria, as the obstacle to real political and economic independence.

5. On spiritual and cultural contributions of resettled liberated slaves to independence movements in the West African subregion, see Emmanuel A. Ayandele, *The Missionary Impact on Modern Nigeria, 1842–1914* (Harlow: Longman, 1966). For their early political involvements, see one of three edited volumes by Toyin Falola, et al., eds., *History of Nigerian, 3: Nigeria in the Twentieth Century* (Ikeja: Longman, 1981), especially Chapter 1.

6. On Youth groups, see Ehiedu E.G. Iweriebor, "Radicalism and the National Liberation Struggles, 1930–1950," in Adebayo Oyebade, ed., *The Foundations of Nigeria: Essays in Honor of Toyin Falola,* (Trenton, NJ: Africa World Press, Inc., 2003), 107–125. See also Iweriebor, "Nationalism and the Struggle for Freedom, 1880–1960," *Foundations of Nigeria*, 79–105.

7. Nationalists' pressure for independence from colonial rule increased with the formation of political parties. Chief Obafemi Awolowo emerged as the leader of the Yoruba-dominated Action Group, based in the Western Region of Nigeria. For more details see Obafemi Awolowo, *Awo: The Autobiography of Chief Obafemi Awolowo* (Cambridge: Cambridge University Press, 1960); and Obafemi Awolowo, *Path to Nigerian Freedom* (London: Faber & Faber, 1947).

8. Nnamdi Azikiwe was the cofounder of the National Council of Nigeria and the Cameroons, (NCNC), with Herbert Macaulay. Dr. Azikiwe became the leader of this nationalist political party. See *The Constitution of the National Council of Nigeria and the Cameroons* (Lagos: Ife-Olu Printing Works, 1945). Also, Nnamdi Azikiwe, *The Development of Political Parties in Nigeria* (London: 1957).

9. The Northern Peoples' Congress was the umbrella political party for the Northern Region, with its leader Sir Ahmadu Sardauna Bello. For in-depth workings of the party in its formative and operational years, see *Ahmadu Bello, My Life* (London: Cambridge University Press, 1962). See also John N. Paden, *Ahmadu Bello: Sardauna of Sokoto-Values and Leadership in Nigeria* (London, England: Hodder and Stoughton Educational Ltd., 1986).

10. Several writers and thinkers have focused attention on the evolution and transformation of Nigeria, from disparate ethnic, religious, and linguistic groupings into a united country, where all the peoples call themselves Nigerians first. The inherent diversities engender conflict, thereby detracting from the formation of a united Nigeria. For more on this, see Adebayo Oyebade, ed., *The Transformation of Nigeria: Essays in Honor of Toyin Falola* (New Jersey: Africa World Press, 2002); and Tekena N. Tamuno, *The Evolution of the Nigerian State: The Southern Phase, 1898–1914* (New York: Humanities Press, 1972).

11. I use leadership communication here to signify the deliberate and pragmatic creation and utilization of all the available means for creating and sharing meanings with the diverse peoples of Nigeria, with the intent to achieve a common goal for the country. The leader communicates to get things done, and that is the performing function of leadership communication, which in my mind is the most significant role for a Nigerian leader. The leader is a manager, a role model, a custodian of the duties and responsibilities of authority, and must be the individual to whom the people look

up to for political, financial, and emotional guidance; and for the protection and safety of the resources of the estate under his or her care. See Robert T. Oliver, *The Influence of Rhetoric in the Shaping of Great Britain: From the Roman Invasion to the Early Nineteenth Century* (Newark, DE: University of Delaware Press, 1986).

12. Political rhetoric here refers to the ability and capacity of the speaker to arouse and sustain the attention of the audience by speaking truthfully about the contexts of speechmaking and the political relevance of the speech to the audience toward achieving a desired goal or goals. See Robert Paine, ed., *Politically Speaking: Cross-Cultural Studies of Rhetoric* (Philadelphia, PA: Institute for the Study of Human Issues, 1981); and Paul E. Corcoran, *Political Language and Rhetoric* (Austin, TX: The University of Texas Press, 1979). Political speaking and speaking politics must merge in the speaker for there to be meaningful relationship between the ruled and the rulers.

13. Lloyd F. Bitzer, "The Rhetorical Situation," *Philosophy and Rhetoric 1:1* (January 1968), 1–10. Bitzer defines exigencies as imperfections that call forth appropriate responses to remedy such situations.

14. Anticolonialist rhetoric is the comprehensive rhetorical strategy and tactics employed by nationalists to draw the attention of the natives to the injustices of colonialism, while simultaneously engaging the colonialists in negotiations, consultations, and compromises that would end control, domination, and imperialist rule, thus enthroning freedom, liberty, and self-rule by the indigenes.

15. Robert T. Oliver, *The Influence of Rhetoric in the Shaping of Great Britain: From the Roman Invasion to the Early Nineteenth Century* (Newark, DE: University of Delaware Press, 1986), 23. See also his companion text, *Public Speaking in the Re-Shaping of Great Britain* (Newark, DE: University of Delaware Press, 1987); and his *Leadership in Asia: Persuasive Communication in the Making of a Nation, 1850–1950* (Newark, DE: University of Delaware Press, 1989). Also see James C. Ching, "Public Address in the Formation of the Democratic Republic of Congo," Quarterly Journal of Speech 51:1 (1965), 1–13.

16. Solomon W. Obotetukudo, "The Rhetorical Constitution of Nigeria: An Examination of the Inaugural and Ascension Speeches of Nigeria's Elected and Military Heads of State, 1960–1985" (PhD Dissertation, University of Southern California, Los Angeles, California, 1992).

17. For an examination of Nazi dictatorial rhetorical style, see Kenneth Burke, *Philosophy of Literary Form: Studies in Symbolic Action, Third Edition* (Baton Rouge, LA: Louisiana State University, 1973) 191–220; see also Ross Scanlan, "The Nazi Party Speaker System, I & II," *Speech Monographs*, 16 (August 1949), 82–97 and (June 1950), 134–148. I am not inclined to equate imperialism with dictatorship. But because both thrive on control, domination, and subjugation, I would crave the liberty to assert analogous communication styles. See Eric Cheyfitz, *The Poetics of Imperialism: Translation and Colonialism from "The Tempest" to "Tarzan,"* *Revised Edition* (Philadelphia, PA: The University of Pennsylvania Press, 1997) especially 227–251. I also want to draw attention to non-Western oratorical traditions where power, status, and influence predetermine who speaks. See Maurice Bloch, ed., *Political Language and Oratory in Traditional Society* (New York: Academic

Press, 1975). On doctrinaire speakers, see Roderick P. Hart, "The Rhetoric of True Believers," *Speech Monographs*, 38:4 (November 1971), 249–261; and Eric Hoffer, *The True Believer: Thoughts on the Nature of Mass Movements* (New York: HarperCollins Books, 1989).

18. Kenneth Cmiel, *Democratic Eloquence: The Fight over Popular Speech in Nineteenth Century America* (New York: William Morrow & Company, 1990); Kathleen Hall Jamieson, *Eloquence in an Electronic Age: The Transformation of Political Speechmaking* (New York: Oxford University Press, 1988); John Dryzek, *Discursive Democracy* (Cambridge: Cambridge University Press, 1990); and George A. Kennedy, *Aristotle on Rhetoric: A Theory of Civic Discourse* (New York: Oxford University Press, 1991).

19. Aristotle, *The Rhetoric and the Poetics of Aristotle*, trans. W. Rhys Roberts, introduction by Edward P. J. Corbett (New York: Modern Library, 1984), 31–34.

20. Aristotle, *The Rhetoric and the Poetics of Aristotle,* 1358b1–1359a 25; see also Karlyn Kohrs Campbell, and Kathleen Hall Jamieson, *Deeds Done in Words: Presidential Rhetoric and the Genres of Governance* (Chicago, IL: The University of Chicago Press, 1990); Wayne Fields, *Union of Words: A History of Presidential Eloquence* (New York: The Free Press, 1996), especially 113–172. See also J. Richard Chase, "The Classical Conception of Epideictic," *Quarterly Journal of Speech,* 47 (1961), 293–300; and Gerard A. Hauser, "Aristotle On Epideictic: The Formation of Public Morality," *Rhetoric Society Quarterly,* 29:1 (1999): 5–23.

21. Solomon W. Obotetukudo, *Presidential Thematics and Communicative Practices in a Plural Nigerian Democracy* (New York: The Edwin Mellen Press, 2010), forthcoming.

22. Solomon W. Obotetukudo, "The Rhetorical Constitution of Nigeria: An Examination of the Inaugural and Ascension Speeches of Nigeria's Elected and Military Heads of State, 1960–1985," (PhD dissertation, University of Southern California, Los Angeles, 1992) 15–18.

23. J. L. Austin, *How to Do Things With Words, Second Edition* (Cambridge, MA: Harvard University Press, 1975), 4–24. The performatory speech is one that performs or evinces an action and not just saying. Many performatory speeches in my interpretation and in relating it to military rhetors refer to a contractual and declaratory statement. For the military orientation, to say is to do, and that makes the words of the military highly regarded and honorable.

24. Oath taking or swearing is a critical component of the African rituals of initiation, trust, loyalty, and honor, and thus evokes an aura of deference, commitment, and sacredness. See Anthony H.M.Kirk-Greene, "On Swearing—An Account of Some Judicial Oaths in Northern Nigeria," *Africa,* 57, (1955): 43–53.

25. Nnamdi Azikiwe, *My Odyssey: An Autobiography* (London: G. Hurst, 1970).

26. Kenneth Burke, *Rhetoric of Motives* (Berkeley and Los Angeles, CA: The University of California Press, 1969) 45–46. Here Burke states that "identification implies division," therefore, rhetoric, the art of using words and symbols to induce actions in other humans, is simply not magical, but humanistic and real; that it fundamentally involves humans in socialization and factionalization, and thus persuasive.

27. Nigeria gained independence from Great Britain on October 1, 1960. However, Her Majesty still had political dominion over Nigeria until October 1, 1963, when that technically ceased. Nigeria became a Republic with all the attendant rights and privileges, thereafter.

28. Solomon W. Obotetukudo, 1992, 21.

29. For a synoptic rendition of the various constitutional developments that predated the October 1, 1960 Independence, see Chika B. Onwuke, "Constitutional Development, 1914–1960: British Legacy or Local Exigency?" in Adebayo Oyebade, ed., *The Foundations of Nigeria* (Trenton, NJ: Africa World Press, Inc., 2003) 153–180.

30. Kenneth Burke, *A Rhetoric of Motives* (Berkeley and Los Angeles, CA: The University of California Press, 1969), 21–22. Here Burke explains the doctrine of consubstantiality as implicitly and explicitly necessary to any way of life. He argues that because it is a way of life, it is an act, as well as "a way of acting-together; and that in acting-together, men have common sensations, concepts, images, ideas, attitudes that make them consubstantial." (p. 21). Consequently, to identify an object, thing, or place A, with an object or thing or place B, is to make A "consubstantial" with B. Both share in the same substantiality, and hence are identifiable with each other. This is critical to understanding the need for a national collective purpose for Nigeria, wherein all Nigerians share in the substance of Nigeria.

31. Rational coordination and cooperation among individuals with similar interests and orientation seem easier than between individuals with dissimilar interests and orientations. See Benedict Anderson, *Imagined Communities: Reflection on the Origin and Spread of Nationalism* (London & New York: Verso Press, 1983); also, Michael Calvin McGee, "A Link Between Rhetoric and Ideology," *Quarterly Journal of Speech,* 66 (1980), 1–16. Usage of similar signs, symbols, codes, and artifacts among members is a clear indicator of identification.

32. Revolutionary rulers and leaders have been known to exploit mob sentimentalism to the detriment of reasonable people in deliberative as well as nondeliberative cultures. Hitler is an example of a leader who mobilized public sentiments by manufacturing hate toward a section of the community. See Peter Gay, *The Cultivation of Hatred, Vol. 3 of the Bourgeois Experience, Victoria to Freud* (New York: 1993).

33. Many Nigerians readily welcome military intervention as "liberators" and "saviors" or even "messiahs" who have come to save the people from the unruliness and excesses of the elected politicians. Eventually, they realize that the military rulers are humans and Nigerians, who are, in fact, products of their society. See Ndaeyo Uko, *Romancing the Guns* (Trenton, NJ: Africa World Press, Inc., 2003).

34. Toyin Falola and Julius Ihonvbere, eds., *The Rise and Fall of Nigeria's Second Republic, 1979–1984* (London: Zed Books, 1985). Several treatises are available narrating Nigerians' despondency with electoral politics. Any book on Nigeria is replete with lamentations and depressing stories and frustrations about corrupt politicians and the hope for a messiah to deliver Nigeria from its selfish politicians. See also Allison A. Ayida, *The Rise and Fall of Nigeria: The History and Philosophy of an Experiment in African Nation-Building* (Lagos & London: Malthouse Press Limited, 1990).

35. I have conceptualized myth here as stories with compelling and widespread probabilities. See Obotetukudo, 1992, 48–146. Walter Fisher's narrative paradigm and Ernst Cassirer's myth of the state influence this thinking. Fisher believes stories have the power to inform and persuade. See his *Human Communication as Narration: Toward a Philosophy of Reason, Value, and Action* (Columbia, SC: University of South Carolina Press, 1987). Cassirer thinks the myth of the state is an anathema to the practical and social life of man who is manipulated by the symbolic state, thus destroying the independent mind, thought of the civilized, and aspiring man. See his *The Myth of the State* (New Haven, CT: Yale University Press, 1946), 3–49. To Cassirer, the state is irrational; and to Fisher, the stories in myths are reasonable, hence all humans are storytellers.

36. Solomon W. Obotetukudo, "The Rhetorical Constitution of Nigeria: An Examination of the Inaugural and Ascension Speeches of Nigeria's Elected and Military Heads of State, 1960– 1985." Ph.D. Dissertation, University of Southern California, Los Angeles, 1992. 67–73. I had discerned the four governing myths in Nigeria as: communalistic, materialistic, venerative, and moralistic. These governing myths dictate the three perpetual ideological dramas on the Nigerian political scene: peripheralism (i.e., neocolonialism), progressivism, and conservativism.

37. Benedict Anderson, *Imagined Communities: Reflections on the Origin and Spread of Nationalism* (New York: Verso Press, 1983); and Benjamin T. Spencer, *The Quest for Nationality* (Syracuse: Syracuse University Press, 1957).

38. Robert T. Oliver, *The Influence of Rhetoric in the Shaping of Great Britain: From the Roman Invasion to the Early Nineteenth Century* (Newark, DE: University of Delaware Press, 1986), 23.

39. Larry Diamond, A. Kirk-Greene, and O. Oyediran, eds., *Transition Without End: Nigerian Politics and Civil Society Under Babangida.* (Boulder, CO: Lynne Rienner Publishers, 1997); and Omo Omoruyi, Tale of June 12, 1993: *The Betrayal of the Democratic Rights of Nigerians* (London: Press Alliance Network, 1999).

40. Solomon W. Obotetukudo, "That We May Be What We Always Wanted: The Communication of Nostalgia and Nigeria's Search for Permanent Democratic Experiences." Forthcoming, 2010. See also, M. Chase and C. Shaw, eds., *The Imagined Past: History and Nostalgia* (New York: Manchester University Press, 1989), especially 1–17 on the dimensions of nostalgia.

41. Solomon W. Obotetukudo, 'Straightforward Ambiguity and Communication in Traditional Societies: Kenneth Burke and Soren Kierkegaard to the Rescue," Paper Presented at the 83rd Speech/National Communication Association, Chicago, Illinois, November 19–23, 1997.

Chapter One

Sir Alhaji Abubakar Tafawa Balewa

BIOGRAPHICAL NOTES ON
SIR ALHAJI ABUBAKAR TAFAWA BALEWA

Sir Alhaji Abubakar Tafawa Balewa was born in a small village by the same name, Tafawa Balewa in 1912, in today's Bauchi State. He attended Tafawa Balewa Elementary School between 1922 and 1925, and the Bauchi Provincal School between 1925 and 1928.

From 1928 to 1933 Balewa attended Katsina Teacher Training College. He later became the headmaster of Bauchi Middle School, his alma mater that had been upgraded in 1933 from an elementary School.

In 1943 he teamed up with Alhaji Aminu Kano to found the Bauchi Discussion Circle to exchange ideas on significant issues of the day. This union did not last; Aminu Kano was more combative and confrontational, while Balewa was more passive and introspective. Balewa continued his educational training by attending the University of London's Institute of Education, from 1945 to 1946. There he earned the teacher's professional certificate.

Back in Nigeria in 1946, Balewa was appointed a native administration education officer. In 1947 he became a member of the reconstituted Legislative Council of Nigeria, as well as a member of the Northern Regional House of Assembly. He was elected vice president of the Northern Teachers' Association in 1948. In the same year, he became a founding member of the Northern Peoples Congress (NPC), a socio-cultural association that was not very far from his involvement in regional and national politics.

When the African Conference was held in London in 1948, Balewa was in attendance as a Nigerian delegate. Also, he attended the 1948 Commonwealth Parliamentary Association, and the 1951 Festival of Britain.

*Sir Alhaji Abubakar Tafawa Balewa.
The First and Only Prime Minister of
Nigeria and Elected Head of State,
October 1, 1960–January 15, 1966.
Born: December 1912 in Bauchi,
Bauchi State, Nigeria. Died: January 15,
1966 assassinated in Lagos, Nigeria.
Source: Courtesy of the federal ministry
of information, Lagos, Nigeria, 1964.*

In 1951, the Northern Peoples Congress became a political party. Balewa was its first deputy president, next in rank to the Sarduana of Sokoto, Sir Ahmadu Bello, the NPC president.

As political fever heated up given Nigeria's nationalists' agitation for independence from Britain, the battle lines were drawn between the radical intellectuals of Southern Nigeria and the cautious and conservative Northern Nigeria. Balewa benefited from the traditionalist feudal system of the North that the British favored. He held several ministerial appointments between 1951 and 1954. Among them were central minister of works and transport, 1951–54; and federal minister of transport, 1954–57. He was appointed member of Governor's Privy Council in 1955.

In September 1957, Sir Balewa as an NPC (Northern People's Congress) member in the House of Representatives became the first prime minster of Nigeria. And when October 1, 1960 was arbitrarily chosen by the British Colonial Government for Nigeria's independence day, Sir Balewa became the prime minister and the de facto head of government following the parliamentary system of government, which was thought to be the best model to accommodate the diversity in size, population, orientation and disposition toward representative democracy.[1] See Figures I.1 and 1.1.

THE FULL TEXT OF THE INAUGURAL SPEECH BY SIR ALHAJI ABUBAKAR TAFAWA BALEWA, NIGERIA'S FIRST AND ONLY PRIME MINISTER, DELIVERED ON NIGERIA'S INDEPENDENCE DAY, OCTOBER 1, 1960 IN LAGOS

Today is Independence Day.[2] The first of October 1960 is a date to which for two years every Nigerian has been eagerly looking forward. At last, our great day has arrived and Nigeria is now indeed an independent, sovereign nation.

Figure 1.1. 1960 Political Map of Nigeria at Independence. Source: Created by the author.

Words cannot adequately express my joy and pride at being the Nigerian citizen privileged to accept from Her Royal Highness the Constitutional Instruments which are the symbols of Nigeria's Independence. It is a unique privilege which I shall remember forever, and it gives me strength and courage as I dedicate my life to the service of our country.

This is a wonderful day, and is all the more wonderful because we have awaited it with increasing impatience, compelled to watch one country after another overtaking us on the road when we have so nearly reached our goal. But now we have acquired our rightful status, and I feel sure that history will show that the building of our nation proceeded at the wisest pace: it has been thorough and Nigeria now stands well-built upon firm foundations.

Today's ceremony marks the culmination of a process which began fifteen years ago and has now reached a happy and successful conclusion. It is with justifiable pride that we claim the achievement of our Independence to be unparalleled in the annals of history.

Each step of our constitutional advance has been purposely and peacefully planned with full and open consultation not only between representatives of all the various interests in Nigeria but in the harmonious cooperation with the administering power which has today relinquished its authority.

At the same time when our constitutional development entered upon its final phase the emphasis was largely upon self-government. We, the elected representatives of the people of Nigeria, concentrated on proving that we are fully capable of managing our own affairs both internally and as a nation.

However, we were not to be allowed the selfish luxury of focusing our interest on our own homes. In these days of rapid communication we cannot live in isolation apart from the rest of the world, even if we wished to do so. All too soon it has become evident that for us Independence implies a great deal more than self-governance. This great country, which has now emerged without bitterness, or bloodshed, finds that she must at once be ready to deal with grave international issues.

This fact has of recent months been emphasized by the startling events which have occurred in this continent. I shall not labour the points but it would be unrealistic not to draw attention first to the awe-inspiring task confronting us at the very start of our nationhood. When this day of October 1, 1960 was chosen for our Independence it seemed that we were destined to move with quiet dignity to our place on the world stage. Recent events have changed the scene beyond recognition so that we find ourselves today being tested to the utmost. We are called upon immediately to show that our claims to responsible government are well-founded, and having been accepted as an independent state we must at once play an active part in maintaining the peace of the world and in preserving civilization. I promise you, we shall not fail for want of determination.

And we come to this task better-equipped than many. For this I pay tribute to the manner in which successive British Governments have gradually transferred the burden of responsibility to our shoulders. The assistance and unfailing encouragement which we have received from each Secretary of State for the Colonies and their intense personal interest in our development has immeasurably lightened that burden.

All our friends in the Colonial Office must today be proud of their handiwork and in the knowledge that they have helped to lay the foundations of a lasting friendship between our two nations. I have indeed every confidence that, based on the happy experience of a successful partnership, our future relations with the United Kingdom will be more cordial than ever, bound together as we shall be in the Commonwealth by a common allegiance to Her Majesty Queen Elizabeth whom today we proudly acclaim as Queen of Nigeria and Head of the Commonwealth.

Time will not permit the individual mention of all those friends, many of them Nigerians, whose selfless labours have contributed to our Independence. Some have not lived to see the fulfillment of their hopes—on them be peace—but nevertheless they are remembered here, and the names of buildings and streets and roads and bridges throughout the country recall to our minds their achievements, some of them on a national scale. Others were confined perhaps to a small area in one division, more humble but of equal values in the total.

Today we have with us representatives of those who have made Nigeria: representatives of the Banking and Commercial enterprises and members, both past and present, of the Public Service. We welcome you and we rejoice that you have been able to come and share in our celebrations.

We wish that it could have been possible for all of those whom you represent to be here today. Many, I know, will be disappointed to be absent but if they are listening to me now, I say to them, "Thank you on behalf of my countrymen. Thank you for your devoted service which helped up Nigeria into a nation." Today we are indeed proud to have achieved our independence, and proud that our efforts should have contributed to this happy event. But do not mistake our pride for arrogance. It is tempered by feeling of sincere gratitude to all who shared in the task of developing Nigeria politically, socially and economically. We are grateful to the British officers whom we have known, first as masters and then as leaders and finally as partners but always as friends. And there have been countless missionaries who have laboured unceasingly in the cause of education and to whom we owe much of our medical service. We are grateful also to those who have brought modern

methods of banking and of commerce, and new industries. I wish to pay tribute to all of these people and to declare our everlasting admiration for their
devotion to duty.

And finally, I must express our gratitude to Her Royal Highness the
Princess Alexandra of Kent for personally bringing to us these symbols of
our freedom, and especially for delivering the gracious message from Her
Majesty the Queen, and so, with the words, "God Save Our Queen" I open a
new chapter in the history of Nigeria, and of the Commonwealth, and indeed
of the world.

NOTES

1. Trevor Clark, *A Right Honourable Gentleman, Abubakar From the Black Rock:
A Narrative Chronicle of the Life and Times of Nigeria's Alhaji Sir Abubakar Tafawa
Balewa* (London: Edward Arnold, 1991); and also, Mike Okoye, ed., *Toward A Better
Nigeria: A Selection of Notable Speeches by Nigerian Leaders* (Ikeja, Nigeria: Times
Books Ltd., n.d.).

2. Sam Epelle, ed., *Tafawa Balewa: Nigeria Speaks-Speeches of Alhaji Sir Abubakar Tafawa Balewa Made Between 1957–1964* (London: Longman Press Ltd., 1964),
59–61.

Chapter Two

Dr. Nnamdi Benjamin Azikiwe

BIOGRAPHICAL NOTES ON
DR. NNAMDI BENJAMIN AZIKIWE

Nnamdi Benjamin Azikiwe was born on November 16, 1904 of Igbo parents in Zungeru, in the present-day Niger State. The father was a clerk in the Nigeria Regiment under the Colonial government. Azikiwe attended Church Missionary School in Onitsha, Methodist Boys' High School in Lagos, and Hope Waddell Institute in Calabar. He discontinued secondary schooling in 1921, but between 1921 and 1924 worked as a clerk in the Nigerian Treasury in Lagos.

In 1925 he departed for the United States. He is recorded as the first Nigerian to ever study in the United States of America. While in the USA, Azikiwe attended Storer College in West Virginia, Howard University in Washington, D.C., and Lincoln University. He received BA (Philosophy and Anthropology) from Lincoln University (1930), MA (Political Science) from Lincoln University (1932), and MA from the University of Pennsylvania (1933).

On his return to Nigeria from the USA in 1934, he was appointed editor of the newly established *African Morning Post* in Accra, (then Gold Coast), Ghana. He returned to Lagos, Nigeria in 1937, and founded the *West African Pilot*. He published his first book, *Renascent Africa* in 1937, a book leaning much toward Pan-Africanism. He joined the Nigerian Youth Movement in 1937. In 1941 he joined the Nigerian National Democratic Party. Between 1937 and 1947, he managed to acquire control and ownership of six dailies in Nigeria: two in Lagos, and one each in Ibadan, Onitsha, Port Harcourt, and Kano. With his fluency in the three dominant Nigerian languages, Igbo,

Dr. Nnamdi Benjamin Azikiwe. 1st Parliamentary-Styled Democratic President of Nigeria and Commander-in-Chief of the Nigerian Armed Forces, October 1, 1960– Janury 15, 1966. Born: November 24, 1904 in Zungeru, Niger State, Nigeria. Died: May 11, 1996 in Enugu, Enugu State, Nigeria Source: onlinenigeria.com/people, 1998.

Hausa, and Yoruba, Azikiwe was ready for the political battle that would take him to the parliamentary presidency in 1963, howbeit ceremonial at that time, but still the highest political office in Nigeria. From 1960 to 1963 he was the governor-general of Nigeria.

In 1944, he founded the African Continental Bank. That same year he cofounded, with Herbert Macaulay, the National Council of Nigeria and the Cameroons (NCNC) with the intent to weld the heterogeneous masses of Nigeria into one social block for political activism against colonialism. He became the secretary-general and later the president of the party in 1946. In 1947 he was elected to the Legislative Council of Nigeria, until 1951. He was elected member of the Western Region House of Assembly, 1952–1953. He left there due to squabbles for being the leader of opposition, to the Eastern Region House of Assembly in 1953. Azikiwe was the premier of Eastern

Region, 1953–1959. He returned to the national limelight as the president of the Nigerian Senate, 1959–1960. Between these appointments, he was a delegate to the London Talks on Nigerian Constitutional Development, 1957–1958.

On October 1, 1960, when Nigeria obtained independence from Great Britain, in a strategic and compromising move for regional balance and ethno-political tolerance and representation in a unity government, Nnamdi Azikiwe was appointed the first indigenous governor-general of Nigeria. See Figures I.1, I.2, 1.1, and 2.1. He was sworn in as governor-general on November 16, 1960, not on the same date as Nigeria's Independence Day, October 1, 1960. In reading the speech, one notices the ethnic, regional, religious, colonial, identity, class, and racial tensions, which early Nigerian leaders and indeed successive leaders have had to live with and sometimes confront. As Governor-General Azikiwe became the head of state of the federation, while the prime minister was the head of government. The inaugural speech as the governor-general and head of state that follows, is instructive as it sets the tone for the public policy on Africa by successive Nigerian governments.[1]

Figure 2.1. 1963 Political Map of Nigeria with Four States. Source: Created by the author.

THE FULL TEXT OF THE INAUGURAL SPEECH BY THE PRESIDENT, HIS EXCELLENCY, DR. NNAMDI BENJAMIN AZIKIWE, TITLED, "RESPECT FOR HUMAN DIGNITY," ON THE OCCASION OF HIS BEING SWORN IN AS THE GOVERNOR-GENERAL AND COMMANDER IN CHIEF OF NIGERIA'S ARMED FORCES ON NOVEMBER 16, 1960

It is with humility mingled with joy that I thank this grand concourse of patriots and friends of Nigeria[2] for congregating here, today, on the occasion of my inauguration as the first African Governor-General and Commander-in-Chief of the Federation of Nigeria. I was appointed to this post of high honour by Her Majesty Queen Elizabeth II, on the advice of the Prime Minister of Nigeria, to succeed my predecessor in office, that accomplished colonial administrator, Sir James Robertson, G.C.M.G., G.C.V.O.

This mighty audience comprises of eminent men and women drawn from all the Regions of Nigeria and different parts of Africa, the United Kingdom and the United States of America. We have in this august assemblage representatives of heads of states and governments, paramount rulers and chieftains, statesmen and politicians, nationalists and freedom fighters, university administrators and professors, trade union leaders and ex-servicemen, local government heads and civil servants, moulders of public opinion in addition to professional men and women in different walks of life, including a select group of invitees who represent various organizations which are interested in Africa and in the orderly progress of our country towards national autonomy.

I am indeed happy that I can count on such an array of well-wishers at home and abroad because the attainment of political independence by our country involved complications which are both national and international, and these require sympathetic and experienced friends to guide us in our honest effort to build a united nation which would be worthy of the respect and collaboration of the comity of nations.

Perhaps it would not be irrelevant for me to call your attention to the fact that in the political history of contemporary Africa, this is the second time that a person of African descent has been inducted into the office of Governor-General. The first occasion was in November, 1940, when General de Gaulle appointed Felix Eboue, a native Cayenne, French Guiana, in the Carribean, to be Governor-General of former French Equatorial Africa, which has now evolved into the Republics of Chad, Gabon, Brazzaville Congo and the Central African Republic.

In the chequered history of our nation, this is the second time that a person of African descent has had the distinction to assume a gubernatorial post. On 8th July, 1960, Sir Adesoji Aderemi, the Oni of Ife, was sworn in as Governor of Western Nigeria. Today, I have had the privilege and the honour of being sworn-in as the first indigenous Governor-General of the sovereign state of Nigeria. It is a distinction to assume such a high office, because during the colonial era, governorship was an instrument of absolute authority; but now it has become an instrument of constitutional authority.

Before the enactment of the Statute of Westminster in 1931, which granted independence to certain countries, which now constitute the Commonwealth of Nations, the Governor-General was an embodiment of power, in that he was both a representative of the Crown and of the Government of his territory by exercising initiative on a number of issues of an executive and administrative nature, and he was vested with reserved powers to veto certain acts of the local government.

The Statute introduced a new element of constitutional importance when the Governor-General ceased to represent the Government of the United Kingdom but continued to represent the Crown, who is the Head of the Commonwealth. In this context, the Governor-General, as Head of State, now holds the same relation to the Government of Nigeria as the Queen does to the Government of the United Kingdom. As a constitutional ruler, the Governor-General exercises power formally and constitutionally in order to reflect the wishes of a democratically constituted authority.

There were substantial reasons for this shifting of emphasis in the exercise of power of Governor-General from an active to a passive role within the framework of the Constitution. Colonial territories not being international persons could not exercise sovereign powers. Their suzerains acted on their behalf but reserved the right to concede to them sovereignty of a restricted nature. This relationship was based on the legal concept that colonial territories were political inferiors; ergo, they were in political servitude until the situation changed.

After a series of Imperial Conferences from 1907 to 1926, it became necessary not only to make a distinction between colonial territories which did not exercise internal and external sovereignty from those which did. Those territories which exercised "responsible government" internally and externally, either partially or wholly or both were regarded as Dominions. The others were Dependencies. Later, the Statute specifically defined "Dominion" to mean Canada, Australia, New Zealand, South Africa, Irish Free State and Newfoundland. It is significant that at the material time these territories, with the exception of South Africa, were inhabited by a great majority of people of European descent. In the case of South Africa, a small European minority had complete control of the government.

In 1926, the Inter-Imperial Relations Committee of the Imperial Conference, under the chairmanship of Lord Balfour, recorded the opinion that the tendency of the Dominions to seek equality of status with Britain was both right and inevitable. Hence, the Dominions were defined as "Autonomous communities within the British Empire, equal in status, in no way subordinate one to another in any respect of their domestic or external affairs, though united by a common allegiance to the Crown, and freely associated as members of the British Commonwealth of Nations."

After the end of the World War II, India, Pakistan, and Ceylon became independent, closely followed, a decade later, by Ghana, Malaysia and Nigeria. The adoption of a republic form of government by three of the above-named States did not affect Commonwealth status materially, but it must be admitted that a fundamental change occurred in its structure; the Commonwealth has evolved from an association of colonial territories settled mainly by persons of European descent to a multi-racial and multi-national community, which has "no ties, no commitments, no obligations, no trace of imperial control or subordinate colonial status."

These great social changes in the structure and outlook of the Commonwealth are basic, hence they have altered the office of Governor-General to become Head of State and representative of the Crown, as distinct from Head of Government. Since colonial rule is authoritarian, the evolution to independence has transformed the situation so that the Governor-General of a Commonwealth country has now become a constitutional ruler. The Imperial Conference of 1926 defined the position in these terms: "That it was an essential consequence of the equality of status existing among the members of the British Commonwealth that the Governor-General of a Dominion is the representative of the Crown, holding in all respects the same position in relation to the administration of public affairs in the Dominion as is held by His Majesty the King in Great Britain, and that he is not the representative or agent of His Majesty's Government in Great Britain."

The fact that British political institutions have influenced the course of our national history, made us in Nigeria to adopt the parliamentary system of government with an active Head of Government, who remains in office, so long as he retains the confidence of the majority of the representatives of the electorate. Hence there is a bifurcation in the exercise of power between the Governor-General, as the erstwhile Head of Government in a colonial regime, and the Prime Minister.

The changes have had an impact also on the nationality of the persons who assume this high office. The Imperial Conferences of 1926 and 1930 agreed that in view of the changes envisaged, the appointment of a Governor-General should be a matter lying solely between the Crown and the particular Commonwealth country concerned. In this connection, the principle was established that is for each State in the Commonwealth to decide whether to appoint distinguished citizens from the United Kingdom or from within its territorial limits or from elsewhere.

In practice, many Commonwealth countries have opted to appoint their own nationals as Governor-General. Since 5th April, 1937, the Crown, on the recommendation of the Prime Minister of South Africa, has always appointed a South African national as Governor-General. In January 1947, the Crown approved the appointment of Sir William John McKell, G.C.M.G., Premier of Western Australia, a Governor-General of Australia. On 15th August, 1947, the Crown approved the appointment of Muhammad Ali Jinnah, leader of the Muslim League, the first Governor-General of Pakistan. After the departure of Lord Mountbatten, the first native Governor-General of India was Chakra-varti Rajagopalachari, former General Secretary of the Indian National Congress. When India became a Republic, the office of President was made analogous to that of Governor-General and Dr. Rajendra Prasad, former Minister of Food and President of the Indian Constituent Assembly, was elected. The present Governor-General of Ceylon, since 1954, is Sir Oliver Goonetilleke, who is former Leader of the Senate and Minister of Finance. It will be noted that all the individuals mentioned above as native Governors-General were active politicians before they assumed their high office.

I have gone to the length of giving this historical background because of the nature of the oaths I have taken today and because of my honest belief that the existence of a state and constitutional government in Nigeria can become a motive power for the revival of the stature of man in Africa and an impelling force for the restoration of the dignity of man in the world. Before the Honourable Chief Justice of the Federation of Nigeria, I have subscribed to two oaths according to the law: the Oath of Allegiance and the Oath of Office.

In making the Oath of Allegiance, I swore that I would be "faithful and bear true allegiance" to the Crown. This oath is consistent with our Commonwealth relationship in view of the implications of Dominion Status. As a member of the Commonwealth of Nations, we are an autonomous community and we are freely associated as such although united by a common allegiance to the Crown. Since Her Majesty is Head of the Commonwealth and the Governor-General is representative of the Queen, it is appropriate that on assuming this honourable office, the appointee should subscribe to the Oath of Allegiance as a visible sign of belief in this association. The Commonwealth is a historic coalition of nations who stand for certain common values and ideals which are generally described as liberal democracy. In this free association of countries, Britain stands supreme as the source of certain spiritual values, such as individual freedom, respect for law and religious toleration. In course of their development from colonial status to independence, the members have been nourished with the concepts of British democratic heritage.

When I subscribed to the Oath of Office, I swore that I would "well and truly serve" in the office of Governor-General. In view of the historical forces at work since the publication of the Durham Report in 1840, and the enactment of the Statute of Westminster in 1931, it is obvious that the evolution of Commonwealth countries have gravitated from authoritarian to constitutional government. In Nigeria this means to me government of the *inhabitants* of Nigeria, with consent of the citizens of Nigeria, through the *accredited representatives* of the *voters* of Nigeria, who are periodically elected secret ballot and by adult suffrage, by a *responsible cabinet* selected from such accredited representatives which remains in office as long as such a cabinet retains the confidence of the majority members of such an elected legislature.

This definition of representative democracy, as it has been adapted to Nigeria, is based on the concepts of the rule of law and respect for individual freedom which have been bequeathed to us during our political association with Britain. These notions are the foundations upon which have been built the pillars of our parliamentary government. Without respect for the rule of law permeating our political fabric, Nigeria would degenerate into a dictatorship with its twin relatives of tyranny and despotism. I hold that the arbitrary exercise of power without restraining influence of the rule of law must be condemned as a fundamental departure from constitutional government. Any justification of such untrammeled exercise of political power is, to me, an outrage on human conscience and a gross violation of basic human rights.

With this concept of the rule of law, we have inherited the idea of individual freedom, which is the sheet-anchor of democratic institutions. The sanctity of the person, the right of a person to fair and public trial, the assumption of innocence of an accused person until he is proven guilty; these are examples of the basic human rights which feature our Constitution and which I have sworn to uphold. But there are other ancillaries to these elements of liberal democracy. I have in mind religious freedom of conscience, freedom of worship, the independence of a responsible judiciary, which is conscious of its responsibilities in a democratic society, and the existence of an untarnishable public service whose members are appointed or promoted strictly on the merits of their qualifications and good character and not on any other extraneous criteria.

What I have analysed, in so far as the kernel of the two oaths taken by me today really can be summed up in four words: respect for human dignity. I submit that respect for human dignity is the challenge which Africa offers to the world. The lack of respect for human dignity has led to the political bondage of man by man in Africa. This act of commission has also accentuated race relations in Africa. Until the conscience of the world has been energetically aroused to solve this problem frankly with absolute honesty, it is safe to predict that the political resurgence which is now sweeping all over Africa is capable of leading to a *revanche* movement which would be disastrous to the peace of the world.

Representative democracy has been tried in Nigeria and it has worked successfully. Parliamentary government has been attempted in Nigeria and we have proved more than equal to the task. Ministerial responsibility is no longer a bugbear to us; it is now part and parcel of our politics. Indeed, the Westminster model of parliamentary government and democracy has been proved by us not only to be capable of being exported to Africa, but practicable in this part of Africa. But these are veneers of a political pattern which is interwoven on a complex social system in a world of which Nigeria is a part. Whilst Nigeria can definitely give assurance of its capacity for self-government and to maintain law and order, as a fully fledged member of the Commonwealth, Nigerians are bound to criticise the scandalous inconsistencies of the world which expose the cloven hoof of certain nations in their attitude towards the darker races.

Whilst it is a fact that the Commonwealth is a voluntary association which is loose, flexible and adaptable, and its members values it "for its very variety and multiplicity of outlook, its member governments sometimes acting in unison, sometimes separately, but always freely exchanging views and information, and always adding something to a common pool of mutual understanding," nevertheless, Nigerians cannot be expected to be supine when such a basic human right as respect for human dignity is violated with impunity in any part of the Commonwealth or any country in the world.

The challenge of Nigeria as a free State in twentieth century Africa is the need to revive the stature of man in Africa and restore the dignity of man in the world. Nigerians believe passionately in the fundamental human rights. We regard all races of the human family as equal. Under no circumstances shall we accept the idea that the black race is inferior to any other race. No matter where this spurious doctrine may prevail, it may be in London or Sharpville or Decatur, we shall never admit that we are an inferior race, because if we accept the Christian or Muslim doctrine that God is perfect and that man was made in the image of God, then it would be sacrilegious, if not heretical, to believe that we are an inferior race.

We cannot concede that it is in our national interest to fraternize with such nations which practice race prejudice and we must not acquiesce in such an outrageous insult on the black race. In fact, we must regard it as a mark of disrespect and an unfriendly act if any country with whom we have a friendly relations indulge in race prejudice in any shape or form, no matter how it may be legally cloaked.

Within the Commonwealth, Nigerians cannot appreciate the equity in denying a national of any part of this free association or multi-racial states and

territories his freedom of movement without due process of law. We cannot
see the justice in restricting the movement of any Commonwealth national
arbitrarily, without due process of law, more so after one had served a long
term of imprisonment as penalty for infraction of the law. We cannot approve
extra-legal acts of this nature because they violate fundamental human rights
and negate the very idea of a rule of law. We cannot refrain from questioning
the expediency of these acts of tyranny and certainly we must denounce them
as an unjustified invasion on the sacred rights of the individual.

Within the rank and file of the United Nations, there are many States who
deny their citizens equality of opportunity and deprive them of fundamental
human rights, for the simple reason that the colour of their skin is black or that
they are natives of Africa. We in Nigeria cannot reconcile with good government the imprisonment of an African who refuses to wear a badge of racial
inferiority which is disguised as an identification card. We cannot see the logic
of a minority group, which controls power, to subvert the ends of government
by punishing representatives of a majority group who refuse to be discriminated
or segregated against, merely on the basis of race and not necessarily on any infraction of a law which is not repugnant to human conscience. Our people find
it extremely puzzling to believe that intelligent people can be so wicked and
inhuman and yet accepted as civilized nations by the international community.

We in Nigeria are non-plussed and we cannot understand why many
member-states in the United Nations looked with disfavor at the idea of pro-
mulgating an international convention on human rights. Why are the leading
nations of the world interested in merely *declaring* their adherence to the ideals of basic human rights, but are not prepared to sign a binding international
convention much more to ratify it in their Parliaments? Could it be that such
nations believe that talks of law and respect for human dignity are outside the
periphery of world politics? Or could it be that such nations merely claim to
be protagonists of democracy but do not believe in this ideology as a practicable proposition and way of life?

We have come a long way in achieving our independence. It was a toughen-
ing school and the experience we gained has armed us with a spiritual weapon
which now enables us to put to test the authenticity of the claims of those who
profess to be democratic and civilized. As such, we ask why is it that after ex-
tracting all its teeth, only Britain and a few members of the Western European
Union dared to sign the European Convention on Human Rights, whilst the
many African Colonial Powers, including France, Spain and Portugal, refused
to endorse in principle, this innocuous but face-saving convention?

If respect for the rule of law and individual freedom must be used as a
yardstick to gauge the progress of civilization among nations, then the world
should be in position to appreciate why we, in Nigeria, have refused to inherit

the prejudices of older European nations by making the basis of our foreign policy, the principle of non-alignment with any power bloc.

As members of a mal-treated race, it would be the highest height of folly for us to hobnob with those who regard the members of our race as inferior. As firm believers in the principle of the brotherhood of man, we would be foolish to pretend that we are happy when the rights of our fellow human beings are wantonly trampled upon by irresponsible rulers and government agencies of undemocratic countries. Having passed through the crucible of political bondage in the furnace of colonial tutelage, how can any reasonable world statesman expect Nigerians to associate in an alliance of mutual security with countries which will regard Africa as a colonial pasture fit for safaris and cattle-grazing and not for the enjoyment of basic human rights.

Our domestic policy is intertwined with our foreign policy. Those who have the responsibility to enunciate these have done so in precise terms. We are more concerned in reviving the stature of man in Africa. We have developed into a stage where we now lead the rest of Africa in the number of elementary and secondary schools and their population. We now have five institutions of higher learning of university standard. About 10,000 of our sons and daughters are attending the leading universities of Europe and America. Our hospitals and health centres outnumber those of any other country in Africa. The total mileage of our tarred and untarred roads measures up with the best in Africa. Our economy is expanding in the agricultural and industrial sectors, and we are busily engaged in stimulating investments so as to increase earning opportunities for our people and thereby increase their purchasing power and raise their living standards. Our population is the highest in Africa, fourth in the Commonwealth and thirteenth in the world.

Since the days of slavery, this continent has been depopulated and exploited. By 1939, that is, on the eve of the World War II, there were only two independent States in Africa: they were the Republic of Liberia and the Union of South Africa. A decade later, this number was increased to four, as a result of the restitution of the Kingdom of Ethiopia and the abandonment of the capitularies which chained the Kingdom of Egypt in political servitude for decades. By the end of 1959, the number of independent African States had reached ten: Liberia, South Africa, Ethiopia, United Arab Republic, Libya, Morocco, Tunisia, Sudan, Ghana and Guinea; that is six republics, three kingdoms and one military dictatorship.

As I speak today, it is with pride that I remind you that this is Africa's year, because sixteen States have already become independent and another will become so later this month, to make it seventeen. The attainment of political freedom by Cameroun, Togo, Senegal, Mali, Malagasy, Somalia, Leopoldville Congo, Brazzaville Congo, Dahomey, Ivory Coast, Upper Volta, Niger,

Chad, Gabon, Central African Republic and Nigeria, this year, is as dramatic and as spectacular as the events in the African continent since the days of the Pharoahs. Mauritania will become an independent Republic before the end of this month, to give sovereign and independent African States a scoreboard of twenty-seven.

As we proceed to the task of nation-building, we cannot avoid taking stock of the hostility against our race by certain sections of humanity, some of whom are now permanently settled on this continent as minorities with great political power. We are bound to take cognizance of a situation where a minority, on account of its superior organization and influence, can usurp power and proceed to bully its minority population to the point of seeking to subdue them by sheer brute force and refined savagery.

If the outside world would be disposed to wink at this extreme form of civilized barbarism, then it is only a matter of time, when the independent African States will come into their own and plan to rescue their kith and kin from this social degradation. It is not yet too late for the European suzerains and associates of these territories to give due warning to their wards and friends in Africa to retrace their steps if they would escape from the wrath that would be inevitable in case they continued to be petulant and incorrigible. The resignation of the Chief Justice of the Central African Federation is very refreshing, for it shows that even among minority groups in Africa there are God-fearing leaders with conviction who have faith in the peaceful co-existence of Africans and non-Africans in Africa. This heroic act is a straw which indicates that the wind of change is bound to sweep away the cobwebs of a venal past.

As Nigeria enjoys its freedom in the world community, its leaders must energetically begin to take an increasing part in matters affecting the destiny of the continent of Africa and the rest of the world. This has become necessary because of the inter-dependence of mankind and because we must unite with progressive forces all over the world so as to fertilize the soil of human relations for the healthy growth and development of democracy. We have been too busy with our self-appointed task of national self-realisation that most of our rank and file have lost all sense of inquiry into the ethics of the prevalent ideologies of the conflicting power blocs.

Only last week, a young student asked me this question: "Can you recommend to me any informative book on Communism?" Out of curiosity I asked her what she wanted to do with such a book, and she replied in all innocence: "Since those who broadcast over the wireless are so afraid of it, I would like to know why they are afraid!" This is typical of the spirit of inquiry which is now surging in our youth and is creating an intellectual ferment among them. I do not advocate the suppression of information nor do I suggest misinformation; but I do hope that our friends in Europe and America will appreciate the incalculable harm they can do to the cause of world peace by crying "Wolf" when no wolf is in sight, and no Nigerian wants to know whether the wolf is a dog or a cat or a cross between a dog and a cat!

Our primary duty with our emergence as an African Power is, in the words of one our learned jurists, "to assert the evolution of a single nation-and to project the personality of that nation.... A constitution is not just legal document to be interpreted as conferring or withdrawing individual rights. A constitution is a way of life and the sacred duty of the courts and the peoples is to interpret it as such and justify its existence by their lives." These thoughts of Mr. Justice Coker deserve serious attention because they contain gems of wisdom that can be used to cement our country in a bond of unity and faith and thereby direct the thoughts of our youth to constructive ends.

In the view of certain observers, here and abroad, my decision to accept and assume the office of Governor-General has been surprising. They thought that since I was leader of a political party which contested the last federal elections, I should continue to fight in order to displace the present Head of Government, instead of supporting the conclusion of a political truce and agreeing to become what one of them euphemistically described as "a prisoner in a gilded cage." Whilst I appreciate the good intentions of these critics, I should make it clear that one important reason why human society is unstable and full of conflicting emotions is because of the tendency to intensify rivalry beyond their normal course. After all, our leaders fought the good fight with all their might because they believed in the righteousness of their cause; and history has proved them right. But they knew that in a team of many players all cannot be elected captains since it is generally accepted that more than one captain cannot run a ship efficiently. That was what Douglas Malloch must have had in mind when he composed these immortal lines:

> If you can't be a prince on the top of a hill
>   Be a scrub in the valley-but be
> The best little scrub by the side of the hill;
>   Be a bush if you can't be a tree.
> If you can't be a bush be a bit of grass,
>   And some highway some happier make;
> If you can't be a muskie then just be a bass—
>   But be the liveliest bass in the lake!
> We can't all be captains, we've got to be crew,
>   There's something for all of us here.
> There's big work to do and there's lesser to do,
>   And the task we must do is the near.
> If you can't be a highway then just be a trail,
>   If you can't be the sun be a star;
> It isn't by size that you win or you fail—
>   Be the best of whatever you are!

I am satisfied that the present arrangement made by those of us, who may be rightly described as the makers of contemporary Nigeria, have ushered freedom into our country and preserved our unity as a nation. I am happy that history has assigned to me an important part to play in order that this unity may have lasting effects and bring home to our people the need to maintain it religiously. I am all the more overjoyed that Nigeria is free and independent without necessarily going the way of certain States in Africa, Asia and Europe, whose instability has been of great concern to the United Nations and the rest of the world.

If am asked whether I am happy—because Nigeria is free, and the Nigerian Government appears to be stable, and the people of Nigeria are apparently satisfied that the prize of freedom and the price our leaders paid for it were worth the sacrifice, I would answer in the affirmative. It is true that other compatriots and I had to scale the craggy heights as we trekked the stony Golgotha of human life. It is true that during the struggle, whose climax was reached after a greater part of a century, our lot was one of vicissitudes and disappointments; nevertheless I am grateful to God that I did not swerve from our objective, in spite of mutilation of facts, amorphous interpretation and deliberate perversion of my actual role. The contest was tough, the encounters were rough, and the foe was implacable; nevertheless we fought tenaciously according to the rules of the game, even when our opponent decided to sneak in a rabbit punch. And we have emerged triumphantly!

I must confess that during the dark and dreary days of our struggle for national freedom, one poem sustained me spiritually and raised my morale so much that I did not bother either to count the cost or to reckon the casualties sustained during our historic conflict for a place in the sun. It was one of Rudyard Kipling's poems and I shall now read it:

> "If you can keep your head when all about you
>   Are losing theirs and blaming it on you,
> If you can trust yourself when all men doubt you,
>   But make allowance for their doubting too;
> If you can wait and not be tired by waiting,
>   Or being lied about, don't deal in lies,
> Or being hated don't give way to hating.
>   And yet don't look too good, nor talk too wise;
> If you can dream—and not make dreams your master;
>   If you can think—and not make thoughts your aim.
> If you can meet with triumph and disaster
>   And treat those two imposters just the same;
> If you can bear to hear the truth you've spoken
>   Twisted by knaves to make a trap for fools,
> Or watch the things you gave your life to, broken,
>   And stoop and build 'em up with worn-out tools;

> If you can make one heap of all your winnings
>> And risk it on one turn of pitch-and-toss,
> And lose, and start again at your beginnings
>> And never breathe a word about your loss;
> If you can force your heart and nerve and sinew
>> To serve your turn long after they are gone,
> And so hold on when there is nothing in you
>> Except the will which says to them: "Hold on!"
> If you can talk with crowds and keep your virtue,
>> Or walk with kings—nor lose the common touch,
> If neither foes nor loving friends can hurt you,
>> If all men count with you, but none too much;
> If you can fill the unforgiving minute
>> With sixty seconds' worth of distance run.
> Yours is the earth and everything that's in it,
>> And—which is more—you'll be a man, my son!"

Independence has come and the world has rejoiced with us. We have proved to be worthy pioneers of human freedom in Nigeria. What remains for us to do now is to dedicate our lives anew to the fascinating task of nation-building. The past is gone with all its bitterness and rancour and recrimination. The future is before us and great events await the leadership of the wise and brave. We have an uphill task to perform and this is not the time for us to undertake a *post mortem* operation in order to allocate blames among our leaders and followers. The issue is not who is right and who is wrong; the main issue is what is right for the Federation of Nigeria and for humanity!

In assuming the office of Governor-General and Commander-in-Chief, I hereby call upon my compatriots to join Alhaji Abubakar and myself in this historic mission of reviving the stature of man in Africa. There is plenty room at the top and there is plenty of work to be done. I call upon Alhaji Ahmadu Bello, the Sardauna of Sokoto, to join us in this Herculean task of national reconstruction. I exhort Chief Obafemi Awolowo to associate with us in this great adventure of restoring the dignity of man in the world. There are many leaders who can give active support and assistance to our nation at this its supreme hour of need: Chief Samuel Ladoke Akintola and Chief Dennis Chukude Osadebay of Western Nigeria, Dr. Michael Iheonukara Okpara and Samuel Grace Ikoku of Eastern Nigeria, Mallam Aminu Kano, Mallam Ibrahim Imam and J.S.Tarka of Northern Nigeria, and countless others.

I appeal to all our leaders, far and near, to forget the wounds which were inflicted in the course of our internecine altercations. The love of our country should out-weigh the love of our petty selves. The enjoyment of individual freedom under the law should mean more to us than our self-centered party programmes and manifestos. Common dangers and common enemies alert us on the need for common security. The British came here in 1851 and found us helplessly divided in tribal compartments. When Britain transferred power to us on 1st October, 1960, we were no longer an expression of geography but a reality of history. During all our years of political vassalage we became socially and economically integrated. We have also developed an identity of interest and we have crystallized common nationality. The process of political integration reached its zenith at midnight of 30th September, 1960, when we lustily sang our National Anthem and our National Flag was hoisted aloft to signal the birth of a new nation.

Come and join Abubakar with me, Sardauna, Awolowo, Akintola, Osadebay, Okpara, Ikoku, Aminu Kano, Ibrahim Imam and Tarka. Let us bind the nation's wound and let us heal the breaches of the past so that in forging our nation there shall emerge on this continent a hate-free, fear-free and greed-free people, who shall be in the vanguard of a world task force, whose assignment is not only to revive the stature of man in Africa, but to restore the dignity of man in the world.

As for me, my stiffest earthly assignment is ended and my major life's work is done. My country is now free, and I have been honoured to be its first indigenous Head of State. What more could one desire in life? I thank God for sparing my life to witness the independence of my nativeland. I am grateful to God for the opportunity to serve and I hereby pledge solemnly to render faithful and loyal service to my country. As in the past, I shall not have considerations for personal comforts or safety or even life itself, if these are the price I must pay for leadership in order to preserve the freedom and unity of my country.

The Independence of Nigeria was doggedly fought and dearly won. During our protracted battles, some of our heroes and heroines fell by the wayside; some went the way of all flesh; some paid with their lives; some were incarcerated; some lost their jobs; some sacrificed their fortunes; some were ostracized; whilst some were victimized and made to suffer indignity because they dared to demand freedom for Nigeria in our life time. Therefore, we must jealously guard our freedom with our lives, if need be. I have made up my mind to do all that lies in my power, so that our newly-won freedom shall endure.

All that remains to be done now is for our leaders and their followers to demonstrate that spiritual resilience which had enabled us to survive the onslaught of the past. With faith in the eventual success of our adventure in the comity of nations, we can look forward to the morrow with hope and charity for our fellow man, knowing that the task has been well done and that prospects of the future are bright. In the words of a distinguished American poet,

Langston Hughes, let us youthfully march together to a greater tomorrow for Nigeria in unity with faith:

> "We have tomorrow
> Bright before us
> Like a flame.
> Yesterday, a night-gone thing,
> A sun-down name.
> And dawn today,
> Broad arch above the road we came.
> We march."

NOTES

1. Zik, My Odyssey: An Autobiography (London, 1973); Mike Okoye, Ed. Toward A Better Nigeria: A Selection of Notable Speeches by Nigerian Leaders (Ikeja, Nigeria: Times Books Ltd., n.d.)

2. F.Chidozie Ogbalu, ed. *Dr. Zik of Africa: Biography and Speeches* (Onitsha, Nigeria: African Literature Bureau, 1955). For content reliability, see also Nnamdi Azikiwe, "Respect for Human Dignity", Inaugural Address by His Excellency, Dr. Nnamdi Azikiwe, Governor-General and Commander-in-Chief of the Federation of Nigeria on November 16, 1960 (Lagos, Nigeria: Federal Ministry of Information, 1960), 1–16.

Chapter Three

Major General Johnson Thomas U. Aguiyi-Ironsi

BIOGRAPHICAL NOTES ON MAJOR GENERAL JOHNSON THOMAS U. AGUIYI-IRONSI

Major General Johnson Thomas U. Aguiyi-Ironsi was born in Umuahia, Abia State, on March 3, 1924. He had his early primary and secondary schooling in Umuahia and Kano. In 1942 he was enlisted into the Nigerian Regiment Seventh Battalion. He was promoted to company sergeant major in 1946. In 1946 he attended the Camberly Staff College in England. He was promoted to second lieutenant of the Royal West African Frontier Force at the completion of his Camberly course in 1949.

In 1953 he became a captain, and a major in 1955. He served as Queen Elizabeth II of England's equerry when she visited Nigeria in 1956. Four years later in 1960, Aguiyi-Ironsi was promoted to lieutenant colonel and was made the commandant of the Fifth Battalion of the Nigerian Army stationed in Kano.

Aguiyi-Ironsi was appointed head of the Nigerian contingent of the United Nations peacekeeping force in Congo (now Zaire) in 1960. Between 1961 and 1962 he was the military attaché to the Nigerian High Commission in London, when he later got promoted to brigadier. While in London, he attended several courses at the Imperial Defence College. He returned to Congo in 1964 to become the commandant of the entire United Nations peacekeeping force there.

In 1965 Aguiyi-Ironsi returned to Nigeria as the most senior indigenous officer. He became the head of the Nigerian Army following the complete Nigerianisation policy of the Nigerian Army, and was promoted to major general. When the troubles with the first Nigerian civilian government escalated beyond the legislative capacity to contain, the Council of Ministers in January 1966 invited the armed forces to take over the reins of government. A group of young army officers, mostly of the Igbo ethnic origin, preempted

Major-General Johnson Thomas Aguiyi-Ironsi. 1st Nigerian Military Head of State and Commander-in-Chief of the Nigerian Armed Forces, January 15, 1966–July 29, 1966. Born: March 3, 1924 in Umuahia, Abia State, Nigeria. Died: July 29, 1966, assassinated in Ibadan, Oyo State, Nigeria. Source: Courtesy of the Nigerian permanent mission at the United Nations, New York, USA.

the official handover and conducted a bloody coup that eliminated members of the legislative class from the non-Igbo ethnic group. Major General Aguiyi-Ironsi became the head of the National Military Government and supreme commander of the Nigerian Armed Forces. He held this position until he was assassinated in a countercoup on July 29, 1966.[1]

THE FULL TEXT OF THE ASCENSION SPEECH BY HIS EXCELLENCY, MAJOR GENERAL JOHNSON THOMAS U. AGUIYI-IRONSI, THE HEAD OF THE FEDERAL MILITARY GOVERNMENT OF NIGERIA, SUPREME COMMANDER AND COMMANDER IN CHIEF OF THE NIGERIAN ARMED FORCES ON JANUARY 17, 1966

The Military Government of the Republic of Nigeria wishes to state that it has taken over the interim administration of the Republic of Nigeria following the invitation of the Council of Ministers of the last Government for the Army to do so.[2]

For some time now there have been escalating political disturbances in parts of Nigeria with increasing loss of faith between political parties, and between political leaders themselves. This crisis of confidence reached a head during the elections in the Western Region in October last year. There were charges by opposition parties of rigging of the elections and general abuse of power by the regional government in the conduct of the elections. Riots, arson, murder and looting became widespread in Western Nigeria since October. The situation deteriorated and certain army officers attempted to seize power.

In the early hours of the morning of January 15, 1966, these officers kidnapped the Prime Minister and minister of Finance and took them to an unknown destination. The revolt was widespread throughout the country and two Regional Premiers and some high-ranking army officers were killed. The whereabouts of the Prime Minister is still unknown. The vast majority of the Nigerian Army under the command of the General Officer commanding the Nigerian Army remained loyal to the National Government and immediately took steps to control the situation.

The Council of Ministers of the National Government met and appraised the immediate need to control the serious situation which threatened the Republic. They also saw quite clearly a possible deterioration of the situation in the light of developments on Saturday, January 15, 1966. On Sunday, January 16, the Council of Ministers unanimously decided to hand over voluntarily the administration of the country with immediate effect, to the Nigerian Army. This was formally done the same day by the Acting President of the Republic.

The Government of the Republic of Nigeria having ceased to function, the Nigeria Armed Forces have been invited to form an Interim Military Government for the purpose of maintaining law and order and of maintaining essential services.

The invitation has been accepted and I, General Johnson Thomas Umunakwe Aguiyi-Ironsi, the General Officer commanding the Nigerian Army have been formally invested with authority as Head of the National Military Government and Supreme Commander of the Nigerian Armed Forces.

The Federal Military Government hereby decrees: the suspension of the provision of the Constitution of the Federation relating to the office of President, the establishment of Parliament, and of the office of Prime Minister; the suspensions of the provisions of the Constitution of the Regions relating to the establishment of the offices of Regional Governors, Regional Premiers and Regional Executive Councils and Regional Legislatures.

The Federal Military further decrees: that there shall be appointed a Military Governor in each Region of the Federation, who shall be directly responsible to the Federal Military Government for the good government of the Region; the appointment as Adviser to the Military Governor of the Region, of the last person to hold the office of Governor of the Region under the suspended provisions of the Constitution.

The Federal Military Government further decrees: that the Chief Justice and all other holders of judicial appointments within the Federation shall continue their appointments, and that the judiciary shall continue to function under their existing statutes; that all holders of appointments in the Civil Service of the Federation and of the Regions shall continue to hold their appointments and to carry out their duties in the normal way, and that similarly the Nigeria Police Force and the Nigeria Special Constabulary shall continue to exercise their functions in the normal way; that all Local Government Police Forces and Native Authority Police Forces shall be placed under the overall command of the Inspector-General.

The Federal Military Government announces, in connection with the internal affairs of the Federation: that it is determined to suppress the current disorder in the Western Region and in the Tiv area of the Northern Region; that it will declare Martial Law in any area of the Federation in which disturbances continue; that it is its intention to maintain law and order in the Federation until such times as a new Constitution for the Federation, prepared in accordance with the wishes of the people, is brought into being.

The Federal Military Government announces, in connection with the external affairs of the country: that it is desirous of maintaining the existing diplomatic relations with other States; and that it is its intention to honour all treaty obligations and all financial agreements and obligations entered into by the previous Government.

The Federal Military Government calls upon all citizens of the Federation to extend their full cooperation to the Government in the urgent task of restoring law and order in the present crisis, and to continue in their normal occupations.

NOTES

1. Mike Okoye, ed., Toward A Better Nigeria: A Selection of Notable Speeches by Nigerian Leaders (Ikeja, Nigeria: Times Books Ltd., n.d.).

2. In view of the panic surrounding Nigeria's first military coup on January 15, 1966, barely five years after independence, the ascension speech of Major-General J.T.U. Aguiyi-Ironsi is reconstructed and validated from the following sources for authenticity and content reliability: The Problem of Nigerian Unity, Appendix 1 (Enugu, Nigeria: Eastern Nigeria Ministry of Information, n.d); O. Ojiako, *13 Years of Military Rule* (Lagos, Nigeria: Daily Times of Nigeria, 1979), 1–25; A. H. M. Kirk-Greene, *Crisis and Conflict in Nigeria: A Documentary Sourcebook, 1966–1970, Vol. 1* (London: Oxford University Press, 1971), 127–129.

Chapter Four

Lieutenant Colonel (Later General) Yakubu Gowon

BIOGRAPHICAL NOTES ON LIEUTENANT COLONEL (LATER GENERAL) YAKUBU GOWON

Lieutenant Colonel (later General) Yakubu Gowon was born in Lur, Pankshin, Plateau State, on October 19, 1934. He attended St. Bartholomew School, Wusasa, near Zaria, from 1939 to 1949. He continued his schooling in the Government College, later renamed Barewa College in Zaria. Gowon started his military career in 1954 as officer cadet in Ghana in the Officer Cadet Training School, Teshie, Ghana. In 1955, he continued training in Eaton Hall, Chester, England; and between 1955 and 1956 was enrolled in the Royal Military Academy in Sandhurst, England. Gowon was commissioned second lieutenant on December 21, 1956.

More military training followed in 1957 at the Young Officers' College, Hythe Warminster, England. On his return to Nigeria, he was posted as second lieutenant in the Fourth Battalion, Nigerian Regiment at Ibadan. Between 1960 and 1961, he was the adjutant of the Fourth Battalion. In that capacity, he was a member of the Nigerian contingent to the United Nations peacekeeping mission in the Congo (now Zaire) between 1960 and 1961.

He became the staff captain-A at the Nigerian Army Headquarters in Lagos in August 1961. By December of the same year through to December 1962, he was seconded to Staff College at Camberly, England. On his return to Nigeria, he was promoted major in December 1962. He returned to Luluabourg in Congo in 1963 as brigade major.

On his redeployment to Nigeria in 1963, Gowon was promoted lieutenant colonel and appointed adjutant general of the Nigerian Army. Lieutenant Colonel Gowon became the first Nigerian to hold that post. In 1965 he attended a Joint Services Staff College in the United Kindgom again, and

Lieutenant-Colonel Yakubu Gowon. 2nd Nigerian Military Head of State and Commander-in-Chief of the Nigerian Armed Forces, July 29, 1966–July 29, 1975. Born: October 19, 1934 in Lur, Pankshin in Plateau State, Nigeria. Source: Courtesy of the federal ministry of information, Lagos, Nigeria, 1967.

became the chief of army, Nigerian Army in January 1966, following the military coup in Lagos, January 1966.

The second military coup of July 29, 1966 catapulted Yakubu Gowon to the head of the Federal Military Government and commander in chief of the Armed Forces of the Federal Republic of Nigeria from August 1, 1966 to July 29, 1975. He was promoted major general in June 1967, and promoted general October 1, 1971.

Under Gowon's leadership, Nigeria was divided into twelve states on May 27, 1967 (see Figure 4.1), thereby depriving the former Eastern Region its vital access to the Atlantic Ocean. The Eastern Region of Nigeria, in a quick reaction to the state creation, seceeded as the Republic of Biafra on May 30, 1967. Also, the state creation cordoned off the minority ethnic residents in that region, thus diffusing their loyalites and support for the Republic of Bi-afra. In June, 1967, Nigeria was plunged into a police action, which foreshad-owed a full-blown civil war of national unity. The three-year civil war ended on January 15, 1970. Nigeria remained united under Gowon's aggressive policies of national reconciliation, rehabilitation, and reconstruction. Gowon was overthrown on July 29, 1975 by another military coup while away in Kampala, Uganda on an Organization of African Unity's (OAU) summit of heads of state.

After losing power, General Gowon went into exile in England. He resumed studies while there to earn degrees in political science, and graduated with the doctorate degree in political science from the University of Warwick, Conventry, England. While in England, Gowon was implicated by a military tribunal that investigated the abortive coup of February 13, 1976, that took the life of General Ramat Murtala Mohammed, the officer who succeeded Gowon in the July 29, 1975 coup. This implication meant that he was dismissed from the Nigerian Army and stripped of his rank and benefits. In 1983, the Second Republic's civilian president Shehu Usman Shagari pardoned Gowon and restored his rank and all his military benefits.

The ascension speech that brought Yakubu Gowon to power on August 29, 1966 followed a countercoup masterminded by Nigerian Army officers of Northern origin, allegedly in retaliation for the first military coup of January

Figure 4.1.   1967 Political Map of Nigeria with Twelve States. Source: Peter P. Ekeh (ed) *Dilemma of Nationhood: An African Analysis of the Biafran Conflict 1972.*

15, 1966 that was reportedly led by Igbo officers of the Nigerian Army, in which mostly Northern civilians and military officers were killed. In the ascension, Gowon called for calm and national unity, and preservation of law and order.[1]

THE FULL TEXT OF THE ASCENSION SPEECH BY LIEUTENANT COLONEL YAKUBU GOWON, HEAD OF THE NATIONAL MILITARY GOVERNMENT AND SUPREME COMMANDER AND COMMANDER IN CHIEF OF THE NIGERIAN ARMED FORCES BROADCAST TO THE NATION ON AUGUST 1, 1966

My Fellow Countrymen,[2]

The year 1966 has certainly been a fateful year for our beloved country, Nigeria. I have been brought to the position today of having to shoulder the grave responsibilities of this country. With the consent of the majority of the Armed Forces and members of the Supreme Military Council, as a result of the unfortunate incident that occurred on the early morning of 29th of July 1966. However, before I dwell on the sad issue of 29th of July 1966, I would like to recall to you the sad and unfortunate incident of January 15th 1966 which bears relevance.

According to certain well known facts which have so far not been disclosed to the Nation and the world, the country was plunged into a national disaster by the grave and unfortunate action taken by a section of the Army against the public. By this, I mean that a group of officers in conjunction with certain civilians decided to overthrow the legal government of the day, but their efforts were thwarted by the inscrutable discipline and loyalty of the great majority of the Army and the other members of the Armed Forces and the Police. The Army was called upon to take up the reins of the government until such time that law and order has been restored.

The attempt to overthrow the government of the day was done by eliminating political leaders and high ranking Army officers, a majority of whom came from a particular section of the country. The Prime Minister lost his life during the uprising. But for the outstanding discipline and loyalty of the members of the Army who were most affected and the other members of the Armed Forces and the police, the situation probably could have degenerated into a civil war.

There followed a period of determined effort of reconstruction ably shouldered by Major-General J.T.U. Aguiyi-Ironsi, but unfortunately certain persons caused suspicion and grave doubts of the Government's sincerity in several quarters. This coupled with the already unpleasant experience of 15th January too fresh in the minds of a majority of the people, certain parts of the country decided to agitate against the military regime which has hitherto enjoyed countrywide support. It was unfortunately followed by serious rioting and bloodshed in many cities and towns in the North. There followed a period of uneasy calm until the early hours of 29th July 1966 when the country was once again plunged into another very serious and grave situation-the second in seven months.

The position on early morning of 29th July was a report from Abeokuta Garrison that there was a mutiny and that two senior and one junior Army officers from a particular section of the country were killed. This soon spread to Ibadan and Ikeja. More casualties were reported in these places. The Supreme Commander was by this time at Ibadan attending the National Rulers Conference and was due to return on the afternoon of July 29th July. The government lodge was reportedly attacked and the last report was that he and the West Military Governor were both kidnapped by some soldiers. Up till now, there is no confirmation of their whereabouts. The situation was soon brought under control in these places.

Very shortly afterwards at about the same time there was a report that there were similar disturbances among the troops in the North and that a section of the troops had taken control of all military stations in the North as well. The units at Enugu and the Garrison at Benin were not involved. All is now quiet and I can assure the public that I shall do all in my power to stop any further bloodshed and restore law, order, and confidence in all parts of the country with your co-operation and good will.

I have now come to the most difficult part but most important of this statement. I am doing it conscious of the great disappointment and heartbreak it will cause all true and sincere lovers of Nigeria and of the Nigerian Unity, both at home and abroad, especially our brothers in the Commonwealth. As a result of the recent event and the other previous similar ones, I have come to strongly believe that we cannot honestly and sincerely continue in this wise, as the basis for trust and confidence in our country in our unitary systems of government has not been able to stand the test of time. I have already remarked on the issue in question. Suffice it to say that putting all considerations to test, political, economic as well as social, the basis for unity is not there, or is so badly rocked not only once but several times. I therefore feel that we should review the issue of our national standing and see if we can help stop the country from drifting away into utter destruction. With the general consensus of opinion of all military Governors and other members of the Supreme and Executive Councils, a decree will soon be issued to lay a sound foundation of this objective.

Fellow countrymen, I sincerely hope we shall be able to resolve most of the problems that have disunited us in the past and really come to respect and trust one another in accordance with all known codes of good conduct and etiquette.

All Foreigners are assured of their personal safety and should have no fear of being molested.

I intend to continue the policy laid down in the statement by the Supreme Commander of the 16th January, 1966 published on 26th January, 1966.

We shall also honour all international treaty obligations and commitments and all financial agreements and obligations entered into by the previous Government.

We are desirous of maintaining good diplomatic relationship with all countries. We therefore consider any foreign interference in any form will be regarded as an act of aggression.

All members of the Armed Forces are requested to keep within their barracks except on essential duties and when ordered from Supreme Headquarters. Troops must not terrorize the public, as such actions will discredit the new National Military Government. Any act of looting or sabotage will be dealt with severely. You are to remember that your task is to help restore law and order and confidence in the public in time of crisis.

I am convinced that with your cooperation and understanding we shall be able to pull the country out of its present predicament.

I promise you that I shall do all I can to return to civil Rule as soon as it can be arranged. I also intend to pursue most vigorously the question of the release of political prisoners.

Fellow countrymen, give me your support and I shall endeavour to live up to expectation.

Thank you and Good Morning.

NOTES

1. Isawa J. Elaigwu, *Gowon: The Bibliography of a Soldier-Statesman* (Ibadan, Nigeria: West Books Publishers, Ltd., 1985); "Yakubu Gowon." *The Columbia Encyclopedia, Sixth Edition,* 2008. http://www.encyclopedia.com/doc/1e1.Gowon-Ya.html,accessed on January 9, 2009. See also, Mike Okoye, ed., *Towards A Better Nigeria* (Ikeja, Nigeria: Times Books Ltd., n.d.).

2. Full Text of Broadcast by Lt. Col. Yakubu Gowon, Head of the National Military Government and Supreme Commander of the Nigerian Armed Forces. *Nigerian Newsletter: A Publication of the Embassy of the Federal Republic of Nigeria, Information Division* (Cairo: Egypt, 1966), 1–3.

Chapter Five

Brigadier (Later General) Murtala Ramat Mohammed

BIOGRAPHICAL NOTES ON BRIGADIER (LATER GENERAL) MURTALA RAMAT MOHAMMED

General Murtala Ramat Mohammed was born on November 8, 1938 in Kano. His primary school education was at Cikin Gida and Gida Makama Primary School in Kano. He later attended Government College (now Barewa College) in Zaria until 1957.

He enlisted into the Nigerian Army in 1958. Mohammed was trained as an officer cadet in Sandhurst Royal Academy in England. In completing his studies, he was commissioned second lieutenant in 1961 and assigned to the Nigerian Army Signals same year.

In 1961 Mohammed was appointed aide-de-camp (ADC) to Chief (Dr.) M.A. Majekodunmi, the Federal Government appointed administrator of the Western Region of Nigeria that was undergoing serious political and cultural upheaval as well as identity crises due to local elections in May 1962. The government of the Western Region was suspended.

In 1963, he became the officer in charge of the First Brigade Signal Troop in Kaduna. He returned to Caterick, England for an intensive course in telecommunications and military signals. On his return to Nigeria in 1964, he was promoted major and appointed officer commanding, One Signal Squadron in Apapa, Lagos. By 1965 Murtala was made the acting chief of Army Signals.

When the January 15, 1966 military coup struck, Mohammed was promoted lieutenant colonel and became the inspector of signals in Lagos until the second military coup of July 29, 1966.

The outbreak of the Nigerian civil war in 1967 saw Lieutenant Colonel Murtala Mohammed as leader of the newly established Second Infantry Division, and he later became the first general officer commanding the

Brigadier (Later General) Murtalla Ramat Mohammed. 3rd Nigerian Military Head of State and Commander-in-Chief of the Nigerian Armed Forces, July 29, 1975–February 13, 1976. Born: November 8, 1938 in Kano, Kano State, Nigeria. Died: February 13, 1976, assassinated in Ikoyi, Lagos, Nigeria. Source: Courtesy of the Nigerian permanent mission at the United Nations, New York, USA.

division in August of that year. He was recalled to Lagos in August 1968 and appointed the inspector of signals and promoted colonel later that year.

Murtala Mohammed attended more courses in the Joint Services Staff College in England, and on his return to Nigeria was promoted brigadier in October 1971. In 1974 August Mohammed was promoted the federal commissioner (minister) for communications. This was his first foray into politics. But he still maintained his post as the inspector of army signals at the Army Headquarters in Apapa, Lagos.

At the official ending of the Nigerian-Biafran civil war on January 15, 1970, General Gowon made a National Day broadcast on Independence Day, October 1, 1970, promising to hand over power to a duly elected civilian government on October 1, 1976. However, during the 1974 Independence Day broadcast, Gowon announced that the 1976 date was unrealistic. Between 1974 and 1975 when he was deposed, there were outcries from all over the country and abroad, deriding him for changing his mind and for not making crucial decisions toward the promised transition to civil rule.

Figure 5.1. 1976 Political Map of Nigeria with Nineteen States. Source: Created by the author.

Then came the July 29, 1975 military coup that catapulted Mohammed to the head of state and commander in chief of the Armed Forces of the Federal Republic of Nigeria, replacing General Yakubu Gowon. In January 1976, Murtala Mohammed was promoted general.

General Murtala Mohammed was married to Mrs. Ajoke Mohammed. He was assassinated in an abortive coup on February 13, 1976. The speech of his ascension the follows has been described by many as one of the most dynamic, concise, and precise speeches of action by any Nigerian leader since independence.[1] He reconfigured the political map of Nigeria with the creation of seven more states in 1976 before his death. See Figure 5.1.

THE FULL TEXT OF THE ASCENSION SPEECH BROADCAST TO THE NATION BY HIS EXCELLENCY, BRIGADIER MURTALA RAMAT MOHAMMED, HEAD OF THE FEDERAL MILITARY GOVERNMENT AND COMMANDER IN CHIEF OF THE NIGERIAN ARMED FORCES, JULY 30, 1975

Fellow Nigerians,[2] events of the past few years have indicated that despite our great human and material resources, the Government has not been able to fulfill the legitimate expectations of our people.

Nigeria has been left to drift.

This situation, if not arrested, would inevitably have resulted in chaos and even bloodshed.

In the endeavour to build a strong, united and virile nation, Nigerians have shed much blood; the thought of further bloodshed, for whatever reason, must, I am sure, be revolting to our people.

The Armed Forces, having examined the situation, came to the conclusion that certain changes were inevitable.

After the civil war, the affairs of State, hitherto a collective responsibility became characterized by lack of consultation, indecision, indiscipline and, even, neglect.

Indeed, the public at large became disillusioned and disappointed by these developments.

The trend was clearly incompatible with the philosophy and image of a corrective regime.

Unknown to the general public, the feeling of disillusion was also evident among members of the Armed Forces whose administration was neglected, but, who, out of sheer loyalty to the nation, and, in the hope that there would be a change, continued to suffer in silence.

Things got to a stage where the head of the administration became virtually inaccessible, even, to official advisors; and when advice was tendered, it was often ignored.

Responsible opinion, including advice by eminent Nigerians, traditional rulers, intellectuals, etc. was similarly discarded.

The leadership, either by design or default, had become too insensitive to the true feelings and yearnings of the people. The nation was thus being plunged inexorably into chaos.

It was obvious that matters could not, and should not, be allowed to continue in this manner and, in order to give the nation a new lease of life, and a sense of direction, the following decisions were taken: the removal of General Yakubu Gowon as Head of the Federal Military Government and Commander-in-Chief of the Armed Forces; the retirement of General Yakubu Gowon from the Armed Forces ; the retirement of General Yakubu Gown from the Armed Forces in the present rank of General with full benefits, in recognition of his past services to the Nation; General Gowon will be free to return to the country as soon as conditions permit; he will be free to pursue any legitimate undertakings of his choice in any part of the country. His personal safety and freedom and those of his family will be guaranteed.

The following members of the Armed Forces are retired with immediate effect: Vice-Admiral J. E. A. Wey, Chief of Staff, Supreme Headquarters; Major-General Hassan Katsina, Deputy Chief of Staff, Supreme Headquarters; Major-General David Ejoor, Chief of Staff (Army); Rear-Admiral Nelson Soroh, Chief of Naval Staff: Brigadier E. E. Ikwue, Chief of Air Staff; and all other officers of the rank of Major-General (or equivalent) and above: Alhaji Kim Salem, Inspector-General of Police; Chief T.A. Fagbola, Deputy Inspector-General of Police.

Also with immediate effect, all the present Military Governors, and the Administrator of the East Central State, have been relieved of their appointments and retired.

As you are already aware, new appointments have been made as follows: Brigadier Olusegun Obasanjo, Chief of Staff, Supreme Headquarters; Brigadier T.Y. Danjuma, Chief of Army Staff; Colonel John Yisa Doko, Chief of Air Staff; Commodore Adelanwa, Chief of Naval Staff; Mr. M.D. Yusufu, Inspector-General of Police.

New Military Governors have also been appointed for the States as follows: Benue-Plateau, Colonel Abdullahi Mohammed; East-Central, Colonel Anthony Ochefu; Kano, Lt. Colonel Sanni Bello; Kwara, Colonel Ibrahim Taiwo; Lagos, Captain Lawal (NN); Mid-West, Colonel George Innih; North-Central, Lt.Colonel Usman Jibrin; North-East, Lt. Colonel Muhammed Buhari; North-West, Lt. Colonel Umaru Mohammed: Rivers, Lt. Colonel Zamani Lekwot; South East, Lt.Colonel Paul Omu; West, Captain Akin Aduwo (NN).

The structure of Government has been re-organized. There will now be three organs of Government, at the Federal Level, namely: the Supreme Military Council; the National Council of State; and the Federal Executive Council.

There will, of course, continue to be Executive Council at the State level.

The reconstituted Supreme Council will comprise the following: the Head of State and Commander-in-Chief of the Armed Forces; Brigadier Olusegun Obasanjo, Chief of Staff, Supreme Headquarters; Brigadier T.Y. Danjuma, Chief of Army Staff; Commodore Adelanwa, Chief of Naval Staff; Colonel John Yisa Doko, Chief of Air Staff; M.D. Yusuf, Inspector-General of Police. General Officers Commanding: 1st Division, Brigadier Julius Alani Akinrinade; 2nd Division, Brigadier Martin Adamu; 3rd Division, Brigadier Emmanuel Abisoye; Lagos Garrison Organization, Brigadier John Obada; Colonel Joseph Garba; Lt. Colonel Shehu Yar'Adua; Brigadier James Oluleye; Brigadier Iliya Bisalla; Colonel Ibrahim Babangida; Lt. Colonel Muktar Muhammed; Colonel Dan Suleiman; Captain Olufemi Olumide (NN); Captain H. Husaini Abdullahi (NN); Mr. Adamu Suleiman, Commissioner of Police; Lt. Colonel Alfred Aduloju; Lt. Commander Godwin Kanu (NN).

All Civil Commissioners in the Federal Executive Council are relieved of their appointment with immediate effect. The composition of the new Council will be announced shortly.

We will review the political programme and make an announcement in due course.

In the meantime, a panel will be set up to advise on the question of new States. A panel will also be set up to advise on the question of the Federal Capital.

With regard to the 1973 population census, it is now clear that whatever results are announced will not command general acceptance throughout the country. It has therefore been decided to cancel the 1973 population count.

Accordingly, for planning purposes, the 1963 census figures shall continue to be used. A panel will be set up to advise on the future of the Interim Common Services Agency (ICSA) and the Eastern States Interim Assets and Liabilities Agency (ESIALA).

The Second World Black and African Festival of Arts and Culture is postponed in view of the obvious difficulties in providing all the necessary facilities. Consultation will be held with the other participating countries with a view to fixing a new date.

Finally, we reaffirm the country's friendship with all countries.

Foreign nationals living in Nigeria will be protected. Foreign investments will also be protected. The Government will honour all obligations entered into by the previous Governments of the Federation.

We will also give continued active support to the Organization of African Unity, the United Nations Organization and the Commonwealth.

Fellow Countrymen, the tasks ahead of us calls for sacrifice and self-discipline at all levels of our society.

This Government will *not* tolerate indiscipline.

This Government will *not* condone abuse of office.

I appeal to you all to co-operate with the Government in our endeavour to give this nation a new lease of life.

This change in Government has been accomplished without shedding any blood; and we intend to keep it so.

Long Live the Federal Republic of Nigeria. Good night!

NOTES

1. Mike Okoye, ed., *Towards a Better Nigeria* (Ikeja, Nigeria: Times Books Ltd., n.d.).

2. Murtala Mohammed, *A Time for Action: Collected Speeches of His Excellency General Murtala Mohammed* (Lagos: Federal Ministry of Information, 1975). See also *News From Nigeria: A Publication of the Nigerian Consulate-General* (New York and San Francisco, October 4 and 26, 1975), 1–4.

Chapter Six

Brigadier (Later General) Olusegun Aremu Obasanjo

BIOGRAPHICAL NOTES ON BRIGADIER (LATER GENERAL) OLUSEGUN AREMU OBASANJO

Brigadier (later General) Olusegun Aremu Obasanjo was born on May 5, 1937 in Abeokuta, in today's Ogun State of Nigeria. He attended Baptist Boys' High School, Abeokuta. In 1958, he joined the Nigerian Army and trained at Mons Officer Cadets' School, Aldershot, England. From there, he attended the Royal Engineers Young Officers' Course in Shrivenham, England.

He was commissioned full lieutenant in 1959 and seconded to the Fifth Battalion of the Nigerian Army in Kaduna. He served in the Congo (now Zaire) in 1960 as part of the United Nations peacekeeping contingent.

In 1963, Obasanjo was promoted to captain, and became the commander of the engineering unit of the Nigerian Army, and attached to the Indian Army Engineering School in Kirkee, India.

General Obasanjo was promoted lieutenant in 1967, and appointed commander Second Area Command of the Nigerian Army the same year. He was made commander Second (Rear) Division in Ibadan in 1967 and later was made the commander of the Ibadan Garrison from 1967–1969.

He was promoted colonel in 1969 and made the commander, Third Marine Commando Division of the Nigerian Army. One noticeable event in the life of Olusegun Obasanjo is that he accepted the surrender of Biafran forces on the battlefield on January 12, 1970. He was made the commander of the Army Corps of Engineers after the end of the Nigerian-Biafran war in 1970.

In 1972, Obasanjo was promoted brigadier. His first political appointment came in January 1975, when he was made the federal commissioner (minister) of works and housing, until July 1975. The July 29, 1975 coup made

General Olusegun Aremu Obasanjo. 4th Military Head of State of Nigerian and Commander-in-Chief of the Nigerian Armed Forces February 13, 1976–October 1, 1979. Born: March 5, 1937 in Abeokuta, Ogun State, Nigeria. Source: Courtesy of the federal ministry of information, Lagos, Nigeria, 1976.

Obasanjo the chief of staff, Supreme Headquarters, Lagos from that date until February 13, 1976, when he became the head of state.

He had just been promoted lieutenant general in January 1976, when the coup that killed his boss, General Murtalla Mohammed catapulted him to the head of the Federal Military Government of Nigeria and commander in chief of the Nigerian Armed Forces. He also became the chairman of the Supreme Military Council. He held these positions until he voluntarily handed over power to a civilian government under Shagari on October 1, 1979.

The ascension speech of General Obasanjo that follows was given during a very somber, trying, reflective, and confusing period in Nigeria, when one of the country's most dynamic and well-admired leaders was assassinated on February 13, 1976, in an abortive coup, just after 205 days in office. Obasanjo had to calm, comfort, and persuade the people to come together and to continue to believe in the hope of a united Nigeria and her potentials and possibilities for greatness, even when despair seemed to be the dominant emotion at the time.[1]

THE FULL TEXT OF THE ASCENSION SPEECH BY HIS EXCELLENCY, LIEUTENANT GENERAL OLUSEGUN OBASANJO HEAD OF THE FEDERAL MILITARY GOVERNMENT AND COMMANDER IN CHIEF OF THE NIGERIAN ARMED FORCES BROADCAST TO THE NATION ON FEBRUARY 14, 1976

Fellow Citizens,[2]

We are once again passing through a critical period in the history of this country; for me personally, this has been one of the saddest moments in my life.

The Supreme Military Council has already announced the assassination of His Excellency, General Murtala Mohammed. We will mourn the passing away of one of the greatest sons of Nigeria.

I had the privilege of serving as the Chief of Staff, Supreme Headquarters, under him and I have no doubt in my mind that the late General Mohammed gave this country a unique sense of direction and purpose.

We are all now obliged to continue with these policies laid down by the Supreme Military Council under the dynamic leadership of General Mohammed.

From the account of the tragic incident gathered so far, the late Head of State was shot yesterday on his way to the office. His aide de camp, Lt. A. Akinsehinwa, his orderly and driver who were with him in the car were also killed.

The Governor of Kwara State, Colonel Ibrahim Taiwo, who was abducted yesterday, was shot dead and his body was found in a shallow grave outside Ilorin.

Colonel Dumuje was shot and wounded in another location in Lagos on his way to the office.

This dastardly act was committed by a few dissident troops organized by Lieutenant Colonel B.S. Dimka of the Nigeria Army Physical Training Corps. Many arrests have already been made and the Supreme Military Council has set up a Military Board of Enquiry to carry out full scale investigations into the incident and the planning of the assassinations.

I wish to assure the nation that the Supreme Military Council has taken a firm decision that all those found to be guilty will be summarily dealt with in a military way.

I therefore appeal to all sections of Nigeria not to take law into their hands. They can be rest assured that the Federal Military Government would see to it that justice is done.

As you have heard in the statement by the Supreme Military Council, I have been called upon against my personal wish and desire to serve as the new Head of State. But I have accepted this honour in the interest of the nation and in memory of the late Head of State.

I know that he would have wished that somebody should continue the task of nation building from where he left off.

I have worked very closely with him and I have shared his beliefs and commitments to the Federal Government's policies and actions.

I believe and feel strongly committed to all we have been doing. I can pay him no better tribute than to continue in the spirit with which he had led this country—that of complete dedication.

All policies of the Federal Military Government continue as before and all Ministries should continue their usual duties.

This tragic incident can only lead to a greater dedication to the upliftment and progress of this nation.

This situation was brought swiftly under control because of the loyalty and dedication of the Armed Forces and the Police. The Armed Forces and Police deserve praise and appreciation from the government and people of this country.

Reports have also reached me from all over the country of public support from various sections of the community. The Federal Military Government is very much gratified by this demonstration of loyalty and support.

At the end of the seven-day mourning period which, was announced earlier, Friday the 20th of February 1976, is hereby declared a public holiday to enable all Nigerians to offer special prayers in all places of worship.

Finally, I will like to appeal to all of you for calm and to avoid any action that might cause a breach of the peace.

This is the period that calls for continued vigilance and it is the duty of one and all to maintain this vigilance in order to preserve the stability of the nation.

NOTES

1. Patrick Avwenagbiku, *Olusegun Obasanjo and His Footprints* (Abuja, Nigeria: Metro Publishers, 2000); also, "General Abubakar Keeps His Word, Obasanjo Takes Over: Nigeria Has High Hopes in Stable Democracy," (Abuja, Nigeria: Publications of the Federal Ministry of Information & Culture, 1999).

2. This speech was published in the London-based magazine as "No Policy Change in Nigeria," *West Africa* (February 23, 1976): 233. See also Mike Okoye, ed., *Toward a Better Nigeria: A Selection of Notable Speeches by Nigerian Leaders, 1957–1989* (Ikeja, Nigeria: The Times Books Ltd., n.d.), 200–201.

Chapter Seven

Alhaji Shehu Usman Shagari

BIOGRAPHICAL NOTES ON
PRESIDENT ALHAJI SHEHU USMAN SHAGARI

Alhaji Shehu Usman Shagari was born in the village of Shagari on February 25, 1925 in Sokoto State. As was common at the time of his birth, Shehu Shagari's very earliest training was in the Quranic schools in his village. His early formal education started at the Yabo Elementary School, 1931–1935 in Shagari. He went from there to Sokoto Middle School, 1936–1940, and then to Kaduna College, 1941–1944. Shagari attended the Teacher Training College in Zaria, from 1944 to 1952.

Between 1953 and 1958, he worked as a temporary or visiting teacher at Sokoto Province. He later veered into politics when he became the secretary of the Northern People's Congress (NPC) in the Sokoto branch from 1951 through 1956. An overlapping assignment and responsibility at this time was as a member of the Federal Scholarship Board, 1954–1958.

His first political appointment was in 1954 when he was elected to the Federal House of Representatives for Sokoto West, 1954–1966. He was the parliamentary secretary to Nigeria's first and only prime minister, Alhaji Sir Abubakar Tafawa Balewa from 1958–1959. In 1958, he was appointed the federal minister of commerce and industries; federal minister of economic development, 1959–1960; federal minister of pensions, 1960–1962; federal minister of internal affairs, 1962–1965; federal minster of works, 1965–1966. With the first military coup in January 1966, Shehu Shagari retired to his home state in Sokoto to a life of a farmer. This short retirement ended in 1967 when he was appointed secretary, Sokoto Province Education Development Fund, 1967–1968. This was followed by the appointment as the commissioner (minister) for establishments, North-Western State, 1968–1969.

Alhaji Shehu Usman Shagari. 2nd Democratic President of Nigeria and Commander-in-Chief of the Nigerian Armed Forces, October 1, 1979–December 31, 1983. Born: February 25, 1925 in Shagari, Sokoto State, Nigeria. Source: Heinemann Educational Books, Ibadan, Nigeria, 2001.

Alhaji Shehu Usman Shagari assumed more important and prominent federal appointments in the succeeding years after the Nigerian-Biafran War. He was made the federal commissioner for economic development, rehabilitation and reconstruction, 1970–1971. He served in the Federal Ministry of Finance and later as commissioner for finance, 1971–1975. Within this period too, he was governor of World Bank as well as member of the International Monetary Fund (IMF) Committee of Twenty.

He was appointed the chairman of the Peugeot Automobile of Nigeria in 1979. His interests in politics peaked again in 1978 when the ban on politics was lifted. He became a founding member of the National Party of Nigeria (NPN) in 1978, and later its presidential candidate in the 1979 and 1983 elections. In both instances, he emerged the winner.

In 1979, Shehu Usman Shagari became the second Nigerian elected president. He was, at this election of 1979, the first Nigerian executive president. Again, in 1983 he won his second term to the presidency, only to be toppled by a military coup in the dying hours of December 31, 1983.

The two inaugural speeches that follow are both historical and political in that both mirror and document the historical exigencies that necessitated the rise and demise of Nigeria's perpetual search for lasting democratic governance.[1]

THE FULL TEXT OF THE OPEN-AIR INAUGURAL SPEECH AT THE TAFAWA BALEWA SQUARE DURING THE FIRST INAUGURATION CEREMONY OF NIGERIA'S EXECUTIVE PRESIDENT AFTER THE SWEARING-IN OF HIS EXCELLENCY, PRESIDENT SHEHU USMAN SHAGARI, HEAD OF THE FEDERAL GOVERNMENT OF NIGERIA AND COMMANDER IN CHIEF OF THE NIGERIAN ARMED FORCES ON OCTOBER 1, 1979

We have just participated in a solemn ceremony marking an important milestone in the history of our nation. Before God and before you all, I have subscribed to a solemn oath of office to serve the country, defend her constitution and uphold the principles of justice without fear or favour. I shall do my utmost to fulfill the oath of my office and discharge its obligations faithfully.

I would like to assure all Nigerians and the whole world that I understand and fully accept the challenges and responsibilities of the office of President. I want to assure you further that I will discharge my obligation to my country to the very best of my ability. In the office of the President I have equal responsibility to all our people irrespective of their political, ethnic or religious persuasion. Accordingly, we should all regard today's celebration as a national event.

I urge all Nigerians to join me in the onerous task of nation building. We all urgently require to harness our resources and energies and to devote them to the development of our country. God has blessed us in abundance with these resources. Let us use them to develop our country. Let us also help our fellow humans who may be less fortunate than ourselves.

It is proper at this juncture to pay tribute to all those who have worked so hard in the past thirteen years, to keep this country together, and to strengthen the foundation for unity, peace and progress. Our military leaders who have been at the helm of affairs since 1966 have done their best for our country. They succeeded in a large measure in unifying us and making us think first as Nigerians. I pay tribute to them and salute them on your behalf.

We must pay our respect and give our thanks to the outgoing Head of the Federal Military Government and Commander-in-Chief of the Armed Forces,

General Olusegun Obasanjo; to Members of the Supreme Military Council; to the Service Chiefs and to all members of the Armed Forces, to the Police and members of the public service for their great contribution in fostering a stronger and more united Nigeria.

Today, we call on all of them again to rise and work with us for the greater glory of our fatherland. On my part, I promise that I will spare no effort to ensure the peace, unity, stability and progress of this nation.

This is not the time and place to spell out the programmes of our government. However, I think it is in order to refer broadly to the responsibilities before us. First, our immediate responsibility is to serve the best interest of Nigeria; to feed and house ourselves better; to educate our children and prepare them to make a fuller contribution towards the building of a more modern society. Next we have a special responsibility for Africa and the African wherever he may be. It will be the cardinal principle of this administration to ensure that all the oppressed peoples of Africa regain their freedom and dignity.

We will extend our whole-hearted co-operation to all African countries and organization to bring about the unity of the African people and the rapid emancipation and development of all the countries of Africa.

It is our strong desire to contribute to world unity, peace, progress and cooperation. We extend our hands of friendship to all the peoples of the world.

At this juncture, let me thank all of you who have participated in this impressive and momentous ceremony. I should like especially to salute the school children for their endurance and patience in preparing for this occasion.

May I take this opportunity also to congratulate all the elected members of the National Assembly and to inform them that the proclamation to convene the first Session of the National Assembly as required of me by the constitution will shortly be made.

Finally, fellow citizens, as we depart from this arena, let us dedicate ourselves anew to move forward in peace, unity and with a strong determination to succeed in meeting the challenges ahead.[2]

THE FULL TEXT OF THE FIRST INAUGURATION ADDRESS DURING THE NATIONWIDE EVENING BROADCAST BY HIS EXCELLENCY, PRESIDENT SHEHU USMAN SHAGARI, CHIEF EXECUTIVE OF THE FEDERAL GOVERNMENT OF NIGERIA, AND COMMANDER IN CHIEF OF THE NIGERIAN ARMED FORCES, ON OCTOBER 1, 1979

Fellow Nigerians,[3]

We have witnessed today the birth of the Second Republic of Nigeria. With the Swearing-in Ceremony this morning, I have formally assumed office as your First Executive President. I want to take this opportunity to thank all of you for your patience and support throughout the period of transition.

The Second Republic has come after almost fourteen years of military rule in the course of which we went through a civil war. Today our new constitution comes into effect; a constitution carefully drawn up by ourselves for ourselves. We are assuming office as a result of a free, democratic and peaceful election. We must be proud of this, and we must be grateful to God and to all those who have worked so hard to make it possible.

This is an occasion which calls for sober reflection on the problem of the First Republic in order to appreciate the magnitude of the tasks ahead.

The problems of creating a national government, a viable economic base and the integration of the various ethnic groups in Nigeria in fairness and without acrimony, overwhelmed the First Republic. These problems are still with us. And it is our determination to do our utmost to contribute to their resolution. This Second Republic is a great challenge and a new opportunity for all of us.

This administration is determined that the slogan of "One Nation, One Destiny," shall be translated into reality. We are not so naïve to think that nationalism is a natural phenomenon which comes about automatically as we grow. It has not been so in any part of the world. National integration requires hard work. There is need for a dedicated leadership and citizenry imbued with faith to cultivate a widespread national feeling for "One Nigeria."

I am convinced that these goals are attainable because we are at this time operating in more auspicious circumstances. Surely, we have learnt great lessons from the past and we have no need to permit divisive factors to continue to undermine our national well-being.

I urge all Nigerians to join me in working with resolution for the attainment of these goals. The first thing is for all those who have participated in the recent elections to work together whether they won or lost.

Now that the elections are over, we must act as good sportsmen, set aside differences and harness our energies to the task of nation building. I would like to enjoin all our State Governors to bear in mind that regardless of their party affiliation, the interest of the nation is supreme. The State which each of them governs is simply a part of Nigeria and a part cannot indeed be greater than a whole. I congratulate them on their new position and sincerely urge them as well as every other citizen of this great country to join hands with me in facing the great task ahead. For my part, I assure you all that the Federal Government will give equal treatment to each State of the Federation regardless of the party in power in that state.

Fellow citizens, great challenges and opportunities are before us. While noticeable achievements have been made, the problems of our economy have become even more complicated. There has been a steep rise in the rate of inflation in Nigeria as is the case all over the world. Nevertheless we are dedicated to building a viable economy by fostering broad mass participation and the utilization of local resources. This way we shall enhance our economic independence.

Our key domestic programmes are in the sectors of agriculture, housing, education, health, industry and the new federal capital. Our first great challenge is agriculture.

Throughout the election campaigns, our party, the National Party of Nigeria, made strong commitments to the people of this country, rapidly to develop and improve agriculture. For centuries, generations of Nigerian farmers have struggled with technologies invented by our ancestors to meet the demands of a long gone age, and to wrest a living from a weary and exhausted soil. I personally spoke many times on our policy for a "Green Revolution." There is need to provide adequate food for every family. There is need to stop the current drain of foreign exchange on the importation of food. We are determined to transform Nigerian agriculture to the point where Nigeria will be self-sufficient in food production, and ensure that the money is more effectively utilized. We shall devote more manpower and technological resources to increase our agricultural productivity and expand our agro-based industries. We shall immediately map out strategies to encourage Nigerians to engage in fruitful agricultural activities. In addition, we shall encourage joint ventures with foreign partners to establish farms as commercially profitable enterprises to produce food as well as raw materials. New emphasis will be placed on modern methods of food storage, distribution and processing.

Because of the importance we attach to housing we shall establish a Ministry of Housing and Environment. Good shelter is recognized by our government as the right of every Nigerian. There is no doubt that to meet acceptable human standards, Nigeria will require millions of additional housing units in the urban as well as in the rural areas. Our current resources and industrial base cannot immediately produce enough housing to meet our current demand. However, we will vigorously attack the problem of housing. In the urban areas we will immediately create new layouts to be serviced by adequate drainage systems, roads, and other infrastructures. Through an improved financing system, urban dwellers will have more credit to build their own houses. In rural areas and small towns, the establishment of rural housing co-operatives will be encouraged. Financial institutions will be encouraged to make loans available to needy low-income families who wish to build or rebuild their own houses.

A primary objective of our housing policy is to create the right atmosphere for a rapid increase in home ownership. We strongly believe that home ownership will lead to family pride and healthy surroundings in every

Nigerian community. Since the cost of building a house is directly related to the cost of building materials, our government will encourage the local production of building materials. Continuous research will be undertaken and factories will be established for the local manufacture of durable and low cost building materials.

Education is our next priority programme:

Fellow citizens, now that the elections are over and October 1 is here, the realities of the problem of education stares us boldly in the face. This government accepts the responsibility for free education at all levels as has been provided for in the constitution. The main problem however is how to make education accessible to all, given the current financial constraints and inadequacy of teachers and educational facilities. We need more schools, more teachers, more laboratories, more books, more desks, more playing fields, and numerous other supplies and equipment all of which are involved with the increase in enrollment. These cannot be found overnight.

My administration is irrevocably committed to making education a priority. We shall immediately expand the educational infrastructure in order to cope with demand at all levels of our educational system. We also plan to make education more qualitative and functional with a sound moral content. To this end, we shall improve the quality of teachers and conditions of service in order to attract them in the right number and quality. We shall encourage individuals and voluntary agencies to open schools as long as they meet government guidelines.

The need for technical manpower, and the rapid development of technology, demand that we maximize the use of all technical and vocational institutions in the country and establish many more. In this connection, we shall establish a Ministry of Science and Technology which will develop policies to be reflected throughout our educational system.

I like to emphasize that our overall policy seeks to provide education which will equip all recipients with the necessary attitudes, knowledge and skill to contribute to national development.

Directly related to these priority programmes both at home and abroad is the need to create a more suitable economic environment. There is need to transform our under-developed country into a modern industrialized society.

To achieve this objective requires the energy of all of us. Our government is determined to release the creative energies of enterprising Nigerians and encourage them to help develop the economy for the good of all.

I particularly call on the labour movement to rise up to the challenge of our time. I am aware of the constraints under which Nigerian workers have had to live in the immediate past. The wage-freeze in the era of biting inflation has had to be maintained in view of the resource constraints of our developing economy; but there are certainly limits beyond which no democratic government will wish to demand sacrifices from workers. The wage-freeze issue, the question of car loans, the question of labour independence and the restoration of free collective bargaining will rank as priorities in the labour policy of my government. Arrangements are on hand for a dialogue between government and the leaders of organized labour at which these issues will be reviewed. Thereafter, I will take the necessary action to effect remedies in the interests of the nation, and of the nation's workers. This Administration stands committed to ameliorate the conditions of Nigerian workers, through appropriate measures including consultation and legislation. However, we must all be determined to see that higher wages and better conditions of service are matched by higher productivity in the interest of national development.

As we develop our economy we shall be in a better position to provide the needed services and amenities for all our citizens. We shall be better equipped to improve our health and other social services programmed for the nation.

In the area of foreign policy, as your President, I will continue to advance and defend the cause of our great country before the world community of nations. It is our national will that Africa shall remain the cornerstone of our foreign policy. Also it is our national will that Africa shall be free, free of racial bigotry, free of oppression and free from the vestiges of colonialism. My government is determined to see the cause of justice and human decency prevail in Namibia, Zimbabwe and South Africa. We shall continue to support all forces of progress and oppose all forces of oppression in Africa and elsewhere. I hereby re-affirm our faith and support for the charter of the United Nations and the Universal Declaration of Human Rights, the charter of the Organization of African Unity, the Economic Community of West African States, and the Organization of Petroleum Exporting Countries. Our watchword shall always be the advancement of mankind and the enhancement of the cause of peace, prosperity and progress through mutual respect and co-operation between nations.

I wish to take this opportunity to pay tribute to members of our armed forces and to our immediate predecessors in office. They have successfully guided the destiny of our nation through most trying conditions. Their discipline, devotion to duty and loyalty to the country have been tested and proved beyond doubt. *I trust they will keep it up.*

You all remember when the government of General Murtala Mohammed and General Obasanjo came to power, they gave a pledge to return this nation to civil rule on October 1, 1979. They have kept their word as true men of honour and today the country has been duly handed over to a democratically elected government. History will indelibly record this nation's gratitude to their exemplary leadership, dedication, statesmanship and courage.

I want to conclude this address by greeting all Nigerians of all walks of life on this historic day. I salute our law enforcement agencies including the police and all those working in the public and private sectors, I salute all our traditional rulers, fathers of our communities and custodians of our cultural heritage. I also salute our religious leaders, custodians of faith and morals.

My fellow citizens, the task ahead is enormous and it is a task for all of us. Our government is committed to building a united, stable and prosperous nation. I need your contribution, co-operation and support. Nigeria can and must become a great and modern nation. Let us with true conscience and determination join hands and re-dedicate ourselves to the service of this great country so that it will be a place we can be, and shall all be, proud of. We cannot afford to fail in this task and by the Grace of God we shall succeed.

May God bless our country and may God bless you all.

A CONTEXTUAL PRELUDE TO THE SECOND INAUGURAL ADDRESS BY PRESIDENT ALHAJI SHEHU USMAN SHAGARI

In 1983, Shehu Shagari was reelected to his second term as the executive president of Nigeria's Second Republic. At this time Nigeria, as other countries then, was undergoing an economic misery. But Nigeria's case was worsened by the contentious reelection campaigns that had introduced mathematical calculations and permutations of what constitutes a two-thirds majority into the lexicon of Nigerian political discourse. But economic hard times plagued the nation the most. The expenses of a presidential system of government meant that the elected officials were drawing their living expenses from a depleting federal coffer, while the majority of Nigerians were hardly making ends meet. Destabilizing currents swept through a demoralized nation, wherein the elected officials seemed to lack redeeming alternatives.

President Shagari gave his second inaugural under the shadow of economic and political uncertainties for his administration and the country as a whole. The following speech is both a rhetorical marker and an artifact of the time and place.

THE FULL TEXT OF THE SECOND INAUGURAL ADDRESS BY HIS EXCELLENCY, PRESIDENT SHEHU SHAGARI, COMMANDER IN CHIEF OF THE NIGERIAN ARMED FORCES, DELIVERED ON THE TWENTY-THIRD INDEPENDENCE ANNIVERSARY AT THE BEGINNING OF HIS SECOND TERM OF OFFICE AS PRESIDENT ON OCTOBER 1, 1983 IN LAGOS.

Fellow Nigerians,[4] four years ago, in accordance with our Constitution, I was sworn in as the President of the Federal Republic of Nigeria and Commander-in-Chief of the Armed Forces. This inauguration ceremony on 1st October 1979 marked the end of almost 14 years of military rule. It marked the beginning of a new presidential system of government based on democracy. At the inception of the civilian administration four years ago, I pledged to uphold our Constitution, to ensure the continued existence of Nigeria as a virile and indivisible entity, and to serve our country to the very best of my ability.

I am happy to say with deep gratitude to Almighty God that we have achieved considerable success in the pursuit of these measures. During the last four years our experiment with the democratic process has been an unqualified success. Our country has enjoyed peace in her pursuit of the policy of self-sufficiency and self-reliance, especially in food production. To this end, we have constituted a green revolution programme, and I know that we are on the right course. We have started to achieve our target. We are providing houses for the people. Our efforts to develop the new federal capital have progressed steadily. In the education sector, we have pursued the policy of qualitative functional education with unremitting vigour. We have therefore increased the number of federal universities from 13 to 21, the latest being the National Open University. To provide a sound basis for our technical development, we have created seven universities of technology. We have completed one steel plant, three rolling mills and at the Ajaokuta complex, whose first phase has already been commissioned, work is continuing on the remaining phases.

Fellow Nigerians, that we have been able to record these achievements, despite the agonizing and harsh economic circumstances witnessed midway through our first term in office as a result of a severe global economic recession, was due to your co-operation and understanding.

As I speak to you today on the 23rd anniversary of our independence, we have just emerged from protracted general elections which have put to the test both our new democratic institutions and our will as a nation to support them in circumstances of severe economic condition. We have passed the test and our electorate has come of age in the sense that it has laid to rest many of the false assumptions about the nature of political loyalties in this country which is supposed to militate against the emergence of a national consensus in our political life. I must congratulate the electorate for exercising its constitutional obligation in a mature manner.

I wish also to place on record my gratitude and that of the entire nation to the Federal Electoral Commission, the law enforcement agencies, and the judiciary for a job well done. These institutions have, in spite of the many difficulties they faced in the performance of their duties, done everything in their power to ensure the success of our new democratic experiment. The elections are now over.

You have given me a clear mandate as your president for another term of four years. I am grateful to you for the honour and I accept the challenges with humility. I trust that with your patient co-operation and God's guidance, we shall succeed in our national endeavour of building a stronger and more prosperous Nigeria.

More than ever before, I ask for your continued co-operation and understanding because the magnitude of the task ahead of us demands nothing less. Although there are brighter prospects in the economic sphere, the situation is still far from normal. The world is still in the throes of the most severe economic depression since the second world war. The Nigerian economy could not be immune to the very adverse effects of the global economic recession. Indeed, our oil export earnings, which reached a peak of 23.4 billion dollars in 1980, declined to an estimated 9.6 billion dollars in 1983. Moreover, the exportable surplus of oil production is being gradually reduced by the growing domestic consumption of refined petroleum products. With the fall in oil revenues, the country is now faced with a growing shortage of foreign exchange. At the same time, our manufacturing sector, which is unhappily import-oriented, continues to weaken.

In the light of this unfavorable economic situation, we intend to reappraise and re-order our priorities. The Federal Government's annual expenditure will therefore be rationalized to reflect the re-ordering of investment priorities with emphasis on consolidating viable on-going projects in agriculture and industries, with the provision of infrastructural facilities. Concurrently, concerted efforts will be made to improve project implementation and monitoring. A number of on-going projects will therefore be reviewed. The proposed additional expenditure on the iron and steel industry will be re-examined with a possible re-phasing of completion dates. We will avoid entering into new commitments with high foreign exchange content. We will only give serious consideration to projects based on locally available resources, such as the petrochemical and LNG projects which will lead to the revitalization and diversification of the economy.

To bridge our yawning resource gap, efforts at internal resource generation will be intensified. In this regard, the exploitation and usage of our local resources have become so important in our quest for self-reliance that it will receive priority attention by the appropriate Ministries. Measures will be taken to ensure that government agencies take a lead in waste reduction in consonance with the dictates of these austere times. In this connection, unprofitable government ventures will be scrapped. Moreover, the recommendations of the various commissions set up to look into the operations of parastatals and other public enterprises will be implemented especially as they relate to the achievement of self-financing and cost-effectiveness. In the allocation of budget funds, greater emphasis will henceforth be placed on maintenance of plants and equipment rather than on purchase of new ones. In this regard, government will encourage the private sector to establish service industries.

To revive and stabilize the economy on a long-term basis, it is imperative that the country now begin the structural re-adjustment process required for renewed economic buoyancy. Macro-economic and sectorial policy changes will have to begin in order to shift resources to the productive sectors of the economy. We therefore intend to adopt a selective expenditure reduction in the 1984 budget so that on-going viable priority projects will not suffer. In pursuance of this objective, I intend to create a national planning commission which will be an expert body for the initiation and co-ordination of economic policy options and to ensure greater planning, discipline and efficiency. This commission which will be located in the presidency will, among other things, serve as the secretariat for the National Economic Council.

At this juncture, I wish to appeal to all governors in the nineteen states to ensure proper discipline and prudence in their general management of public funds. This is because no matter how well we establish planning, discipline at the federal level, imprudent and uncoordinated budgeting at the state level will have an almost equally negative effect on the national economy.

In the light of the present economic situation, I have also decided to re-structure and rationalize the machinery of government to facilitate improved performance. To reduce costs, and make for greater efficiency through better co-ordination, the number of federal ministries and departments will be reduced.

Henceforth, renewed emphasis will be placed on a prudent management of men and materials. I wish, therefore, to stress that, under the new dispensation, all government functionaries, especially ministries, special advisors and top government officials, will be expected to demonstrate not only competence, resourcefulness and dedication but also an exemplary standard of probity and integrity.

In the spirit of the on-going ethical revolution, proven cases of abuse of office and corruption will attract immediate sanctions. Indiscipline and inefficiency will similarly be punished while a system of rewarding competence and efficient delivery will be evolved. In answer to the demands of our times, only competent and trustworthy men and women, able and willing to deliver, will be put at the helm of affairs.

In addition to the reduction in the number of ministries and political appointments, I am convinced that we have now gained sufficient awareness of the type of civil service which we require under the presidential system of government which we now operate. Our civil service which is a product of the parliamentary era has adapted itself reasonably well to the demands of the new system. I would therefore like to commend the civil service for the support it has given to the outgoing administration. I trust I can count on its continued support during my second term of office.

However, like any other organisation, the civil service is not perfect. It has therefore become necessary to re-examine it in terms of structure and organization in order to make it more efficient and responsive to the requirements of the new presidential system. In order to ensure that its adaptation is systematised, I intend to set up a panel to re-examine the concept and structure of the civil service commission and to review the operations procedures, methods of organizations, recruitment, control and discipline of the civil service in relation to the responsibilities of the civil service commission to it and to make appropriate recommendations for improving its efficiency and productivity.

Our 1983 manifesto has promised free, functional and qualitative education at all levels. In fulfillment of that objective, I have set up a high-powered technical committee to work out the details of the financial and other implications of the scheme and advise government on how best to achieve these policy objectives. This approach has become imperative to enable us to arrive at long-term solutions to the problems of financing education in all its ramifications. Pending the completion of this exercise, all states currently implementing the free education policy should continue to do so without prejudice to whatever recommendations the committee may make on this issue.

At this juncture, I wish to extend my hearty congratulations to all those who have been elected into the various elective offices in our constitution. I offer them my hand of fellowship. I ask them to join me in this task of making Nigeria great. To their other opponents as well as mine, I congratulate them on putting up a good fight. I ask them not to allow their spirit to be dampened by defeat but to co-operate with us and give the best of their services to our fatherland. Now that elections are over, I wish to appeal to all Nigerians to go about their legitimate business peacefully. I must warn, however, that lawlessness will not be condoned. And any attempt by anybody or group to cause a breach of the peace will be adequately dealt with by the law enforcement agencies. To our brothers and friends in the international community, I once more offer our hands of continued fraternity and friendly relations, our special commitment to Africa as the centerpiece of our foreign policy will continue. The struggle for the achievement of freedom for all the oppressed people of Africa will continue to attract our sympathy and support. Nigeria will strive to encourage other African countries to emulate our democratic experiment and learn from our democratic experience. No sacrifice will be considered too great in the achievement of real freedom and democracy in Africa.

Fellow Nigerians, we have spent the last four years in establishing and consolidating our new system of government. In the difficult days ahead, I will need all your support and understanding to bring about economic stabilisation and prosperity for all our people. I will need all your support to generate and sustain a high standard of national ethics. I will need all your support to enable Nigeria to assume an even more dynamic and purposeful role in the achievement of Africa unity, international peace and security. Your massive mandate freely given to me in the just concluded elections makes me confident that this support will not be denied. On my part, I wish to renew my pledge to uphold the constitution and to serve you all to the very best of my ability.

May God bless you all.

NOTES

1. Shehu Shagari, *Beckoned to Serve: An Autobiography of Shehu Shagari* (Ibadan, Nigeria: Heinemann Educational Books, 2001); A. Okion Ojigbo, *Shehu Shagari: The Biography of Nigeria's First Executive President* (Lagos, Nigeria: Tokion Publishing, 1992); David Williams, *President and Power in Nigeria: The Life of Shehu Shagari* (London, Frank Cass & Co., Ltd. 1982).

2. Aminu Tijjani and David Williams, eds., *Shehu Shagari: My Vision of Nigeria* (London: Frank Cass and Co., Ltd., 1981), 5–7.

3. Aminu Tijjani and David Williams, eds., *Shehu Shagari-My Vision of Nigeria,* 8–14.

4. The British Broadcasting Corporation: Summary of World Broadcasts Section 4: The Middle East, Africa and Latin America (October 4, 1983), 5–12. For content reliability, See also *The New Nigerian* (October 3, 1983), 3 and 29 for the full text of the National Day Broadcast.

Chapter Eight

Major General Muhammadu Buhari

BIOGRAPHICAL NOTES ON MAJOR GENERAL MUHAMMADU BUHARI

Major General Muhammadu Buhari was born in Daura, Katsina State, on December 17, 1942. He attended the Central Primary School, Daura. He later continued his early schooling in Katsina Middle School from 1953 to 1956. Between 1956 and 1962, he attended Government College, Katsina. Buhari started his early military training in 1962 at the Nigerian Military Training College in Kaduna. He had additional training at Mons Officers' Cadet School, Aldershot in England from 1962–1963.

Buhari returned from England in 1963. In January 1963, he was commissioned lieutenant and assigned to the Second Infantry Battalion in Abeokuta as platoon commander. He received platoon leadership training at the Platoon Commanders' Course at the Nigerian Military Training College, Kaduna from November 1963 to January 1964. He also trained at the Mechanical Transport Officers' Course at the Army Mechanical Transport School, Bordon, United Kingdom.

During the Congo (now Zaire) crises in the 1960s Buhari served in the Second Battalion of the Nigerian Army.

Between January 1964 and January 1965, he was mechanical transport officer of the Lagos Garrison Transport Company. He was transport commander in the Second Infantry Brigade Transport Company, from January to July 1965. From August 1965 to April 1967, he was at the Second Infantry Battalion. He later became its adjutant and then the battalion commander in the same period. From April 1967 to July, Buhari was the brigade major in the Second Sector of the First Infantry Division.

General Muhammadu Buhari. 5th Nigerian Military Head of State and Commander-in-Chief of the Nigerian Armed Forces, January 1, 1984–August 27, 1985. Born: December 17, 1942 in Daura, Katsina State, Nigeria. Source: Courtesy of the federal ministry of information and culture, Abuja, Nigeria, 1984.

Buhari was the brigade major of the Third Infantry Brigade from July 1967 to October 1968 in the depths of the Nigerian Civil War. From November 1968 to January 1970, he was the brigade major/commandant of the Fourth Sector, organized to fight the enemy in Awka. Between January 1970 and December 1971, he was commandant, Thirty-First Infantry Brigade.

He served as assistant adjutant-general in the First Infantry Division Headquarters from December 1971 to December 1972. From then to December 1973, he attended more training at the Defence Service Staff College in Wellington, India.

Between January and September 1974, Buhari was made the colonel general staff in the Third Infantry Division Headquarters. Between September 1974 and June 1975, he served as acting director of supplies and transport at the Headquarters of the Nigerian Army Corps of Supplies and Transport.

General Buhari was appointed the federal commissioner (minister) for petroleum and energy, between January 1976 and January 1978. Under his tenure, the Ministry of Petroleum and Nigerian National Oil Corporation merged to form the Nigerian National Petroleum Corporation (NNPC). Buhari became the first chairman of NNPC, from July 1978 to June 1979.

Buhari was the Nigerian Army military secretary headquartered at the army headquarters and a member of the Supreme Military Council from 1978 July to June 1979. In 1979, when the military disengaged from active politics, General Buhari attended the United States War College. On his return to Nigeria, he was posted as the general officer commanding (GOC) to the Headquarters of the Fourth Infantry Division of the Nigerian Army, Ibadan, from August 1980 to January 1981.

From January to October 1981, Buhari was the general officer commanding (GOC) of the Second Mechanised Infantry Division of the Nigerian Army, headquartered in Ibadan.

From November 1981 to December 31, 1983, he was the GOC of the Third Armoured Division in Jos. After the coup was announced, Buhari became the head of state and commander in chief of the Nigerian Armed Forces following the end of the Nigerian Second Republic. He was promoted major general in March 1983.

The ascension speech that follows tells the story of Nigeria under the Second Republic. As the economic crises worsened and the political atmosphere under the Second Republic became more polarized along party, ethnic, and religious lines, the military struck again in the dying hours of December 31, 1983.

Again, the first official words of this new leader inform the reader about the problems of good governance, accountability, legitimacy, respect for authority, and the rule of law in a plural society like Nigeria.[1]

THE FULL TEXT OF THE ASCENSION SPEECH BY HIS EXCELLENCY, MAJOR GENERAL MUHAMMADU BUHARI, HEAD OF THE FEDERAL MILITARY GOVERNMENT AND COMMANDER IN CHIEF OF THE NIGERIAN ARMED FORCES, BROADCAST ON JANUARY 1, 1984

Fellow Nigerians,[2] you are aware of the change in the government of the Federal Republic of Nigeria which was announced early this morning. In pursuance of the primary objective of saving our beloved nation from total collapse, I, Major General Muhammadu Buhari of the Nigerian Army, after due consultations among the services of the armed forces, have been formally invested with the authority of the Head of the Federal Military Government and Commander-in-Chief of the armed forces of the Federal Republic of Nigeria. It is with humility and deep sense of responsibility that I accepted this challenge and call to national duty.

As you must have heard in the announcement, the Constitution of the Federal Republic of Nigeria 1979 has been suspended except those sections of it which are exempted in the constitution suspension and modification decree to be issued in due course.

The change became necessary in order to put an end to the serious economic predicaments and crisis of confidence now afflicting our nation. Consequently the Nigerian armed forces have constituted themselves into a Federal Military Government comprised of a Supreme Military Council, a National Council of State, a Federal Executive Council at the centre, and State Executive Councils to be presided over by a military governor in each state of the States of the Federation. Members of these bodies will be announced soon.

The Nature of Politics Since 1979:

The last Federal Government drew up a programme with the aim of handing over political power to the civilians in 1979. That programme, as you all know, was implemented to the letter. The 1979 constitution was promulgated. However, little did the military realize that the political leadership of the Second Republic would sacrifice most of the checks and balances in the constitution and bring us to the present state of general insecurity. The premium of political power became so exceedingly high that political contestants regarded victory in election as a matter of life and death struggle and were determined to capture or retain power by all means.

Mismanagement of the Economy:

It is true that there is worldwide economic recession. However, in the case of Nigeria it in fact was aggravated by mismanagement. We believe that appropriate government agencies gave good advice, but their advice was disregarded by the leadership. This situation could have been saved if the legislators were alive to their constitutional responsibilities. Instead, the legislators were preoccupied with determining their salary scale, fringe benefits and unnecessary foreign travel, et cetera, which took no account of the state of the economy and the welfare of the people they represented.

As a result of their inability to cultivate financial discipline and stringent management of the economy, we have come to depend largely on internal and external borrowing to execute government projects with attendant domestic price pressure and soaring external debts.

Thus, given the propensity of the outgoing civilian administration to mismanage our financial resources, Nigeria was already condemned to live perpetually with the twin problems of heavy budget deficit and weak balance of payments with little prospect of building a virile and viable economy.

The 1983 Elections:

The last general elections could be anything but free and fair. The only political parties that could complain of election rigging are those that lack the resources to rig. There is ample evidence that rigging and thuggery were relative to the resources available to the parties. This conclusively proved to us that the parties have not developed confidence in the presidential system of government on which the nation invested so much material and resources.

Corruption and Indiscipline:

While corruption and indiscipline had been associated with our state of underdevelopment, these twin evils in our politics have attained unprecedented height over the past four years. The corrupt, inept and insensitive leadership in the last four years has been the sources of immorality and impropriety in our society. Since what happens in any society is largely a reflection of the leadership of that society, we deplore corruption in all its facets. With no corruption in all its processes, this government will not tolerate kickbacks, inflation of contracts and over-invoicing of imports, et cetera. Nor will it condone forgery, fraud, embezzlement, misuse and abuse of office and illegal dealings in foreign exchange and smuggling.

Arson has been used to cover up fraudulent acts in public institutions. I am referring to the fire incidents that gutted the P and T building in Lagos, the Anambra State Broadcasting Corporation, the Republic Building at Marina, the Federal Ministry of Education, the Federal Capital Development Authority's account office at Abuja, and the NET (Nigerian External Telecommunications) building. Most of these fires occurred at a time when Nigerians were being apprehensive of the frequency of fraud scandals and the government's apparent incapacity to deal with them. Corruption has become so pervasive and intractable that a whole ministry has been created to tame it.

Moment of Truth:

Fellow Nigerians, this indeed is the moment of truth. My colleagues and I in the Supreme Military Council must be frank enough to acknowledge the fact that at the moment, an accurate picture of the financial position is yet to be determined. We have no doubt that the situation is bad enough. In spite of this, every effort will be made to ensure that the difficult and degrading conditions under which we are living are ameliorated.

Let no one, however, be deceived that workers who have not received their salaries in the past eight or so months will receive such salaries between today and tomorrow, or that hospitals, which have been without drugs for months, will be provided with drugs immediately. We are determined that with the help of God we shall do our best to settle genuine payments to which government is committed, including backlog of workers' salaries after proper scrutiny.

We are confident, and we assure you, that even in the face of the global recession and the seemingly grim and disturbing financial picture, given prudent management of Nigeria's existing financial resources and our determination to substantially reduce waste, it will be possible to clear the accumulated domestic payment arrears, to reduce and eventually narrow down rising budgetary deficit and weak balance of payments position.

Priority Programmes:

The Federal Military Government would reappraise policies with a view to paying greater attention to the following areas:

The economy will be given new impetus and better sense of direction; corrupt officials and their agents would be brought to book; in view of the drought that affected most of the parts of the country, the Federal Military Government will, within the available resources, import food stuff to supplement the shortfalls suffered in the last harvest; payment of salary arrears to workers.

Our foreign policy will be both dynamic and realistic. Africa will of course continue to be the centre piece of our foreign policy.

The morale and combat readiness of the armed forces will be given high priority. Officers and men with high personal and professional integrity will have nothing to fear.

The Judiciary, the Civil Service, and the Police, Et Cetera:

The Chief Justice of Nigeria and all other office holders of judicial appointments within the Federation shall continue to function under existing laws subject to such exceptions as may be decreed from time to time by the Federal Military Government.

All holders of appointment in the Federal Civil Service, the police, the national security organization, shall continue to exercise their function in the normal way subject to changes that may be introduced by the Federal Military Government. All board chairmen and members of corporations and parastatals and other existing departments are hereby relieved of their appointments with immediate effect.

External Relations:

The Federal Military Government will maintain and strengthen existing diplomatic relations with other states and with international organizations and institutions such as the OAU, the United Nations and its organs, the OPEC, ECOWAS, and the Commonwealth of Nations, et cetera.

The Federal Military Government will honour and respect all treaty obligations entered into by the previous governments. And we hope that such nations and bodies will reciprocate this gesture by respecting our country's territorial integrity and sovereignty.

Fellow Nigerians, finally we have dutifully intervened to save this nation from imminent collapse. We therefore expect all Nigerians, including those who participated directly or indirectly in bringing the nation into present predicaments, to cooperate with us. This generation of Nigerians and indeed future generations have no other country than Nigeria. We shall remain here and salvage it together.

May God be with us all. Good morning.

NOTES

1. Mike Okoye, ed., *Toward A Better Nigeria* (Ikeja, Lagos: Times Books Ltd., n.d.).

2. "Buhari's New Year Broadcast." *West Africa* (January 9, 1984): 56–57. For content reliability, see *Foreign Broadcast Information Service Daily Report, Middle East and Africa* 5:001 (January 3, 1984): T2–T3.

Chapter Nine

General Ibrahim Badamosi Babangida

BIOGRAPHICAL NOTES ON GENERAL IBRAHIM BADAMOSI BABANGIDA

General Ibrahim Badamosi Babangida was born on August 17, 1941 in Minna, Niger State. His early primary school started from 1950 and went through to 1956. He attended the Government College, Bida, from 1957 to 1962.

Babangida began his military training at the Nigerian Military Training College, in Kaduna. He was commissioned second lieutenant later in 1963. In 1964, he attended Indian Military Academy. After his graduation from the Academy, Babangida was made the commanding officer of the First Reconnaissance Squadron, from 1964 to January 1966.

From January through April, 1966, he attended the Young Officers' Course at the Royal Armoured Center in the United Kingdom. After the course, he returned to Nigeria, and was promoted lieutenant. In 1968, he was promoted captain. He founded and was appointed commandant, 44 Infantry Battalion, which was nicknamed The Rangers. He made major in 1970.

On his return from the company commanders' course at Warminster in the United Kingdom in November 1970, Babangida was made the instructor and company commander at the Nigerian Defence Academy, from 1970 to 1972.

He attended American Armoured School for the advanced armoured officers' course between August 1972 and June 1973, in the United States. On his return to Nigeria, he was appointed commandant four Reconnaissance Regiment (RECCE) and was promoted lieutenant colonel. This position led to his appointment as the inspector, and subsequently, commandant of the Nigerian Army Armoured Corps. Again, between January and June, 1980, he attended the Naval Post-Graduate School in the United States for the senior international defence management course.

*General Ibrahim Badamosi Babangida 6th Nigerian Military Head
of State and Commander-in-Chief of the Nigerian Armed Forces,
August 27, 1985–August 28, 1993. Born: August 27, 1941 in Minna,
Niger State, Nigeria. Source: BBC Africa Services, 1987.*

Ibrahim Babaginda was promoted brigadier in 1979 and was the commandant of the armoured corps. Prior to that, he attended senior officers' course
at the Command and Staff College, Jaji, Nigeria. Between August 1, 1975
and September 30, 1979, Babangida was a member of the Supreme Military
Council, and again from December 31, 1983 to August 27, 1985.

He was promoted major general on March 1, 1983. On December 31,
1983, he became the chief of army staff, when a military coup toppled the
Second Republic under President Shehu Shagari. Babangida remained in that
post until he became the first Nigerian military president and commander in
chief of the Nigerian Armed Forces as well as chairman of the Armed Forces
Ruling Council (AFRC), when he masterminded the coup of August 27,
1985, that overthrew General Buhari.

He was promoted full general in 1987. Babangida is married to former
Miss Maryam King. They both have four children.

Many Nigerians described the military regime of General Buhari as reactionary and draconian as far as civil liberties and freedom of the press were concerned. Nevertheless, the regime earned high marks for its War on Discipline crusade. As a restless country of diverse peoples, no one leader seemed to be able to have the magic formula to govern Nigerians. Therefore, Buhari was overthrown by one of the plotters of the earlier coup that enthroned him. The ascension speech of Babangida marks the first time that a succeeding ruler scapegoats his predecessor by name in the public discourse suffused with blaming theme. Such a violation of the rules of decorum, decency, and politeness in political discourse was a testimony to the degradation rituals in military power, authority, and legitimacy, as evident in the speech that follows.

Besides the scapegoating routines, the general atmosphere of economic stagnation, and legal affronts to the civil rights of Nigerians, the ascension did not point to any magic formula to bring back happy days to Nigerians. Audacious rhetoric demanded that the country face the economic problems. What follows is an example of a military rhetor in a politician's garb and very short on specifics.[1]

THE FULL TEXT OF THE ASCENSION SPEECH BY MAJOR GENERAL IBRAHIM BABANGIDA, HEAD OF THE FEDERAL MILITARY GOVERNMENT AND COMMANDER IN CHIEF OF NIGERIAN ARMED FORCES, BROADCAST ON AUGUST 27, 1985

Fellow Nigerians,[2] when in December 1983 the former military leadership headed by Major General Muhammandu Buhari assumed the reins of government, its ascension was heralded with the most popular enthusiasm accorded any new government in the history of this country. With the nation then at the mercy of political misdirection and on the brink of economic collapse, a new sense of hope was created in the minds of every Nigerian. Since January 1984, however, we have witnessed a systematic denigration of that hope. It was stated then that the mismanagement of the economy, lack of public accountability, insensitivity of the political leadership and a general deterioration in the standard of living which had subjected the common man to intolerable suffering were the reasons for intervention.

Nigerians have since then been under a regime that continued with the same trends. Events today indicate that most of the reasons to justify the military take over of the government from civilians still persist. The initial objectives were betrayed and fundamental changes do not appear on the horizon. Because of the present state of uncertainty, suppression and stagnation which have resulted from the perpetuation of a small group, the Nigerian armed forces could not as a part of this government be unfairly committed to take responsibility for failure. Our dedication to the course of ensuring that our nation remains a united entity, worthy of respect and capable of functioning as a credible and viable part of the international community, dictated the need to arrest the situation.

Let me at this point attempt to make you understand the premise upon which it became necessary to change the leadership. The principles of discussion, consultation, and cooperation, which should have guided the decision-making process of the Supreme Military Council and the Federal Executive Council, were disregarded soon after the government settled down in 1984. While some of us thought it appropriate to give a little more time anticipating a conducive atmosphere would develop in which affairs of state could be attended to with a greater sense of responsibility, it became increasingly clear that such expectations could not be fulfilled. Regrettably it turned out that Major-General Buhari was too rigid and uncompromising in his attitude to issues of national significance. Efforts to make him understand that a diverse polity like Nigeria requires recognition and appreciation of differences in both cultural and individual perceptions only served to aggravate his attitude. Major-General Tunde Idiagbon was similarly inclined in that respect. As the Chief of Staff, Supreme Headquarters, he failed to exhibit the appropriate disposition demanded by his position. He arrogated to himself absolute knowledge of problems and solutions and acted in accordance with what was convenient to him, using the machinery of government as his tool. A combination of these characteristics in the two most important persons holding the nation's vital offices became impossible to contend with. The situation was made worse by a number of other government functionaries and organizations, chief among them was the Nigerian Security Organization. In fact this body will be overhauled and reorganized.

And it came to be that the same government which received a tumultuous welcome now became alienated from the people. To prevent a complete erosion of our given mandate therefore, we need to act so that hope may be renewed. Let me now address your attention to the major issues that confront us, that we may as one people chart a future direction for our dear country. We do not claim to have all the answers to all the questions which our present problems have put before us as a nation. We have come with a stronger determination to create an atmosphere in which positive effort will be given the necessary support for lasting solutions.

For matters of the moment which require immediate resolution, we intend to pursue a determined programme of action. Major issues falling into this category have been identified and decision taken on what should be done. Firstly, the issue of political detainees and convictions of the Special

Military Tribunals. The history of our nation has never recorded the degree of indiscipline and corruption as in the period between October 1979 and December 1983. While this government recognizes the bitterness created by the irresponsible excesses of the politicians, we consider it unfortunate the methods of such a nature to cause more bitterness were applied to deal with past misdeeds.

We must never allow ourselves to lose a sense of natural justice. The innocent cannot suffer the crimes of the guilty. The guilty should be punished, only as a lesson for the future. In line with this government's intention to uphold fundamental human rights, the issue of detainees will be looked into with dispatch. As we do not intend to lead a country where individuals are under fear of expressing themselves, the Public Officers Protection Against False Accusation Decree Number Four of 1984 is hereby repealed with immediate effect. All journalists who have been in detention under this decree are hereby unconditionally released. The responsibility of the media to disseminate information shall be exercised without undue hinderance. In that process, those responsible are expected to be forthright and to have to the nation's interest as the primary consideration. The issue of decrees has generated a lot of controversy. It is the intention of this government to review all decrees.

The last 20 months have not witnessed any significant changes in the national economy. Contrary to expectations we have so far been subjected to a steady deterioration in the general conditions of living and intolerable suffering by the ordinary Nigerians has reached unprecedented heights. Prices of goods and equipment have risen higher, scarcity of commodities has increased, hospitals still remain mere consulting clinics, while educational institutions are on the brink of total decay. Unemployment has stretched to critical dimensions.

Due to the stalemate which arose in negotiations with the International Monetary Fund the former government embarked on a series of a countertrade agreements. Under the countertrade agreements, Nigerians were forced to buy goods and commodities at higher prices than obtained in the international market. The government intends to review the whole issue of countertrade.

A lot has been said and heard about our position with the International Monetary Fund. Although we formally applied to the Fund in April 1983, no progress has yet been made in the negotiations as a stalemate has existed for the last two years. We shall break the deadlock that frustrated the negotiations with a view to evaluating more objectively both the negative and the positive implications of reaching a mutual agreement with the Fund. At all times in the course of discussions, our representatives will be guided by the feelings and aspirations of the Nigerian people.

It is the view of this government that austerity without structural readjustment is not the solution to our economic predicament. The present situation whereby 44 percent of our revenue earnings is utilized to service debts is not realistic.

To protect the danger this poses to the poor and the needy in our society, steps will be taken to ensure a comprehensive strategy of economic reforms. The crux of our economic problems have been identified to centre around four fundamental issues: One: A decrease of our domestic production while our population continues to increase. Two: Dependence on imports for both consumer goods and raw materials for our industries. Three: a grossly unequal gap between the rich and the poor. Four: The large role played by the public sector in economic activities with hardly any concrete result to justify such a role. These are the problems we must confront.

Nigeria's foreign policy in the last 20 months has been characterized by inconsistencies and incoherence. It has lacked the clarity to make us know where we stood on matters of international concern to enable other countries to relate to us with seriousness. Our role as Africa's spokesman has been diminished because we have been unable to maintain the respect African countries had for Nigeria.

The ousted military government conducted our external relations by a policy of retaliatory reaction. Nigeria became a country that reacted to given situations, rather than taking the initiative as it should and as it had always been done. More so, vengeful considerations must not become the basis for our diplomacy. Africa's problems and their solutions shall constitute the premises of our foreign policy. The revitalization of the Organization of African Unity's Lagos Plan of Action for self-sufficiency and constructive co-operation in Africa shall be our primary pursuit.

The Economic Community of West African States must be revamped with a view to achieving the objectives of regional integration. The problems of the drought-stricken areas of Africa will be given more attention and sympathy and our best efforts will be made to assist in their rehabilitation within the limits of our resources. Our membership in the United Nations Organization will be made more practical and meaningful. The call for a New International Economic Order which lost its momentum in the face of the debt crisis will be made once again.

Nigeria hereby makes a renewed request to the Non-Aligned Movement to regroup and reinvigorate its determination to restructure the global economic system. While we propose to the industrialized nations to positively consider the dire plight of developing countries and assist responsively to the dangers that face us, we shall remain members of the various multilateral institutions and inter-governmental organizations we belong to and do what must be done to enhance our membership and participation in them.

Fellow Nigerians, this country has had since independence a history mixed with turbulence and fortune. We have witnessed our rise to greatness followed with a decline to the status of a bewildered nation. Our human potentials have been neglected, our human resources put to waste. A phenomenon of constant insecurity and overbearing uncertainty have become characteristic of our national existence. My colleagues and I are determined to unite this country. We shall not allow anything to obstruct us.

We recognize that a government, be it civilian or military, needs the consent of the people to govern if it is to meet its objectives. We do not intend to rule by force. At the same time we should not be expected to submit to unreasonable demands. Fundamental rights and civil liberties will be respected but their exercise must not degenerate into irrational expression or border on subversion. The War Against Indiscipline shall continue but this time in the minds and conduct of Nigerians, and not by way of symbolism or money consuming campaigns. This government on its part will ensure that the leadership exhibits proper example.

Criticism of actions and decisions taken by us will be given necessary attention, and where necessary, changes made in accordance to what is expected of us. Let me reiterate what was said in 1984, and I quote: "This generation of Nigerians and indeed future generations have no other country but Nigeria. We must all stay and salvage it together." This time it shall be pursued with deeper commitment and genuine sincerity.

There is a lot of work to be done, by every single Nigerian. Let us all dedicate ourselves to the cause of building a strong, united and virile nation for the sake of our own lives and the benefit of posterity. Finally, I wish to commend the members of the Armed Forces and the Nigeria Police for their mature conduct during the change.

I thank you all for your cooperation and understanding.

God bless Nigeria.

NOTES

1. Gabriel E. Umoden, *The Babangida Years: The First Authoritative Biography of Nigeria's Most Visionary Leader* (Lagos, Nigeria: Gabumo Publishing Co., 1992); and Mike Okoye, ed., *Towards A Better Nigeria* (Ikeja, Nigeria: Times Books, Ltd., n.d.).

2. Towards New Goals, New Directions: Maiden Speech by His Excellency, General Ibrahim Babangida, Head of the Federal Military Government and Commander in Chief of the Armed Forces on August 27, 1985 (Lagos: Federal Ministry of Information, Domestic Publicity Division, Ikoyi, 1985). For content reliability, see also the cover story "Our Mission," *Africa* 169 (September, 1985): 14–15; and "Deeper Commitment," *West Africa* (September 2, 1985): 1791–1793.

Chapter Ten

Chief Ernest
Adegunle Shonekan

BIOGRAPHICAL NOTES ON
CHIEF ERNEST ADEGUNLE SHONEKAN

Chief Ernest Adegunle Oladeinde Shonekan was born May 9, 1936 in Lagos. He was educated at the CMS (Church Missionary Society) Grammar School in Lagos. He attended and received his law training from the University of London, and was later called to the bar at the Inns of Court Council of Legal Education, in the United Kingdom.

He joined the United African Company (UAC) in 1964 on his return to Nigeria. He spent all his professional life in that company, starting first in the legal department, as the assistant legal adviser, and the deputy legal adviser after two years. Later he became a member of the UAC Board.

In 1980, Ernest Shonekan was made the chairman and Chief Executive Officer of UAC, thus becoming the Chief Officer of the largest African controlled company in Sub-Saharan Africa.

Chief Shonekan was thrown into the political corridor in January 1993 when General Babangida, the self-acclaimed military president, appointed him to head the transitional team, in one of Babangida's last machinations to hand over power to an elected civilian government of the long-awaited Third Nigerian Republic on August 27, 1993. But the June 12, 1993 election annulment by Babangida made that dream, only a pipe dream. Instead, Babangida set up the Interim National Government and unilaterally installed Shonekan its interim head of state. Shonekan described his ascension as circumstantial, thus giving birth to a government he called "a child of circumstance" in his first television broadcast to the nation. In that capacity, Ernest Shonekan was to supervise the conducting

Chief Ernest Adegunle Shonekan. 1st Interim National Government President and Commander-in-Chief of the Nigerian Armed Forces, August 28, 1993–Novemebr 16, 1993. Born: May 9, 1936 in Lagos, Nigeria. Source: Maxsiollum.wordpress.com, 2008.

of another presidential election six months later. By this time, Nigeria was on the brink of explosion. Calls for Babangida's disengagement became most vociferous all over the country.

When General Babangida stepped aside from active governance on August 26, 1993, Ernest Shonekan assumed office as the head of the Interim National Government, thereby becoming a de facto appointed civilian president. In his first maiden address to the nation, Shonekan attempted to rationalize the shattered dreams of millions of Nigerians who had turned out in millions to elect a civilian government after nine years of military rule.[1]

THE FULL TEXT OF THE MAIDEN ADDRESS BY CHIEF ERNEST SHONEKAN, THE INTERIM PRESIDENT OF NIGERIA'S INTERIM NATIONAL GOVERNMENT AND COMMANDER IN CHIEF OF THE NIGERIAN ARMED FORCES ON HIS ASCENSION SPEECH BROADCAST AS NIGERIA'S FIRST INTERIM HEAD OF STATE, ON AUGUST 31, 1993

Fellow Nigerians,[2]

Following the annulment of the June 12 presidential election, a broad-based national committee comprising representatives of the two parties, National Republican Convention, the Social Democratic party and government representatives recommended the formation of an Interim National Government as the most viable stop-gap arrangement pending the time a fresh presidential election will be held by the Babangida administration.

That the Interim National Government is a child of circumstance is an incontrovertible fact. It is however, the best solution in the difficult circumstances in which the country found itself. It turned out to be the only way by which a peaceful end could be put to the military leadership of the government of our country, given the firm determination of the military to annul the June 12 and the obvious lack of a consensus among the political class in their response.

The rationale for the Interim National Government is the imperative to move forward as a united and indivisible nation. The country cannot afford to get bogged down much longer in the post-election quagmire which was leading progressively to a catastrophe. A solution had to be found since we all know that the long-run benefits of staying together as one nation far outweigh the intermittent pains of learning to grow together.

We simply cannot afford to fritter away the gains and experience of thirty-three years of independence. The path of wisdom is to consolidate our gains and build on our strengths while striving hard to correct our shortcomings.

This is precisely what the Interim National Government is determined to do during its short tenure.

It is true that we have been passing through a particularly difficult period of our history lately. However, the Interim National Government is the positive proof of our enduring capacity to devise our own solutions to our peculiar problems. As a home-grown innovation, the Interim National Government ought, therefore, to re-assure the cynics and detractors, both at home and abroad, of our resolve to stay together as one nation with a common destiny.

I want to assure you all my fellow countrymen and women that the best is yet to come. June 12 has now become part of the political history of this country and it is advisable that we let it remain so. However, government will put together the records of the events in detail for posterity.

Fellow Nigerians, our recent wrenching experiences remain a most painful reminder of our civil war which lasted three and a half years with most traumatic consequences. Keen observers of events of the last few weeks would have wondered whether we learnt any lessons from the civil war. Upon sober reflections, such observers would after August 26 and 27, have concluded that we have indeed learnt that an all or nothing approach to a political crisis usually leads to disaster. Politics should not be a zero-sum game. Indeed, what we have just been through teaches us an additional lesson that we should not take our unity and corporate existence for granted. We must work hard at it and jealously protect and nurture it. In this regard, the travails of the recent past should further strengthen the fabric of our national experience.

Generally, the duties and responsibilities of the Interim National Government are quite enormous and challenging. We have been charged with the responsibility of ensuring effective administration of the country by steering the ship of state in all national and international circumstances and to effectively protect all our citizens.

Our task also includes giving priority attention to the material well-being of our citizens. In addition, we are to oversee the local government elections due later this year. Most importantly, we have an onerous duty of bringing to its logical conclusion the political transition programme by overseeing the conduct of the presidential election and putting in place all necessary apparatus and processes which will ensure a smooth handing-over of power to a democratically elected president at the end of the interim period.

The general direction of our policy during the interim period will be towards promoting national reconciliation and healing the deep wounds inflicted on our collective psyche by recent political events. We intend to soothe frayed nerves and seek to enhance the tone and quality of public discourse. We also wish to adopt a people-oriented approach in policy formulation in order to rekindle hope of a bright future in the generality of our people. Our charity will begin at home and our style will be simple enough, but our resolve to do the right things for the greater majority of our people will be firm.

The existence of the Interim National Government terminates on March 31, 1994, which makes it a seven-month tenure. You will all agree with me that in order to successfully carry out our brief and make a positive impact we must be properly focused. Given the constraint of time, we must give priority to the conclusion of the political transition programme by overseeing the conduct of the presidential election and ensuring a smooth hand-over of power to a democratically elected president at the end of our tenure.

I have been assured that preparations for the local government elections which are due to take place in the last quarter of this year are on course. I shall give instructions immediately to the National Electoral Commission to consult with the two political parties with a view to establishing a timetable within the next one week for the presidential election.

On the political front we are still groping in the dark for a generally acceptable and workable formula. The problems we confront in this sphere derive largely from the multi-ethnic, multi-religious and multi-national nature of our society. Since we cannot run away from this fundamental characteristic of our society we have to learn to understand our differences so that we can deal with them realistically. It would not serve useful purpose to pretend that we do not confront serious problems in fusing together the various segments of our society into a cohesive nation. This is a major challenge of leadership in the political life of our beloved country.

In order to solve the fundamental problem of unity and douse the political storm brewing we must put in place a credible conflict resolution mechanism, fashioned to reflect our peculiar experiences and aspirations. If anything, events of the recent past had revealed poignantly in us as severely limited in crisis-solving capacity. Our leaders of thought must meaningfully address this area of urgent need.

Crises are an integral part of nation-building, more so in our highly complex type of society. There are two critical factors to note in our search for a workable crisis resolution mechanism. First, we must accept the principle of dialogue, backed by a spirit of give and take and second, we ought to widen our margin of tolerance in the debate on national issues.

Politicians have been assigned a prominent role in the Interim National Government and the two political parties are well represented in the new cabinet. More importantly, the powers of the National Assembly to legislate have been restored. Thus, the Interim National affords an opportunity for a befitting rehearsal of the Third Republic in terms of co-operation among the three key arms of government, that is, the executive, the legislative and the judiciary.

The ball is now in the court of our politicians and I fervently hope that they will rise to the occasion and prove the "doubting Thomases" wrong. Additionally, I call upon the political parties to restore harmony and discipline within the various levels of party leadership. Without these, they will find it difficult to fulfill the requirements and provide a conducive atmosphere for a free and fair election.

Fellow Nigerians, I am aware that the recent political unrest has taken a heavy toll on our economy. I do not intend to pretend otherwise. Reports reaching me about the movements and sufferings of our people across the country, consequent upon the political firestorm make my heart ache indeed. Uncertainty and gloom remain on the horizon. Economic activities are generally depressed and investor confidence at home and abroad is all but eroded. It behooves us, therefore, to prevent further deterioration of our economy and the collapse of the standard of living of our citizenry. However, given the short tenure of the Interim National Government and the daunting tasks it confronts, we must prioritise and manage our resources and time most efficiently. Hence, the political problem will rank highest in the hierarchy of issues to be addressed in the next seven months, although we will not and cannot neglect economic issues.

We have decided to declare our priorities now to avoid being misunderstood later. During the life of the Interim national Government, we intend to run an open government with an emphasis on the twin concepts of accountability and transparency. We shall encourage a consensus approach to policy-making, often consulting as widely as possible with various segments of our society on issues of national importance.

To this end, I am hereby appealing to our traditional rulers, political and religious leaders, the private sector and labour organizations, academicians and students to come forward and offer ideas as to how best to accomplish our tasks and move ahead.

Fellow Nigerians, the total disregard for uprightness in our society, which has enthroned wealth by all means, is quite worrisome to me. Thus, not only are those who defraud our public treasuries honoured, even armed robbers and drug barons are able to buy respectability. Rampant corruption and get-rich-quick mania, therefore, have become cankerworms in all spheres of our national life.

Having given these problems a serious thought, I have come to the painful conclusion that to forge ahead as a society we must extirpate corruption from our public life. I am also convinced that to accomplish this very important task the battle must begin with the leadership of our country.

Therefore, I am serving notice here and now of the determination of the Interim National Government to launch a crusade against corruption in our public life. To this end, I shall strive to lead by personal example. The ING will also ensure that the laws against corruption are enforced without fear or favour. The role of the populace in fighting the cankerworm of corruption cannot be over-emphasized. Each and everyone should resolve to join the crusade. Each and everyone must be determined to expose corruption wherever it exists.

The twin problem of corruption is social indiscipline which is also widespread in our country today. It is indiscipline which breeds corruption and the other social problems afflicting us. Therefore, we must join hands together to uproot indiscipline in all its ramification from our society. In this respect, parents, teachers and religious leaders have an important role to play.

In addition, leaders of government must by their personal acts be a shining example of discipline. I am seizing the opportunity of this occasion, therefore, to charge the members of the ING to demonstrate the virtues of discipline and integrity at all times. On this score, I pledge to take the lead.

I want to appeal to our media as members of the fourth estate of the realm for full cooperation and patriotic understanding during the tenure of the ING. We have all been living witnesses of the turbulent events of the recent past in which the media have by no means been passive observers. Experience, it is said, is the best teacher, therefore, I expect that the media practitioners are much wiser now.

There is a thin line connecting the orderly and the disorderly, hence, it behooves our media practitioners to report and analyse issues of national importance with utmost circumspection and a sense of patriotism.

It is a widely accepted fact that democracy cannot thrive without a free press and it is equally widely acknowledged that Nigeria can boast of the most vibrant and freest press in Africa. I feel proud about this observation and I want to enjoin our media to maintain their good image. Ours is a government of reconciliation seeking to heal the wounds of the nation and the media should co-operate in this important task. To this end, our newspapers, radio and television must seek to inform, educate and entertain in the best tradition of their noble profession.

They should at all times be objective in their reporting and seek to promote among Nigerians a sense of shared perspective on national and international issues. They should avoid the abuse of their privileged position by campaign of calumny and outlandish imaginative reporting calculated to bring into disrepute public figures and their families. To say the least this smacks of an utter disregard for professionalism and respect for privacy.

More importantly, this runs counter to African tradition which accords respect to elders. The media should become a partner in progress and be carried along in the arduous task of nation-building.

Fellow countrymen and women, the government has noted with grave concern the crisis that has engulfed our tertiary education since July 1992. Currently, most of our higher institutions are under closure following the strike embarked upon by members of the academic staff of the various institutions since early May. However, the foundation for progress and rapid transformation of the society comes from education. Indeed, development of human capital is a necessary if not sufficient condition for future growth and development of our national economy.

I wish to reiterate that within the limits of available resources the ING is determined to provide succour for our institutions. This is a matter close to my heart personally. Let me add, however, that in the face of dwindling national resources, it is necessary for tertiary institutions to evolve ways and means of managing well with less. It is important to continue to place emphasis on generating independent revenue as well as prudent management of available resources. I fervently appeal to all sections of the higher education sector to urgently set in motion the machinery for the resumption of normal academic activities as part of the process of healing the nation's wounds.

I have noted with dismay the series of strikes and work stoppages which have characterised most of the current year. It particularly gives cause for concern that the country has been losing valuable man-hours at a time when the requirement of our weak economy is increased productivity.

I should emphasise that it is our national economy which suffers for it and ultimately the common man who bears the brunt of it all. I am hereby calling for a moratorium on labour unrest, work stoppages and stay-at-home orders in the greater interest of our fatherland. Consequently, I plead to enter into series of dialogue with various interest-groups so that together, we can find lasting solutions to our problems.

It is now recognised that an important element in our present political crisis is the reaction of foreign countries. Though basically an internal affair such has democratisation become a major element of the evolving new world order that the Nigerian evolving democratic experiment is of universal interest. We have to admit that our tortuous path to democratisation has been at once a source of admiration and of bewilderment to the outside world.

We began our process well before democratisation became the fashion. However, let us not ascribe ill-will to our foreign friends. Rather, let us call upon them to quickly re-assess our relations in light of the recent changes that this country has witnessed in its governance. The withdrawal of General Babangida as President, Commander-in-Chief of the Armed Forces on August 26, signalled the final disengagement of the military from government. This is a major step whose primordial significance should not be lost on our well wishers.

I should like to restate particularly for the benefit of our foreign partners that the ING is not a military-led government either overtly or covertly. I have spent all my adult life working for and promoting free market economy. In order for it to thrive, such a system requires free expression of political opinions and government freely elected by the people.

Therefore, I cannot be a party to the perpetuation of military rule which by its nature is not based on democratic principles. In accepting to be part of the transitional government in January 1993 it was on the understanding that it was the final stage scheduled to terminate in August 1993. With the complication that arose after June 12 and the annulment of the presidential election an interim arrangement became the most realistic option for making the military respect the target date of August 27 for their disengagement. Even in the environment of the new world order, the first step of any form of crisis resolution remains the encouragement of local initiatives. I call upon our foreign partners therefore to give us credit for fashioning out a Nigerian solution and to show their goodwill in our efforts at implementation.

Nigeria's population and resources have thrust on her regional leadership responsibilities in Africa. The commitment of our country to maintenance of international peace and stability on the continent in general and the ECOWAS sub-region in particular which we intend to continue has often demanded a lot of sacrifice of our resources. We have gladly made the sacrifice to the admiration of the international community. Nigeria's well-being, therefore, should be seen by our foreign partners in a broader perspective. The continuation of Nigeria's policy of being its brother's keeper requires a sound economic base. The support and co-operation of our industrialised partners in our efforts at revamping our national economy become therefore of mutual interest. I would hope that the ING can count on such support.

There is no doubt that our economy has suffered because of our peace-enforcement operations as part of ECOMOG in Liberia. Mercifully, the fratricidal war is now over and Liberians have at last begun the process of establishing a national government which will reconstruct the war torn country, and rehabilitate the war-weary populace. I call upon the United Nations and other international agencies to come to the assistance of Liberia.

We in this sub-region have done enough. Now is the time to bring the boys home. I have, therefore, directed the Secretary of Defense to work out a withdrawal plan immediately, so as to bring the boys home before the end of the tenure of ING. I intend to discuss this plan at an ECOWAS summit meeting to be specially convened for this purpose.

Fellow Nigerians, in this concluding part of my first address to you as Head of the ING, I should like to emphasise a number of points.

First, you should not ignore or under-rate the significance of August 26, the date on which General Babangida stepped down as president and Commander-in-Chief of the Armed Forces. How many of you believe when in his address to the joint session of the National Assembly on August 17, he offered to "voluntarily step aside"? In the days after that address a thousand interpretations were made of his assertion to "step aside" both in and outside Nigeria all showing signs of disbelief. As it turned out, he did, in fact, not only step aside but stepped down on August 26.

If I, Ernest Shonekan, accepted to take over from him the mantle of leadership of our country, albeit temporarily, it is a sacrifice I felt able to make in order to make August 26 happen. I am neither unaware of the personal risk nor the possible misunderstanding of my motives. Let me assure you, fellow Nigerians, that if there had been an alternative way of making the military disengage and our march to full democratisation as an indivisible entity assured, I would have embarked on a long deserved vacation. But, as events unfolded my patriotic zeal could not have made me walk away when it became clear that I had a crucial and historic role to play in the only solution viable under the circumstances.

Secondly, let it be said loud and clear that the challenge of leadership in our country has never been more than it is now. The political climate is poisoned, economic activities are at a low ebb while corruption, indiscipline and other social ills reign supreme. Our leadership should not allow the beautiful dream of a great country at independence to become a burden just after three decades. It would be tantamount to an unpardonable indictment of the present generation of leaders to allow the labours of our heroes past to be in vain. Therefore, our country cries out now for a leader who has a vision and the moral courage to translate that vision into reality. This is the way to debunk the myth of an ever-bungling leadership, incapable of building a modern society, in spite of the generous endowment of nature in terms of human and material resources.

Thirdly, the way forward for all of us is to pull in the same direction towards clearly defined objectives. The ING is irrevocably committed to conclude the democratisation process and to hand over power to an elected president at the end of its tenure. We must not lose sight of the urgent need to stem further deterioration of our economy and to implement measures for recovery and reform. It is equally important that we strive to improve the quality of governance, accept transparency and accountability in the management of public finance and carry out a crusade against corruption.

Fourthly, I want to assure the international community that Nigeria will continue to honour her obligations. During the tenure of the interim national government, we will do all that is necessary to strengthen the structures that will guarantee to all Nigerians the fundamental human rights as enshrined in our constitution and in the relevant international instruments to which Nigeria is a party. In fact, we have clearly indicated our intentions in this direction by releasing some human rights activists a few days ago.

Lastly, I urge you, good people of Nigeria, to see the events of the past several weeks as nothing more than a passing phase in the life of our country. Please give this government a chance to live up to its promise by keeping and maintaining the peace as well as going about your lawful duties without let or hindrance.

Thank you and God bless.

Long live the Federal Republic of Nigeria.

NOTES

1. Ernest A. Shonekan. http://en.wikipedia.org/wiki/Ernest_Shonekan. Accessed March 12, 2008.

2. Chief Ernest Adegnle Shonekan, "State of the Nation" Address, (Ministry of Foreign Affairs, Abuja, Nigeria, August 31, 1993).

Chapter Eleven

General Sani Abacha

BIOGRAPHICAL NOTES ON
GENERAL SANI ABACHA

General Sani Abacha was born on September 20, 1943. He had his early military training at the Nigerian Military Training College, Kaduna, and Mons Defence Officers Training College, Aldershot, United Kingdom. In 1963 he was commissioned a second lieutenant. With several other military trainings in the School of Infantry in Warminster, the Command and Staff College, Jaji, and the National Institute for Policy and Strategic Studies, NIPPS, Jos, Abacha had many military command responsibilities.

In 1984, he was appointed the general officer commanding the Second Division of the Nigerian Army, with headquarters in Ibadan, Oyo State. During the General Buhari 605–day-old military administration, Abacha was a member of that Supreme Military Council, as well as member of Babangida's eight-year rule by the Armed Forces Ruling Council.

Other high-profile military positions General Abacha held included that of the former chief of army staff, minister of defence, and chairman, Joint Chiefs of Staff. On November 17, 1993, he forced the resignation of a Babangida installed Interim National Government under Chief Ernest Shonekan, and assumed power as the head of state, and commander in chief of the Armed Forces of the Federal Republic of Nigeria. With that stroke of the military whip, Abacha earned himself the dubious honor of being the seventh military ruler of Nigeria since independence from Britain in 1960.

In the wake of the annulment of the June 12, 1993 presidential election results, and the subsequent appointment by Babangida of Ernest Shonekan as the head of state of the Interim National Government, there was no credibilty or any shade of legitimacy to Nigeria as a country across the globe. The

General Sanni Abacha. 7th Nigerian Military Head of State and Commander-in-Chief of the Nigerian Armed Forces, November 17, 1993–July 9, 1998. Born: September 20, 1943 in Kano, Nigeria. Died: June 9, 1998 in Abuja, Nigeria. Source: Courtesy of the Nigerian permanent mission at the United Nations, New York, USA.

eighty-two days of administrative caretaker government by Chief Shonekan was just that. And when General Abacha seized the reins of political power on November 17, 1993, it was not a surprise that in the words of the famous Nigerian novelist Chinua Achebe things had really fallen apart in a diverse thirty-six-state country where the center could barely hold itself together. See Figure 11.1. A strong hand needed to intervene to restore law and order. The ascension speech that follows is General Abacha's first on-air broadcast on the evening of November 18, 1993.[1]

THE FULL TEXT OF THE ASCENSION SPEECH OF GENERAL SANI ABACHA ON NOVEMBER 18, 1993, AS THE MILITARY HEAD OF STATE AND COMMANDER IN CHIEF OF THE NIGERIAN ARMED FORCES, AFTER THE SUDDEN RESIGNATION OF CHIEF ERNEST SHONEKAN AS THE HEAD OF THE INTERIM NATIONAL GOVERNMENT

Fellow Nigerians,[2] sequel to the resignation of the former Head of the Interim National Government and Commander-in-Chief of the Armed Forces, Chief

Figure 11.1. **2010 Political Map of Nigeria with Thirty-Six States. Source: Created by the author.**

Ernest Shonekan and my subsequent appointment as head of state and commander-in-chief, I have had extensive consultations within the armed forces hierarchy and other well meaning Nigerians in a bid to find solutions to the various political, economic and social problems which have engulfed our beloved country, and which have made life most difficult to the ordinary citizen of this nation.

Chief Ernest Shonekan took over as head of state and commander-in-chief of the Nigerian Armed Forces at a most trying time in the history of the country. Politically, economically, and socially, there were lots of uncertainties. Things appeared bleak and the atmosphere was heavy with uncertainties. However, driven by a belief in himself, his countrymen, and love for his country, he accepted to face the challenges of our time. I will, therefore, like to take this opportunity to pay tribute to him for his selfless service to the nation. He showed great courage at taking on the daunting task of heading the Interim National Government and even greater courage to know when to leave.

Many have expressed fears about the apparent return of the military. Many have talked about the concern of the international community. However, under the present circumstances the survival of our beloved country is far above any other consideration. Nigeria is the only country we have. We must, therefore, solve our problems ourselves. We must lay a very solid foundation for the growth of democracy. We should avoid any ad hoc or temporary solutions. The problems must be addressed firmly, objectively, decisively and with all sincerity of purpose. Consequently, the following decisions come into immediate effect:

- The Interim National Government is hereby dissolved.
- The National and State Assemblies are also dissolved.
- The State Executive Councils are dissolved. The Brigade Commanders are to take over from the Governors in their States until Administrators are appointed. Where there are no Brigade Commanders, the Commissioners of Police in the State are to take over.
- All Local Governments stand dissolved. The Directors of Personnel are to take over the administration of the Local Governments until Administrators are appointed.
- All former Secretaries to Federal Ministries are to hand over to their Directors-General until Ministers are appointed.
- The two political parties are hereby dissolved.
- All processions, political meetings and associations of any type in any part of the country are hereby banned.
- Any consultative committee by whatever name called is hereby proscribed.
- Decree 61 of 1993 is hereby abrogated.

A Provisional Ruling Council (PRC), is hereby established. It will comprise:

- The Head of State, Commander-in-Chief of the Armed Forces of the Federal Republic of Nigeria as Chairman
- The Chief of General Staff as Vice-Chairman
- The Honourable Minister of Defence
- The Chief of Defence Staff
- The Service Chiefs
- The Inspector General of Police
- The Attorney General and Minister of Justice
- The Internal Affairs Minister
- The Foreign Affairs Minister
- The National Security Adviser

Legislative powers will reside in the Council.
States will be governed by civilian administrators to be appointed later.
Also, a Federal Executive Council will be put in place.
Our security system will be enhanced to ensure that lives of citizens, property of individuals are protected and preserved. Drug trafficking and other economic crimes such as 419 must be tackled and eliminated.

On the current strike throughout the nation following the increase in the price of fuel, I appeal to all the trade unions to return to work immediately. We cannot afford further dislocation and destruction of our economy.

On the closed media houses, government is hereby lifting the order of proscription with immediate effect. We, however, appeal to the media houses that in this spirit of national reconciliation, we should show more restraint and build a united and peaceful Nigeria.

Fellow Nigerians, the events of the past months, starting from the annulment of the June 12 presidential election, culminating in the appointment of the former Head of State, Chief Ernest Shonekan, who unfortunately resigned yesterday, are well known to you. The economic downturn has undoubtedly been aggravated by the ongoing political crisis.

We require well thought-out and permanent solutions to these problems if we are to emerge stronger from them. Consequently, a constitutional conference with full constituent powers will be established soon to determine the future constitutional structure of Nigeria. The constitutional conference will also recommend the method of forming parties, which will lead to the ultimate recognition of political parties formed by the people. While the conference is on, the reorganisation and reform of the following major institutions will be carried out:

• The Military
• The Police
• The Customs
• The Judiciary
• NITEL
• NNPC
• NEPA
• The Banking Industry
• Higher Educational Institutions

This regime will be firm, humane, and decisive. We will not condone nor tolerate any act of indiscipline. Any attempt to test our will will be decisively dealt with. For the International Community, we ask that you suspend judgment while we grapple with the onerous task of nation building, reconciliation and repairs. This government is a child of necessity with a strong determination to restore peace and stability to our country and on these foundations, enthrone a lasting and true democracy. Give us the chance to solve our problems in our own ways.

Long Live the Federal Republic of Nigeria.

NOTES

1. Sani Abacha, Presidential Profile, from www.nigeriaonline.com. (Accessed March 26, 2009).

2. General Sani Abacha, *Maiden Broadcast to the Nation* (Abuja, Nigeria: Federal Ministry of Information and Communications Document, November 18, 1993).

Chapter Twelve

General Abdulsalami Abubakar

BIOGRAPHICAL NOTES ON
GENERAL ABDULSALAMI ABUBAKAR

General Abdulsalami Abubakar was born in Minna in today's Niger state on June 13, 1942, to Alhaji Abubakar Jibrin and Hajiya Fatikande Mohammed. He attended Minna Native Authority Primary School between 1950 and 1956. He attended secondary school at Government College, Bida, also in Niger state, from 1957 to1962. In 1963, he briefly attended Kaduna Technical College from January to October, when he enlisted in the Nigerian Air Force on October 3, as an officer cadet.

Between June 1964 and July 1966, he was trained in Germany as a flying pilot. When he returned to Nigeria in 1966, he was seconded to the Nigerian Army. He underwent several military trainings at the Nigerian Defence Academy, Kaduna, as an officer cadet of Emergency Combatant Short Service Course 2. On the successful completion of the cadet training, Abubakar was commissioned on October 20, 1967 as second lieutenant and posted to infantry. He was promoted major general October 1, 1991.

Among his outstanding service commendations in various capacities in the Nigerian Army and Defence Headquarters are: general staff officer 2, Second Garrison (1967–1968), commanding officer, 92 Infantry Battalion (1969–1974), brigade major, 7 Infantry Brigade (1974–1975), commanding officer, 84, Infantry Battalion (1975) and assistant adjutant general, 3 Infantry Division 1979. He was commanding officer, 145 Infantry Battalion (NIBATT II) of the United Nations Interim Force in Lebanon (1978–1979), chief instructor, Nigerian Defence Academy (1980–1982), and colonel Administration and Quartering, 1 Mechanised Division (1982–1984). He was commander, 3 Mechanised Brigade, between 1985 and 1986.

General Abdulsalami Abubakar 8th Nigerian Military Head of State and Commander-in-Chief of the Nigerian Armed Forces, June 8, 1998-May 29, 1999. Born: June 13, 1942 in Minna, Niger State, Nigeria. Source: Courtesy of the Nigerian permanent mission at the United Nations, New York, USA.

General Abubakar served as the military secretary of the army, 1986–1988. His first command of an infantry division came in January 1990. He served in that capacity till September 1990 when he was appointed as general officer commanding 1 Mechanised Division (1990–1991). From 1991–1993 he was appointed principal staff officer in the Defence Headquarters as chief of policy and plans (army).

As a professional soldier, he has availed himself of changes in military technology and tactical rules of warfare. He has attended military management and professional excellence courses in the United States. Among such courses are: The Infantry Officers Advanced Course, USA, 1975–1976; Airborne Course, 1976, Command and General Staff Officer Course, USA, 1976–1977, and the International Defence Management Course, USA, 1982. In 1985 he attended the Senior Executive Course at the National Institute for Policy and Strategic Studies (NIPSS), Kuru, Jos.

General Abubakar became chief of defence staff, Defence Headquarters on December 1, 1993. He was promoted to full general and appointed head of state, commander in chief of the Armed Forces, Federal Republic of Nigeria on June 9, 1998, by the country's Provisional Ruling Council following the death of General Sani Abacha.

General Abubakar is married to the Honourable Justice Fati Lami Abubakar. They have six children.

The rise to power and leadership by General Abdulsalami Abubakar was circumstantial upon General Abacha's sudden death on June 8, 1998. As Abubakar was thrust into the position of the head of the Nigerian Government, he had to summon the courage and the discipline demanded of a trained military professional, to rise to the occasion. For fifteen years, Nigeria had been plagued by military rule that did not seem better than the civilian governments. The two immediate preceeding rulers had been described as the worst military rulers Nigerians ever had. The general conclusion and the psychology of the Nigerian was that the military had no useful purpose in politics. Abubakar was senstive to this, and in his ascension speech he laid down the conditions for rapid military disengagment from Nigerian politics. Besides the announcement of the mourning protocols for the deceased ex-military ruler, the speech was a call for honour and courage from the military, and service from all Nigerians, as well as a patriotic call to all Nigerians at one of those several trying moments in her history as a plural and ethnically diverse country.[1]

THE FULL TEXT OF THE ASCENSION SPEECH BY GENERAL ABDULSALAMI ABUBAKAR, THE HEAD OF STATE AND COMMANDER IN CHIEF OF THE NIGERIAN ARMED FORCES, BROADCAST ON JUNE 9, 1998

Fellow Nigerians,[2]

The Provisional Ruling Council met at an extra-ordinary session yesterday following the sudden death of the Head of State, Commander-in-Chief of the Armed Forces of the Federal Republic of Nigeria, General Sanni Abacha, GCON and appointed me as the new Head of State, Commander-in-Chief.

Like other Nigerians, I received the sad news with great shock and, in accepting the burden of history now placed upon me as Head of State, I pray that Almighty God will give us the fortitude to bear the irreparable loss.

It is not in question that General Sanni Abacha died on very active and patriotic service of our beloved fatherland. We shall forever remember him for his innovative leadership and transparent stewardship to the nation at the most trying period of our nascent history.

We salute his honesty, resoluteness, fearlessness and total commitment to the preservation of Nigeria as a united, stable and prosperous entity. The most befitting way to honour his memory is for all Nigerians to uphold those ideals, ethos and lessons he tried to infuse into our national consciousness.

Fellow Nigerians, I enjoin you to bear this national tragedy with courage and faith in God. This is time for reflection and national prayers. The Almighty God in His Infinite mercies and compassion will soothe our grief and strengthen our collective resolve and aspiration for peace, stability and socio-economic development of our country.

My fervent appeal also goes to the international community for their understanding and cooperation. Nigeria demands a fair hearing and constructive engagement and not isolation. We remain an important member of the international system through the frame-work of the United Nations, a veritable instrument of international cooperation and inter-dependence.

We shall honour all our international obligations and maintain our national commitment to international peace and security, especially in the West African sub-region. Similarly, we intend to continue to have friendly relations with all nations of the world. However, in spite of the recent developments in the country, we shall resolutely defend our sovereignty, independence and territorial integrity.

Fellow Nigerians, we remain fully committed to the socio-political transition programme of General Sanni Abacha's Administration and will do everything to ensure its full and successful implementation. In this regard, I am holding consultations with all relevant agencies at the highest level.

We shall need the full cooperation of all Nigerians to succeed in this sacred endeavour and wish to extend invitation to all those Nigerians in self-exile to return home to join the process of reconstruction, reconciliation and the conclusion of the transition programme.

One-month period of national mourning starting June 9, to July 7, 1998 has been declared to solemnise the occasion. In addition, Condolence Registers will be opened in strategic places in Abuja, State Capitals and Local Government Headquarters throughout the country.

Once again, may God Almighty inspire us and guide us to manage this national tragedy and pray that General Abacha's gentle soul may rest in perfect peace. Amen.

NOTES

1. "General Abubakar Keeps His Word, Obasanjo Takes Over: Nigeria Has High Hopes in Stable Democracy." (Abuja, Nigeria: Publications of the Federal Ministry of Information & Culture, 1999).

2. General Abdulsalami Abubakar, Maiden Broadcast by the New Head of State, and Commander-in-Chief of the Armed Forces of Nigeria, June 9, 1998 (Washington, D.C.: The Nigerian Embassy, Information Department Document).

Chapter Thirteen

Olusegun Aremu Obasanjo

BIOGRAPHICAL NOTES ON
PRESIDENT OLUSEGUN AREMU OBASANJO

President Olusegun Aremu Obasanjo was born in Abeokuta, Ogun State, on March 5, 1937. He was educated at Baptist Boys' High School, Abeokuta. In 1958 he enlisted in the Nigerian Army. His earlier military training included: Mons Officers Cadet School, Aldershot, England; Royal College of Military Engineering, Chatham, England; School of Survey, Newbury, England; Indian Defence Staff College; Indian Army School of Engineering, Poona; Royal College of Defence Studies, London, 1974.

His military service included the Fifth Battalion, Nigerian Army, Kaduna and the Cameroons, 1958–1959, after which he was commissioned a second lieutenant, Nigerian Army in 1959. He was promoted lieutenant in 1960. He served in the Nigerian contingent of the United Nations force in the Congo (now Zaire) in 1960. He later joined the then only Engineering Unit of the Nigerian Army and became its commander in 1963. Obasanjo was promoted captain, Nigerian Army in 1963. He was attached to Indian Army Engineering School, at Kirkee, India, in 1965. He earned a promotion to major in 1965, and became lieutenant colonel in 1967.

In 1967 Obasanjo became commander, Second Area Command, Nigerian Army, and commander, garrison, Nigerian Army in Ibadan, 1967–1969. He was promoted colonel in 1969. He became the general officer commanding Third Infantry Division, Nigerian Army, 1969–1970. During the Nigerian-Biafran Civil War, Obasanjo was commander, Third Marine Commando Division, South-Eastern State.

Between 1970 and1975, he was the commander, Engineering Corps of the Nigerian Army. He was promoted brigadier of the Nigerian Army in 1972.

General Olusegun Aremu Obasanjo. 4th Military Head of State of Nigerian and Commander-in-Chief of the Nigerian Armed Forces February 13, 1976–October 1, 1979. Born: March 5, 1937 in Abeokuta, Ogun State, Nigeria. Source: Maxsiollum.wordpress.com, 2004.

Obasanjo was appointed federal commissioner (now called minister) for works and housing, January–July 1975.

Obasanjo was appointed chief of staff Supreme Headquarters, Nigerian Army, 1975–1976, and was promoted lieutenant general in 1976. He was a member and later chairman of the defunct Supreme Military Council (SMC), from 1975 to 1979. On the assassination of General Murtalla Muhammad on February 13, 1976, Obasanjo was appointed head of state and commander in chief of the Nigerian Armed Forces, February 13, 1976 through September 30, 1979 when he handed over the reins of Nigerian democratic presidential administration to a duly elected civilian successor, Alhaji Shehu Usman Shagari. He was promoted army general in 1979. He voluntarily retired from the Nigerian Army October 1979, but remained a member of the Advisory Council of State since 1979. He has been a fellow of the Institute of African Studies, University of Ibadan, since 1979; member, UNESCO Commission for Peace in the Minds of Men, 1981–1986; member, Independent (Palme)

Commission on Disarmament and Security issues, since 1983; member, WHO Committee of Experts on Effects of Nuclear Weapons; member, Executive Committee, Inter-Action Council of Former Heads of State and Government. He was member and cochair, Commonwealth Leaders on the security needs of Commonwealth Frontline States and Mozambique; and founder/organiser, African Leadership Forum, Otta, Ogun State, 1988. He was appointed special adviser to the International Institute of Tropical Agriculture (IITA), May 1989.

In 1980, Obasanjo was honoured with the Grand Commander of the Order of the Federal Republic of Nigeria (GCFR). He has been conferred with several honorary degrees from universities in and outside of Nigeria. He has also published several books, among which are: *A March of Progress* (1979), *My Command* (1980), *Nzeogwu* (1987), *Africa Embattled* (1988), and *Constitution for National Integration and Development* (1989).

He established private business ventures in retirement. One of such is the Obasanjo Farms Nigeria Limited in Otta, Ogun State.

Obasanjo is married with many children.

Since the last time General Obasanjo handed over political power to an elected civilian government in 1979, Nigeria only knew civil democratic governance till December 31, 1983. Between then and 1999, the country was awash with military dictators with different shades of authority and legitimacy as well as personal ambitions. It was under this shadow of self-doubt and frustrations with Western-styled democratic government and authoritarian dictatorships, that Obasanjo was recruited to run for the next democratic experiment in Nigeria, as a retired army general who in retirement had become a successful farmer, writer, and political commentator and critique of the military regimes in Nigeria. He ran and won the election. On this his second coming to the Nigerian political leadership as a civilian President, Obasanjo had many skills and knowledge to share in the rudiments of successful leadership and political management of a plural democratic society. In the following inaugural speech, Obasanjo is conscious of his place in history and the role he can play to usher Nigeria into a new century with a much-desired system of government all Nigerians would be proud to call their own.[1]

THE FULL TEXT OF THE INAUGURAL SPEECH OF PRESIDENT OLUSEGUN OBASANJO AND COMMANDER IN CHIEF OF THE NIGERIAN ARMED FORCES ON THE OCCASION OF BEING INAUGURATED ON MAY 29, 1999 AS THE THIRD DEMOCRATICALLY ELECTED NIGERIAN PRESIDENT SINCE INDEPENDENCE

Your Royal Highness, the Prince of Wales, Your Excellencies, Visiting Presidents, Your Excellencies, Visiting Heads of Government, Your

Excellencies, Visiting Special Representatives, Your Excellencies, Heads of Diplomatic Missions, Your Excellency, the Vice- President of Nigeria, My Lord, the Chief Justice of the Federal Republic of Nigeria, Your Excelencies, Former Presidents and Heads of State of Nigeria, My Lords, Spiritual and Temporal, Distinguished Senators and Honourable Members of the House of Representatives, Distinguished Guests, Ladies and Gentlemen, Fellow Nigerians,[2]

We give praise and honour to God Almighty for this day specially appointed by God himself. Everything created by God has its destiny, and it is the destiny of all of us to see this day. Twelve months ago, no-one could have predicted the series of stunning events that made it possible for democratic elections to be held at the local government level, the state level, and culminating in the National Assembly elections. Thereafter, you the good people of Nigeria elected me, a man who had walked through the valley of the shadow of death, as your president to head the democratic civilian administration. I believe that this is what God Almighty has ordained for me and for my beloved country, Nigeria, and its people.

I accept this destiny in all humility and with the full belief that with the backing and support of our people, we shall not fail. I wish at this point to thank all you good Nigerians for the confidence reposed in me. I wish to pay tribute to the great and gallant Nigerians who lost their lives in the course of the struggle for liberty, democracy and good governance. They held the beacon of freedom and liberty high in the face of state terrorism and tyranny. We thank God that their sacrifice has not been in vain. We will surely always remember them.

Our thanks go also to the friends of Nigeria in many lands for the commitment and unrelenting support they gave throughout the dark ominous days of the struggle. Nigerians living in foreign lands deserve special tribute for not forgetting their fatherland, and for making their voices heard persistently in defence of freedom; and I must commend you, my home-based fellow Nigerians for the way you bore unprecedented hardship, deprivation of every conceivable rights and privileges that were once taken for granted.

I commend General Abdulsalami Abubakar and members of the Provisional Ruling Council, PRC, for the leadership they gave the country in the last 11 months, and for keeping meticulously to their announced time-table of handing over to a democratically elected government today. As officers and gentlemen, they have kept their word. The Independent National Electoral Commission, INEC, also deserve the thanks of all of us. In the face of doubt and scepticism and great time constraints, the chairman and his commissioners conducted the elections, right from local government level to the presidential level. They acquitted themselves creditably and they deserve our gratitude.

Nigeria is wonderfully endowed by the Almighty with human and other resources. It does no credit either to us or the entire black race if we fail in managing our resources for quick improvement in the quality of life of our people. Instead of progress and development, which we are entitled to expect from those who govern us, we experienced in the last decade and half and particularly in the last regime but one, persistent deterioration in the quality of our governance, leading to instability and the weakening of all public institutions. Good men were shunned and kept away from government while those who should be kept away were drawn near. Relations between men and women who had been friends for many decades and between communities that had lived together in peace for many generations became very bitter because of the actions or inaction of government. The citizens developed distrust in government, and because promises made for the improvement of the conditions of the people were not kept, all statements by government met with cynicism. Government officials became progressively indifferent to propriety of conduct and showed little commitment to promoting the general welfare of the people and the public good. Government and all its agencies became thoroughly corrupt and reckless. Members of the public had to bribe their way through in ministries and parastatals to get attention and one government agency had to bribe another government agency to obtain the release of their statutory allocations of funds. The impact of official corruption is so rampant and has earned Nigeria a very bad image at home and abroad. Besides, it has distorted and retrogressed development. Our Infrastructures—NEPA, NITEL, roads, railways, education, housing and other social services were allowed to decay and collapse.

Our country has thus been through one of its darkest periods. All these have brought the nation to a situation of chaos and near despair. This is the challenge before us. Fellow Nigerians, let us rise as one to face the task ahead and turn this daunting scene into opportunities in a new dawn. Let us make this the beginning of a genuine renaissance.

Fellow Nigerians, the entire Nigerian scene is very bleak indeed; so, bleak people ask me: Where do we begin? I know what great things you expect of me at this new dawn. As I have said many times in my extensive travels in the country, I am not a miracle worker. It will be foolish to underrate the task ahead alone. You have been asked many times in the past to make sacrifices and to be patient. I am also going to ask you to make sacrifices and to exercise patience. The difference will be that in the past, sacrifices were made and patience exercised with little or no results. This time, however, the results of your sacrifice and patience will be clear and manifest for all to see.

With God as our guide and with 120 million Nigerians working with me with commitment, sustained effort and determination we shall not fail. On my part, I will give the forthright, purposeful, committed, honest, and transparent leadership that the situation demands. I am determined, with your full cooperation to make significant changes within a year of my administration. Together we shall take steps to halt the decline in the human development indices as they apply to Nigeria. All the impacts of bad governance on our people that are immediately removable will be removed while working for medium and long-term solutions. Corruption, the greatest single bane of our society today, will be tackled head-on at all levels. Corruption is incipient in all human societies and in most human activities, but it must not be condoned. This is why laws are made and enforced to check corruption so that society will survive and develop in an orderly, reasonable, and predictable way. No society can achieve anything near its full potential if it allows corruption to become the full-blown cancer it has become in Nigeria.

One of the greatest tragedies of military rule in recent times is that corruption was allowed to grow unchallenged and unchecked even when it was glaring for everybody to see. Rules and regulations for doing official business were deliberately ignored, set aside, or by-passed to facilitate corrupt practices. Beneficiaries of corruption in all forms will fight back with all at their disposals. We shall be firm with them.

There will be no sacred cows. Nobody, no matter who and where will be allowed to get away with the breach of the law or the perpetration of corruption and evil.

Under this administration, therefore, all the rules and regulations designed to help honesty and transparency in dealing with government will be restored and enforced. Specifically, I will immediately reintroduce civil service rules and financial instructions and enforce compliance. Other regulations will be introduced to ensure transparency. The rampant corruption in the public service and the cynical contempt for integrity that pervades every level of the bureaucracy will be stamped out. The public officer must be encouraged to believe once again that integrity pays and self-respect must be restored and his work must be fairly rewarded through better pay and benefits—both while he is in service and in retirement.

I am very aware of the widespread cynicism and total lack of confidence in government, arising from the bad faith, deceit and evil actions of recent administrations. Where official pronouncements are repeatedly made and not met by action, government forfeits the confidence of the people and their trust. One of the immediate acts of this administration will be to implement quickly and decisively measures that will restore confidence in governance. These measures will help to create the auspicious atmosphere necessary for the reforms and the difficult decisions and the hard work required to pull the country back on the path of development and growth.

The issue of crime requires as much attention and seriousness as the issue of corruption. Although the police are in the forefront of fighting crimes and ensuring our security, it is our responsibility to help the police to be able to help us. The police will be made to do their job, all Nigerian citizens and residents in our midst are entitled to the protection of life and property. A determined effort will be made to cut down significantly the incidence of violent crimes.

I believe that this administration must deal with the following issues even in these difficult times of near economic collapse: the crises in the oil-producing areas, food supply, food security, and agriculture, law and order with particular reference to armed robbery and cultism in our educational institutions, exploration and production of petroleum, education, macroeconomic policies, supply and distribution of petroleum products, the debt issue, corruption, drug, organized fraud called 419, and crimes leading to loss of lives, properties, and investment; infrastructure, water supply, energy, telecommunications, ports, airways, national shipping and Nigeria railway; resuscitation of the manufacturing industry, job creation, poverty alleviation, housing both for civilian population and barrack refurbishment and new constructions for the armed forces and the Police; ECOMOG, health services, political and constitutional dialogue, women and youth empowerment.

In pursuit of these priorities, I have worked out measures which must be implemented within the first six months. Details of the focus and measures of this administration on these and other matters will be announced from time to time. I shall quickly ascertain the true state of our finances and the economy and shall let the nation know. In the light of resources available, I shall concentrate on those issues that can bring urgent beneficial relief to our people. I will need good men and women of proven integrity and record of good performance to help me in my cabinet. I appreciate that the quality and calibre of the members of my cabinet and top appointments will send a positive or negative signal to Nigerians and the international community as to the seriousness of the administration to make salutary changes. In a difficult and abnormal situation, great care and circumspection are called for in appointments to the cabinet and high public positions.

To be appointed a minister, or to any other public office is not a license to loot the treasury. It is a call to national service. It is one of the best ways of rendering dedicated service to humanity. In this administration, being a minister or holding any other public office will not deprive you of what you have before you come into office, but you will not be allowed to have conflict of interest, abuse of office, or illicit acquisitions. Service to be satisfying must entail certain amounts of sacrifice. A regular weekly meeting of cabinet will be reintroduced to enrich the quality of decisions of government through open discussions of memoranda in council. Before any issues are introduced to the cabinet, the time-tested procedure of inter-ministerial consultation will have been made.

The conclusion of council, circulated to all ministers and permanent secretaries, will, as used to be the practice in the past, be the authority for executive action and for incurring expenditure of public fund. This will help the cohesion of the government, ensure discipline, and hinder corrupt intentions since all major contracts must go to council for open consideration.

A code of conduct for ministers and other public officers will be introduced. Other measures for individual and collective self-control and self-discipline of ministers and other public officers will also be introduced. I am determined to stretch my hand of fellowship to all Nigerians, regardless of their political affiliations. I intend to reconcile all those who feel alienated by past political events and I will endeavour to heal divisions and to restore the harmony we used to know in this country. A bill will be forwarded within weeks of the inception of the administration to the National Assembly for a law providing for 13 per cent derivation in revenue allocation to be used for ecological rehabilitation, infrastructure, and other developments. A competent group will be set up immediately to prepare a comprehensive development plan for the Niger Delta area. Dialogue will be held at all levels with the real representatives of all sections of the oil-producing communities to improve communication and better mutual understanding. Responsibility and initiative for resolving the crisis in the Niger Delta rests with the government.

Nigeria has over the years played a very active role in the ECOMOG for the restoration of peace in Liberia and Sierra Leone. Our national interests require the establishment and maintenance of peace and stability in the West African sub-region. Specifically, in the case of Sierra Leone, we shall endeavour to ensure a quick resolution of the crisis by dialogue and diplomatic means, by increasing activity on the second track of peace and reconciliation. This will enable us reduce our commitments in both theatres, but particularly in Sierra Leone.

Nigeria, once a well-respected country and a key role player in international bodies, became a pariah nation. We shall pursue a dynamic foreign policy to promote friendly relations with all nations and will continue to play a constructive role in the United Nations and the Organization of African Unity, the Commonwealth, and other international bodies. We shall continue to honour existing agreements between Nigeria and other countries. It is our firm resolve to restore Nigeria fully to her previous prestigious position in the comity of nations.

Let me once again thank our international friends who fought for democracy alongside with us. Today, we are taking a decisive step on the path of democracy. We will leave no stone unturned to ensure sustenance of democracy because it is good for us, it is good for Africa, and it is good for the world. We call on the world, particularly the Western world, to help us sustain democracy by sharing with us the burden of debt which may be crushing and destructive to democracy in our land.

The incursion of the military into government has been a disaster for our country. The esprit de corps among military personnel has been destroyed. Professionalism has been lost. Most youths go into the military now not to pursue a noble career but with the sole intention of taking part in coups and to be appointed as military administrators of states and chairmen of task forces. As a retired officer, my heart bleeds to see the degradation in the proficiency of the military. A great deal of re-orientation has to be undertaken and a redefinition of roles, retraining, and re-education will have to be done to ensure that the military submits to civil authority and regains its pride, professionalism, and tradition. We shall restore military cooperation and exchanges with our traditional friends and we will help the military to help itself. It is my resolve to work harmoniously with the legislature and the judiciary to ensure that Nigeria enjoys good and civilized governance.

I am also determined to build a broad consensus amongst all parties to enhance national harmony and stability and, thus, ensure success in the long struggle ahead. Politicians have a duty in whatever capacity they may find themselves, whether as legislators or ministers, to be committed and be seen to be committed to the public good. Politicians must carefully examine the budget to ensure that public funds are judiciously spent. They must avoid damage to their own credibility and not vote for themselves special privileges. They must join in the campaign against corruption and help re-establish integrity in the conduct of public affairs. I assure you all that it is the policy of this government to ensure fair remuneration in service and in retirement to public servants, which includes legislators, civil servants, the police, and members of the armed forces, parastatals and public-owned educational institutions. I call on all Nigerians, but particularly our religious leaders, to pray for moral and spiritual revival and regeneration in our nation.

I shall end this address by stressing again that we must change our ways of governance and of doing business on this eve of the coming millennium. This, we must do to ensure progress, justice, harmony, and unity, and above all, to rekindle confidence amongst our people, confidence that their condition will rapidly improve and that Nigeria will be great and will become a major world player in the very near future.

May the Almighty help us all.

THE FULL TEXT OF HIS EXCELLENCY PRESIDENT OLUSEGUN OBASNAJO'S FIRST INAUGURAL ADDRESS TO THE JOINT NATIONAL ASSEMBLY SESSION ON JUNE 4, 1999

Let us thank God for this great moment in the life of our country[3] as we take this decisive step in our democratic renewal. I take the opportunity of this occasion to welcome you all to this milestone on our journey toward nationhood and sustainable democracy.

I also want to seize this opportunity to congratulate each and every one of you for your success at the polls. It is my sincere hope that the confidence reposed in you by our people, and their expectation of you in terms of selfless service shall constitute the motivation force in all your deliberations and activities over the next four years.

Unfortunately, our recent contemporary circumstances have put our nation at the crossroads, such that we all talk of "a new beginning." The inauguration last Saturday has been compared with the birth of the nation nearly four decades ago when we adopted a Coat of Arms with the words UNITY AND FAITH.

If we had adhered to these precepts, we would not now be talking of "a new beginning." Hence the imperative that we make the "new beginning" of today the last one, and we can only do this by laying a durable foundation for continuous evolution of democratic governance in this country.

Unity means recognizing our obligations to common destiny and working together along the best route to that destiny. Faith implies hope and confidence in ourselves and in the future. And above all, trust in the Almighty.

We are from different social backgrounds, we belong to different ethnic groups, we hold different religious beliefs, and our political affiliations are not all the same. But our common problems, which dictate the need for common solutions, in pursuit of the common good, demand that as Senators and Members of the House of Representatives, you must constantly remind yourselves of our new national motto: Unity and Faith, Peace and Progress.

Peace means understanding and agreeing on the need for common solutions. Progress means doing what we have to do for the common good.

It is in pursuit of these objectives that I wish here to outline to you the agenda for our Administration.

Reconciliation:

We are a nation of many ethnic groups joined together by God and historical circumstances. In the early fifties, the founding fathers of our nation recognized the imperative of federalism with the Richards Constitution.

Since then, our people have come to understand and appreciate the extent of historical links within the geographical area housing our nation. We have accepted the bonds binding us within the federalist structure. And despite an unfortunate civil war, we have demonstrated our willingness to co-exist, co-habit and continue as one people.

In reaction to the political turmoil of the past few years, various groups and communities have been advocating their perceptions of "true federalism":

- Some talk of "restructuring of the federation" with separate defense and law enforcement commands;
- Others demand the application of a revenue allocation formula based only on the princple of derivation;
- There are those who want the country carved into six geopolitical zones.

These demands are mostly borne out of deep frustration and despair over the persistent failure of central governments to meet the hopes and aspirations of the people.

An inventory of our grievances would reveal that without exception all sections have felt marginalised in the last fifteen years. In a situation where all groups complain of marginalisation, the question is begged: who is doing the marginalisation?

This whole nation has been traumatized by misrule. It is perhaps understandable that in the absence of a trustworthy, transparent and just central authority, each one feels a victim and suspects the other of being the oppressor.

While in no way condoning the misguided decsions or tactical miscalculations of the past, I will, at this time, appeal for calm and mature reflections. We have come a long way as one Nigeria. As much as we have rejoiced together in times of triumph, let us reconcile our misunderstandings in times of disappointments. The imperative of stability and progress demands nothing less.

The issues arising are important enough to warrant thorough and careful assessments. I thus propose to work with the National Assembly, State Governments and our Traditional Authorities and all other forms of representative bodies and institutions within the Nigerian polity to achieve practicable and workable solutions within the next four years.

Economic Recovery:

Nigeria's most valuable asset is the population of dynamic and versatile men, women and youths who only need to have their energies harnessed and channeled to productive use. They yearn for honest, transparent and accountable leadership that they can trust and from which they can derive inspiration for hard work and fulfilling application of their talents and capabilities.

Let me pledge here that I shall spare no effort for the ultimate success of the Nigerian nation.

Our march towards economic recovery will require strict discipline, tight and responsible finanacial management. The resources available to discharge government business is meager and dwindling. The action to save the economy will demand sacrifice that will be extensive and painful.

Let me give you some insight into our financial situation. The projected budgetary deficit for the end of May 1999 was 163 billion Naira, but our administration has found that this figure had been exceeded by 93 billion Naira, an increase of over 57 percent, bringing the actual budget deficit to 256 billion Naira. We simply cannot sustain this level of expenditure pattern. And yet we have to add the extra cost of democracy in terms of capital and recurrent cost of the National Assembly.

With regard to our foreign reserves, the balance as at the end of May 1999 stood at .75 billion US dollars, compared with the sum of 7.1 billion US dollars at the beginning of January this year. At this rate of depletion the country will be in the red to the tune of 246 million US dollars by the end of the year.

The situation is dire and calls for immediate action. And we have started that action. The recently announced freeze on payments of extra-budgetary commitment is expeced to save the nation 50 billion Naira and 1.1 billion US dollars in foreign exchange.

Here are the other necessary measures we will have to take:

• Bloated public institutions have to be rationalised. We have started consultations with the IMF, World Bank, and other major donor organisations, to assist us with retraining of people who will be affected by the rationalisation. We intend to provide conducive economic environment for the retrained people to find gainful employment.
• The problem of ghost workers will have to be urgently and seriously tackled.
• All those who have served their time will be honourably retired and adequately compensated to permit them speedy and comfortable resettlement.
• Government expenditure will from now on be according to the financial rules and regulations, in order to ensure that every kobo that this Government earns will be used to serve the best interest of the common man in Nigeria. The Presidency in conjunction with the office of the

Accountant General and Auditor General of the Federation, will ensure that every item of expenditure is carefully monitored and fully accounted for, and it will all be done in accordance with the Financial Instructions.

You in the National Assembly will shortly be presented with the salaries and allowances attached to each public office, for approval as part of the details of the budget. Incomes will be reviewed periodically to ensure that officials are always remunerated sufficiently for their performance and not distracted or tempted into fraudulent acts or divided interests.

The Federal Tenders Board and the Ministerial Tenders Board will be reactivated and given wider powers to determine and ensure that contracts are only awarded to those competent enough to execute them. All Government contracts from now on will be processed through these two bodies. This procedure, with the implicit transparency and competitiveness, will eliminate the so-called 'Nigerian Factor' that adds as much as 50 per cent to costs of contracts.

Our objective is to put in place cost saving measures and stringent financial management as the starting point to economic recovery. At the end of the exercise we hope to demonstrate the extent to which mismanagement has cost us dearly all these many years.

For the above measures to be effective and achieve the intended aims, all officials and members of government institutions must heed the warning that mechanisms will be put in place for permanent and constant surveillance to ensure probity and accountability.

You may have heard this before, but I will say it again: This administration will not, under any circumstance, condone corruption or protect corrupt officials of Government. The Government will be watchful for fraud and misappropriation of public funds. It will expose and severely punish those who do not heed this admonition.

I implore you to join me in the fight against corruption and crime. To that end, I shall, within the next fortnight, be presenting to this Honourable House a bill for a law to prevent and punish corruption.

The current budget will be reviewed to reflect reordering of priorities in accordance with the agenda of our administration and the realities of the national economy. Details will be presented to the National Assembly as soon as posible. I expect you to treat the consideration of the budget with maximum dispatch.

Development Issues:

We all know the extent of the destruction and decay of almost all aspects of our national institutions and infrastructures. Rather than waste time repeating the familiar litany of our woes, I will move on to outline our Administration's strategy for rehabilitation, resuscitation and revitalization.

Transport is the lifeline of the economy and social interaction. An inefficient transport system implies stagnation in all sectors.

Our priorities in this sector will be:

- Design and implement a new policy on road maintenance.
- Design and implement a new rural roads development programme, with emphasis on the use of direct labour to engage a large number of our able bodied young men.
- Rehabilitate, modernize and expand our railways so that this national asset can once more become relevant to our economic development.
- Improve air travel by upgrading and revamping a good network of airports, airstrips across the country, and installing up-to-date navigational aids.
- Our practically defunct national airline will be critically examined to see the best means of resuscitating it.
- Private airlines will be encouraged.
- Optimally utilize the network of rivers for water transport inland.
- Encourage the development of effective and true mass transit system in certain urban areas.

Food and agriculture: Our goal is food security which is classically defined as access by all people at all times to enough food for an active healthy life. It is in this regard that this administration's priorities will be as follows:

- Farmers will be given maximum necessary support to cultivate and produce more per hectare per season, by such measures as timely supply of agriculture inputs.
- Rehabilitation and reactivation of irrigation facilities and encouragement of small size irrigation facilities by farmers.
- We will support and encourage livestock production with a view to making the country self-sufficient in meat products within the life of this Assembly.

Solid Minerals are to be found in different parts of Nigeria and they constitute a natural endowment with which we are also blessed. Our Administration will re-examine thoroughly our policies in respect of solid minerals development, with a view to identifying the forces militating against investments in this sector. We will remove such impediments.

Petroleum is presently our most important source of foreign exchange. Sadly, and very tragically, despite the position it occupies in our economy, this sector has suffered not only neglect as other national assets have, but has been subjected to the most unpatriotic abuses.

Our priorities in this sector will be:

- To urgently review our policies, giving top priority to the rehabilitation of our refineries.
- Design a programme for the regular and efficient maintenance of our refineries, flow stations, pipelines and depots.
- Ensure the observance and enforcement of all laws that govern the procurement, storage and distribution of all petroleum products.
- Ensure that the observance and enforcement of all laws that govern the procurement and distribution of all petroleum resources is only by competitive bidding, thereby maximising the revenue accruing to the government.
- Enhance all serious private ventures and efforts towards encouraging investments to expand exploration activities and development of new fields.
- The government will be more active in the implementation of Joint Venture Agreements so as to better protect our national interests.

Petrochemicals and natural gas are sub-sectors in this area which require the utmost attention. We have a duty to do all that is necessary to maximize our endowment advantages of these potential revenue earners. We will pursue such policies that by the end of four years, the annual revenue from this sector should be close to the annual revenue from petroleum sub-sector.

Education:

There is no home in this country which is not concerned about the state of our education. The structure is in a disgraceful condition. Teachers are now producing thousands of functionally illiterate young people for a life of joblessness and despondency.

Our administration will embark on a thorough exercise of reviving, revamping, improving and updating our education system. We shall pay special attention to science and technology. We will seek the cooperation of the international community and non-governmental agencies in designing and executing our programmes. Measures will be taken to encourage education in areas of the country where educational awareness and facilties are low. Then we will relaunch Universal Primary Education and make it compulsory.

Privatization and Foreign Investment:

Our administration looks foward to an economy of vibrant partnership between government and business. It shall be one of cooperation and non-confrontation. Government shall not seek to do that which experience has proved it is least competent to handle. Business will be encouraged to be conscious of socal responsibilities. Private profit must look to promote public purpose and public good.

In this vein our Administration will pursue the policy of privatising all parastatals when it is judged that their performance will be enhanced and their subsequent status will be of overall benefit to the nation.

The privatization process will not be rushed, and will only follow a full and detailed management and valuation audit of the targeted establishments. After we have determined the value of the assets, the method of sale will be open, transparent and accessible to all Nigerians who may have the capital to invest.

This privatization process must be such that it gains and retains the confidence of both Nigerians and the international community.

We are also hoping that the international concern for democratic governance does not stop with the installation of our Adminstration. All Nigerians are expecting democracy to yield dividends that they can perceive in their lives. It is in this regard that we are hoping to count on further support from our international friends.

Our national circumstances are far from easy, so our message to our international well-wishers has to be blunt. The euphoria today could quickly evaporate if it is not followed by massive inflow of foreign investment and a more realistic reappraisal of the crushing debt burden.

Our Administration promises to provide a stable and secure enabling environment for all those seeking to do legitimate business within Nigeria.

We are also keen to discuss meaningfully all aspects of our foreign debts with a view to achieving a level of relief that matches our harsh realities.

Rich Nigerians at home and abroad must be seen to have faith in the country by investing in long term industrial projects and thereby confirming confidence in their own country.

The National Assembly has a duty to be part of this effort in every way it can, as one element promoting public-private sectors partnership. The signals emanating from this Honourable Assembly will go a long way towards the realization of our hopes and aspiration for our country.

Distinguished Senators and Honourable Members of the House, together we have to further the cause of democracy. It is thus vital that you immediately set in motion the process to repeal or amend all laws which are inconsistent with democratic ideals, practices and principles.

The expectation of Nigerians is high that the enthronement of democracy will usher in an era of prosperity. Prosperity will come after we have demonstrated our ability to confront the challenge of national re-awakening.

We Nigerians must decide and do what is necessary.

EXPLANATORY NOTES ON THE SECOND INAUGURAL ADDRESS BY PRESIDENT OLUSEGUN OBASANJO

Given the excitement of a return to civil rule, the first term of president Obasanjo was fast-paced, exciting, and pregnant with great expectations. One would not say that Nigerians were lethargic, or that the politicians were lacking of ambition. But the challenge to the president was to bring these anxious, impatient, and disparate Nigerians with diverse needs and wants, to come to appreciate the slow hands of democratic governance. Nigerians had been governed by the military's mantra of "governance with immediate effect," whereby decisions were brisk and devoid of elaborate deliberations and counter-arguments that had come to be associated with Nigerian politicians.

But Obasanjo managed a second victory at the polls. He was sworn in to a second term on May 29, 2003. This inaugural speech, being his last in the presidency, takes stock of his first term and lays down the continuing policies in his second term, toward democratic institutionalization as well as economic and socio-cultural rejuvenation of the country in the twenty-firsrt century.

THE FULL TEXT OF THE SECOND INAUGURAL ADDRESS BY HIS EXCELLENCY, PRESIDENT OLUSEGUN OBASANJO AND COMMANDER IN CHIEF OF THE NIGERIAN ARMED FORCES DELIVERED AT THE EAGLE SQUARE, ABUJA, ON HIS RESUMPTION OF SECOND TERM ON MAY 29, 2003, AS THE THIRD DEMOCRATICALLY ELECTED CIVILIAN PRESIDENT OF NIGERIA SINCE INDEPENDENCE

Fellow Nigerians,[4]

Let us thank God for this great day in the history of our nation. Let us praise the Almighty for guiding us through many weeks of difficult but successful electoral process, culminating in today's milestone event of civilian-to-civilian transition, as we continue on our political journey towards sustainable democracy in a truly united nation.

Exactly four years ago to this day, I humbly accepted the mantle of leadership of this country, as determined by the mandate offered to me by the results of the preceding elections. It will be recalled that our campaign slogan had been "the leadership you can trust." This was meant in the fullest sense, and I immediately embarked, with all resources at my disposal, to work hard in order to earn that trust, I am indeed delighted to regard the renewed mandate as affirmation that our leadership has been accepted as trustworthy.

Furthermore, I am humbled by the confidence reposed in our leadership by the overwhelming response to our campaign for continuity, stability, and progress. Let me assure you that, for as long as God gives me strength, I will not spare any effort in rising to this challenge of building firmly and decisively on our achievements in the last four years. By the Grace of God Almighty, we will draw on the lessons learnt so far, and, with your patriotic support, we will confidently advance towards our vision of a united Nigeria, a strong Nigeria, a prosperous Nigeria, a peaceful Nigeria, a just Nigeria, indeed a great Nigeria. This is the Nigeria of our God-ordained destiny. This is the Nigeria that is the permanent goal in our leadership vision.

I would like to offer this day, which is also the fourth National Democracy, Human Rights and Thanksgiving Day, as a prize for every man, woman and child who in their various ways, directly and indirectly, have contributed to the march of democracy and good governance over the last four ears. All Nigerians deserve commendation for their patience with a learning curve that began with the transition from the darkest episode of our history to the dawn of hope. Of course, there have been numerous bumps in the process, but we have taken them in our strides. Whereas there are a few who may have suffered as a result of the bumps, we are pleased to note that there are more Nigerians who are openly acknowledging that they have gained democracy dividends.

For all of us, today is a day to celebrate the fact that Nigeria has not only remained intact, but also that the nation is getting stronger, with institutions that are firming up, and a society that is no longer in despair because in many respects the future is looking much much brighter.

My special appreciation goes to Vice President and the members of the Federal Executive council. The collective dedication and hardwork of these men and women, have been the driving force for moving Nigeria forward to the point that today, we can be confident in our ability to move Nigeria forward.

Let us acknowledge with deepest appreciation the National Assembly where Senators and Members of the House of Representatives have put in their best to legislatively steer the ship of nation over largely uncharted waters. The learning process for them has not been easy, but thanks to the efforts of some of them, the next four years should hold better prospects for law-making in this country, not to mention the prospects of higher degree of harmony between the Executive and the Legislature, which is a sine qua non for the efficient and effective democratic management of affairs of this nation.

Let us thank the members of the National Council of State for their prompt and regular regard for their constitutional responsibilities.

We must appreciate that our democratic machine could only move this far because of the supportive role of all elected officials at State and Local Government levels. These officials have made vital contributions to the nurturing of grassroots democracy, which indeed is the base for our national democracy.

We acknowledge, with deep appreciation the consistent support of our foreign partners over the last four years. Beginning with expression of faith in our transition, these partners have since welcomed us back into the comity of nations, where our honour has been fully restored, and we are now fully respected, as we discharge our obligations consistent with our foreign policy. We thank those foreign investors who have followed with substantial investment in our future and raised our profile for many others who are yet to come in.

Let me once again commend the INEC [Independent National Electoral Commission] Chairman, his fellow Commissioners, his staff and officials who have done remarkably well in managing the last elections. The sheer scale of the logistics of moving huge quantities of materials, coordinating and conducting the voting process in thousands of polling stations across this relatively huge country, should earn INEC a place of honour in our history and among other electoral bodies in the world. INEC have not claimed perfection, and no human action can ever be described as perfect, nevertheless the post-election reviews should stand them in good stead to strengthen our democratic practice.

Fellow Nigerians, you do not need reminding that this inauguration has completed the task for which we have all fervently prayed and worked hard , namely civilian-to-civilian transition. Sceptics, basing their prediction on electoral antecedents had predicted the worst possible scenario for our elections. Let us thank God that they have been proven wrong. And that with your mandate, I pledge to provide leadership that will consolidate this new democratic foundation and ensure that future elections will not only be successful but expedite the maturing of our nation as a truly democratic country in which Nigerians can choose their leadership without rancour.

In this context, I would like to commend the Election Tribunals for their decisions in settling disputes arising from the elections brought before them. All over the world, elections manifest various degrees of imperfection. It is for this reason that Election Tribunals were instituted as an avenue for all those who may have grievances to seek redress. We thus note with satisfaction that the Election Tribunals are indeed serving to add credibility and faith to the electoral process.

Now is the time to once more commend all participants in these elections, including leaders of all Parties and their supporters, and of course the candidates for all parties. Every participant in every way has added value to the democratic principles that propelled the elections. Let me extend my hearty congratulations to all the winners into the various elected offices. I sincerely hope that you will remember always that those who elected you will continue to look up to you for leadership. To those who may not have won this time, the nation owes you appreciation for your input of dynamism into our electoral process, thus setting us firmly on the path of democracy.

Fellow Nigerians, while we celebrate today as the crowning moment of the elections, we must not forget that the process has entailed fighting on numerous fronts, especially for the political contestants who tend to see the electorate as a battleground where opponents are to be vanquished. Naturally the electioneering has meant times of heightened passion for individuals as well as groups and communities who pushed for victory. A large number of people came out of the election experience feeling hurt with mostly emotional injuries, but in some instances, regrettably, there had been physical wounds, and even death.

But at the end of it all, we should—and we must—be able to look back with the satisfaction that it had been for a good cause, since we all aimed to serve the cause of democracy, through exercising our democracy right to persuade our fellow citizens to vote for us.

This is why I see my initial assignment as president in trying to heal the wounds from the elections. As clearly expressed and implied in my oath of office, I intend to use my mandate to provide quality leadership for all of Nigeria and for all Nigerians regardless of their political persuasions. Anything less would be unconstitutional, morally inadequate, and contrary to the will of God whose wishes are my command. Above all, in adherence to my leadership vision of a greater Nigeria, the only way to advance this country that belongs to all of us, is through solidarity and hard work.

Fellow Nigerians, the coincidence of this day, with the anniversary of National Human Rights, Democracy and Thanksgiving Day, gives us opportunity once again to reflect on the journey since May 29th 1999, which marked the end of fifteen years of undemocratic military rule.

We can all recall how the entire nation breathed a sigh of relief when we greeted the new dawn with a collective cry of "never again!"

As the in-coming administration, we were fully conscious of the high expectations by which the rot would immediately be put to an end, our infrastructure would resurrect from its ruins and our comatose public service would function again.

Nigerian society was free to dream of a social organisation that would be free of rampant corruption and pervasive indiscipline. The citizens dreamt of a restoration of social values and the reinstatement of self-pride. Most of all, the feeling of despair and trauma had been such that 29th May 1999 was perceived by many as virtually the last opportunity to rescue the nation from the edge of a precipice of demise.

In answering the challenge, we declared, without intending to dampen people's expectations, that it be borne in mind that we did not possess a magic wand with which we could achieve instant transformation.

In answering the call to service, our fundamental assumption was that Nigeria can indeed be saved and that it must be saved by Nigerians themselves for whom this country is the only they can call their own. Personally, I saw the retrogression as a failure of leadership and I was emboldened by my earlier experience whereby we had left legacies of what is achievable under good leadership.

Four years ago, we had no illusions that it would be easy to put right in a few years the destruction of two decades, but we did not allow the enormity of the task to force us into a retreat. Instead we took it on as a challenge and duty for the kind of leadership we believe can save Nigeria.

Mindful of the hopes and aspirations that Nigerians had in our vision for the country, our first strategy was to itemise the content of that vision into concrete steps for progressive action. The overriding consideration was that our social systems desperately needed to be rationalised and made wholesome. We identified as imperative the need to restore the rule of law. Our social institutions had to be firmly based on principles of equality, justice and peaceful coexistence. We recognised that we must enshrine the ethics of transparency, accountability, and responsible leadership. And we also recognised that, in order to reduce poverty and improve the quality of life, we had to put in place an economic regime that was efficient, productive and capable of delivering perceptible results.

I can say that to the best of my knowledge, our Administration has been consistent in staying focused on our vision. To the best of our ability, that vision had informed our thoughts, our policies and our actions.

Statistics of social indices show considerable improvements in the quality of life, as measured by higher income and stronger purchasing power. The greatest gain of all is the increase in the social capital, as measured by the amount of faith and trust that citizens now have in their social system. There is ample evidence that hopelessness and despair have been replaced by enthusiasm, hope, and faith in brighter prospect for the country.

We have good reasons to take pride in our records in specific areas. In the oil and gas sector, for instance, the improvement in the last four years dwarfs the totals of activities in the previous 30 years! The quantum leap in this sector has brought us closer to our target of earning substantial revenue from gas, in comparison to crude oil, during the next four years.

Our persistent drive to attract foreign investment has resulted in an increase in the number of foreign investors who have either invested in the country or are planning to do so. We have markedly improved the conditions of service of public sector employees. The private sector is reporting significant increase in business activities and legitimate profits.

On good governance, we note with satisfaction that the democratic process which commenced four years ago, is in various ways thriving, along with our democratic institutions which are showing signs of steadily maturing. The heart of good governance is a function of the Federal Executive Council, which we are proud to put on record has met regularly to make collective and transparent decisions for the running of the affairs of the country.

I am happy to note that the efforts to truncate the anti-corruption law, which forms the pillar of the light against corruption, has been so far unsuccessful. And Due Process has made its impact on costs of contracts, supplies and purchases.

We are aware of the expectations to see rapid results from our anti-corruption crusade. Our leadership regards corruption as the antithesis of development and I would like to assure you that we are determined to fight this evil to a standstill. For starters, we have been able to put in place an Anti-Corruption Commission which, unfortunately has had to cope with legislative and constitutional hurdles. The Commission had brought 39 cases of corruption to court for prosecution; this is in stark contrast with none at all in the preceding 20 years. After the court battle on the anti-corruption law, we will seek to amend the initial law for expeditious handling of corruption cases in the court.

Our leadership has meant the end of governance through the instruments of intimidation and coercion, because we strictly believe in participation and adherence to the rule of law. We are pleased to note that this has been welcomed by all Nigerians, who no doubt relish such freedoms as freedom of speech, freedom of political expression and freedom of political association.

We have cause to be proud of the fact that there are no political prisoners in Nigeria today. No Nigerian asylum seekers. We are proud of the freedom and independence of the judiciary, manifested in landmark judgments by the Supreme Court on issues that are fundamental to the existence and survival of our country.

Within this year, Nigeria's image is set for a tremendous boost with the hosting of two key international events, namely, the All Africa Games and the Commonwealth Heads of Government Meeting. Our image as a pariah nation is erased for good! In four years, our status as a respected nation has grown, as we have participated in and hosted a number of key summits in the international forum. And now, the success of the civilian-to-civilian transition should dispel any lingering doubts about our stability, strength and credibility as a nation to be reckoned with at all times.

We will work to strengthen the democratic process and eliminate all forms of electoral malpractices so that future elections will generate less tension and enhance the quality of governance and leadership in our country.

Fellow Nigerians, in asking you to vote for continuity, stability and progress, we took due cognisance of the fact that much of the last four years, have been devoted to laying the foundation for the rebirth of our nation. As architects of that foundation, we desired the opportunity to advance the re-construction to the point where we can all have confidence in the stability of our social system. Thus we recognise, with due humility, that there is considerably a lot more that needs to be done, to get us closer to our ultimate goal of a truly re-born and truly great Nigeria.

Although we have in place policies in the direction of our objectives, we intend to intensify and consolidate progress in many areas.

On infrastructure, our vigorous policy of investment in roads, energy and water supply has begun to yield noticeable results. We intend to construct more roads and maintain old ones, to improve transportation and ease movement of goods throughout the country.

Power supply:

It is our determination to improve the quality of power supply and to expand output to at least 10,000 Megawatts by the end of our second term in office. This is in recognition of the fact that our aspiration to industrialise will remain impaired for as long as there is not enough energy.

Healthcare:

More resources will be put into our hospitals and health care delivery system, not just to improve but to stop preventable deaths and raise the national life expectancy.

Education:

The introduction of UBE as a priority policy underlines our commitment to provide opportunity for the education of all citizens in order to develop their innate abilities and empower them to fully participate in the development of the country.

The UBE Programme will be completed and the Nigerian Society can enjoy the privilege of having in school, all children of school age. We plan to complete the refurbishment of our educational institutions at all levels in order to make them fully operational, qualitatively and quantitatively, so as to meet the educational needs and skill development of our society.

Agriculture:

Production has continued to increase year by year as a result of an agricultural policy to ensure food security for this nation through increased crop production, improved livestock husbandry as well as new marketing strategies for better returns for farmers.

We intend to pursue the various strands of agricultural policies to the level of food security when we can begin to claim that the average Nigerian is eating enough of balanced diet from food that is available and affordable.

Industry:

The ongoing privatisation should advance considerably and government would be able to concentrate on its assignment of providing an enabling environment for optimal productivity in manufacturing. We note with appreciation that our efforts to encourage small and medium scale industries have so far attracted a substantial amount of funds from commercial banks. We will press ahead with our plans to make this sector of the industry a vital segment for jobs and income for a large number of Nigerians.

Politics:

These last general elections have finally laid to rest the beast of ethnic politics after over fifty years of its influence on the Nigerian political scene. Let us praise God Almighty and commend Nigerian voters for making this possible. We note, however, with apprehension that, while we celebrate the apparent demise of ethnic politics, there is the tragic appearance of religion in our national politics. It is imperative that we nip this in the bud, because religion mixed with politics, in a multi-faith country like ours, portends destruction and devastation of our social fabric and our entire structure.

Foreign Policy:

It is pertinent to observe that our elections are not important to us alone but to all democrats in the world. Much as the success of our elections strengthens our democracy, it also adds significantly to the democratic process throughout the world. We believe that human nature is essentially the same, even though behaviour might differ according to environment and custom. Africans, in their quest for development, do indeed need to modernise their social systems, but we must remain firm and focused on our Africanness, in terms of uniqueness of customs, socal values, orientation and progressive culture.

We note with satisfaction, the progress being made in ECOWAS. Nigeria is proud to be in the forefront for fast tracking programmes of integration in the sub-region.

The New Economic Partnership for African Development (NEPAD) has been successfully launched and has taken off. It is the African Union's sustainable continental strategy for Africa's political and socio-economic redemption, through good governance, sound economic reforms, respect for human rights, investment in indigenous human and material resources, environmental protection and international cooperation, based on shared values, peace, common security and development.

The African Union itself is moving ahead in its new mission of programmes for economic integration, together with measures towards economic stability and unity. Here again, Nigeria will be in the forefront of actions to advance the progress of these programmes.

We in Nigeria, are fully aware of the recent events in the world, from which would appear that a new paradigm is evolving for a new world order. There is a clear indication that the assumptions of post second world war order that gave hope, confidence, and security to all nations, big and small, are undergoing significant changes. We in Africa, must take note of these trends, and we must prepare adequately and accordingly, otherwise there is a serious risk that the marginalisation that we have hitherto suffered, may become complete de-linkage.

We must aim to fully assess all aspects of international affairs, while we cultivate new friends and cherish old ones who have supported us, but never forgetting that our objective is to be master of our fate, captains of our destiny and architects of our future.

There is a limit to which we can depend on outside help, as illustrated in our campaign for debt relief for over four years, with hardly any tangible results. But we will not give up, because we believe that there is great inequity and injustice in the debt issue which requires global attention.

Federal Executive Council:

In order to assist me in my executive tasks, I plan to assemble some of the best men and women as ministers and members of the executive council. The appointment criteria will be: ability, integrity, competence, shared vision and good character. The performance of all ministers who will have targets, will be carefully monitored and assessed to ensure effective implementation of policies in their respective ministries. The present structure of the Presidency will be critically reviewed to include a Monitoring Unit that will follow up and report on the effective implementation of policy decisions.

Fellow Nigerians, we share your hopes for a better Nigeria, we identify with your expectations that the government should be able to bring about requisite changes. I can assure you that Nigeria is not just the number one item on our agenda. And your aspirations will remain top priority in all our policy decisions.

But all our efforts, all our material inputs will come to naught if they are not complemented with a change in our attitudes. Four years ago, we identified and warned against the attitude of "business as usual" as a potential enemy to our vision. Our experience has confirmed this, such that some have regarded me as a loner in my belief that Nigerians can change. But I am not daunted. I have repeatedly called for moral rectitude, and I will continue to repeat the message. I simply refuse to accept the cynical view that Nigerians prefer chaos to order. I cannot endorse the view that Nigerians are innately corrupt. I cannot believe that Nigerians would, in preference for a decent and civilized society, opt for one in which law and order is disregarded, and regulations are circumvented as the norm. I am a firm believer in the good nature of the Nigerian, and I will continue to appeal to that good nature. My unshaken and unshakeable faith, belief in and commitment to Nigeria is anchored in my equally strong belief in the intrinsic good nature of humans, and that, given the right environment and impetus, man can change for the better.

We all have a stake in Enterprise Nigeria and each of us stands a better chance in getting optimum dividends if, instead of asking "What's in it for me," ask "what's in it for Nigeria," to determine our choice of action when our sense of duty and service is called upon. Among other things, this is the only way to ensure replenishment of that proverbial national cake, which we all love so much to partake of. This is the ultimate solution for combating such negative social tendencies as corruptibility, ethnicity, lack of patriotism, lawlessness, inefficiency, diminished sense of justice, and lack of dignity and mutual respect for fellow citizens.

Today, I ask all Nigerians to come along with me in the Nigeria-craft; let us pilot and move it in the next four years, let us keep it at a cruising level that is beyond turbulence, and let us sustain an optimum cruising speed in the direction of our dreams. Let this be our hope. And let this be the challenge for all of us.

May God bless the Federal Republic of Nigeria.

THE FULL TEXT OF PRESIDENT OLUSEGUN OBASANJO'S SECOND INAUGURAL ADDRESS TO THE JOINT SESSION OF THE NEWLY CONSTITUTED NATIONAL ASSEMBLY, IN ABUJA, JUNE 5, 2003

All thanks be to Almighty God for bringing us to this critical juncture in the life of our country.5 It gives me much pleasure to welcome you all, Distinguished and Honourable members of the National Assembly, to the ceremony marking the formal opening of our Federal Legislature, after the recent and successful general elections, the second in this Republic.

Only last week, the Executive arm, that is the Vice President and myself, as well as all the state governors and their deputies, were sworn-in at ceremonies here in Abuja and in all the respective state capitals. Even as we renew our gratitude to God, all of us in this country have every reason to be proud of this moment in our history. The successful general elections, and the enduring formalities of making civilian-to-civilian transition, testify to the fact that our renewed effort at building a united, strong and democratic country is being well nurtured. Democracy is taking firm root in our land and Nigerians are collectively and confidently moving our country forward, according to the National Anthem injunction: "to serve with heart and might, one nation bound in freedom, peace and unity."

Let me congratulate all of you, Distinguished Senators, and Honourable Members of the Houses of Representatives, on your election or re-election, as the case might be. It is a great honour to be chosen to serve your country in this exalted capacity, of being a member of your nation's law making body. Each of us, electorally mandated officials, carries the heavy burden of the sacred trust given by the electorate. We are laden with the challenge to discharge that trust efficiently and as completely as possible, with due diligence, intellect, patriotism, humility, and leadership by example, and with team spirit that accords with democratic values. Our target must be the highest expectations of our respective electorates, and indeed of all our people.

The beacon of light that will guide us on our path of duty and service will, among other attributes, encompass a democratic instinct, a keen sense of justice and compassion, due process and an unwavering focus on the goal of serving our country.

The last four years, and the recent general elections have convinced me of the validity of my strategy of a single-item agenda: Nigeria. Contrary to the views of those who are inclined to highlight our differences as a people, and emphasise the mistaken notion of our diversity as a source of structural weakness, instead of being a rich source of strength, the trend of events, especially in the recent General Elections, is that our people are happily settled on Nigeria as united and indivisible country, with a bright future and the potential for world greatness. What remains now, is how not to betray that bright future, while we actualise the potential for greatness. The hope of realising the greatness of Nigeria has never been higher!

Distinguished and Honourable Members of the National Assembly, the last elections have been rather drastic on both chambers. More than seventy percent of the senators did not return, and more than two-thirds of the representatives are new. While experience has its premium, and we would have wished for more retention of experience, I, however, respectfully urge you to consider the radical turnover of membership as a kind of rejuvenation, and possibly a blessing in disguise. Please join me in expressing appreciation to those who left, for their service to the Assembly. We wish them all the best for the future.

Let me raise some observations on the Executive-Legislative relations in the last four years. With all due respect, distinguished legislators, the best that could be said about that relationship was that it had been a learning curve, with both sides having ample opportunity to assess and understand each other. It is most regrettable that the process has meant much work was left undone in the form of Bills waiting to be legislated upon. I look forward to you expediting action on such outstanding bills. Equally regrettable is the fact that public wrangling pertaining to the unwholesome aspects of this relationship had cast doubts in the minds of many, at home and abroad, about the future prospects for our newly instituted democracy.

A new attitude and a new orientation is definitely called for. The electorate who voted us into office are expecting nothing less. Let us not disappoint them. All we need to do is pay due respect to the sanctity of the ground rules of behaviour appropriate to the leadership status conferred on us by our various mandates, because those ground rules are themselves predicated on such fundamental principles as: national interest, patriotism, public interest, integrity, social responsibility, code of conduct, as well as loyalty to the party whose ideology is our political platform.

I believe that everyone here is aware of our anti-corruption crusade. The Executive will not condone corruption in any way or form. The Executive will not compromise on this evil that continues to deal damaging blows to our efforts to achieve economic development and social progress. In this regard, Nigerians, and indeed friends of Nigeria throughout the world, are expecting this National Assembly to quickly restore credibility to law-making, by tidying up the circumstances surrounding the previous ill-motivated attempts to counter our battle against corruption. The existing Anti-Corruption Act, whose Bill was first to be sent to National Assembly, is our article of faith that corruption in Nigeria can be combated, its provisions express our seriousness about being accountable and transparent. Let us use it. Let us enforce it. And there should be no sacred cows. To expedite court action on persons found corrupt, there is need to amend the Act. I intend to forward the Bill to effect such amendment, to the National Assembly this month.

I especially appeal to and invite this National Assembly to join hands with me in fighting against corruption anywhere it rears its ugly head in this country. Such a patriotic act will enhance the prestige and reputation of this national law-making body.

It is only fair to say that I look forward to reciprocation by the National Assembly, to the gestures and undertakings, so that we can put the recent past behind us and begin anew for the benefit of the country. I fully identify with the majority of Nigerians who are hoping this refreshed and renewed National Assembly will move away from actions that are obstructive to effective management of the affairs of this nation. You can always count on me for regular briefing and consultation.

The definition and the use of the instrument of oversight function to mean attempts to extort and blackmail, will simply not work. Furthermore, impeachment, or even the threat of it, as a means of arm-twisting and not as a result of some patent constitutional breach on the part of the Executive, will destabilise not only the President, but the entire country, whilst making a mockery of our notion of democracy and democratic processes.

And let me say it here and now, this Executive will not succumb to blackmail, threats or intimidation, under any circumstance. I offer an open arm of cooperation, consultation and dialogue.

Urgent National Issues:

Parties and candidates who lost at the polls during the recent general elections, tended on the whole to have behaved well, in spite of allegations of irregularities. But, a few others have been threatening the peace and stability of the country, and, by extension, our current success in reinstating democracy as the only legitimate and viable system of government.

The elections are over. Those who are aggrieved have numerous-honoured facilities for legally pursuing their grievances, including election tribunals. But we have a duty to maintain national security and public order. We will be restrained, but we will not succumb to harassment and threat to national security, by those who are finding it difficult to demonstrate sportsmanship in the face of defeat. The full force of the law, but only the law, shall be brought to bear on those who run foul of it. I therefore, appeal here and once more, to our defeated opponents to take their defeat philosophically and bear in mind that next elections are only four years away. In the meantime, there are special judicial processes available to anyone unwilling to accept the verdict of the INEC on his or her candidature. We are fully committed to do everything possible to look into alleged malpractices because, among other reasons, we regard it as our duty to guard against future recurrence so as to enable us to strengthen our future practice of democracy.

Meanwhile to you victors here, I would like to express my profound concern with escalating cost of elections in this country to contestants. I have no doubt that your recent experiences will support my observation that these costs are reaching proportions that are prohibitive for the ordinary Nigerian. With this excessive influence of money, our brand of democracy runs the risk of being out of reach and inaccessible for the active participation of very many Nigerians. This would be a distortion of the core values of democracy. I am thus hoping that the National Assembly and the Executive will work together to find ways of correcting this unsavoury development in our politics.

The Rule of Law:

If we all were to observe the rule of law, most of our problems as nation would varnish almost instantly. This is because rule of law is the backbone of the social organization needed to make good use of what God has given us in the land, the people and material resources to conquer poverty, entrench prosperity, and achieve accelerated socio-economic development. It is no coincidence that eminent world economists are known to have concluded that the rule of law is the invisible architecture of economic growth. Our administration is committed to establishing the rule of law in every aspect of our national life. Apart from the moral dimensions, observance of the rule of law increases productivity because it protects the domestic worker and encourages the foreign investor to invest in our economy. Thus, the rule of law is an imperative for setting up an efficient and prosperous state.

The Economy:

The economy needs urgent attention everywhere. But it is more in our case because of structural distortions, which have resisted attempts at corrective measures, such as the Structural Adjustment Programme, on-and-off import control and export drives, as well as deregulation. Addressing the economy will have to be wholesale. And while not ignoring the international rules of the game, we must be guided by our overriding national interests.

In contemplating our renewed effort to move the economy forward, some specific areas must receive special attention. They include:

- unemployment, especially among the young, and acquisition of skills;
- rural poverty, especially among rural women;
- fiscal policy with new initiatives on taxation and cost of sharing;
- monetary policy with sustainable growth;
- greater controls or moderation of inflation and interest rates;
- managing the burdensome pension bills while giving future security to workers and their families;
- value addition to all of our exports;
- attack on consumerism and expensive acquired tastes;
- poor maintenance and lack of protection of government properties;
- the issue of production and productivity.

I look forward to working positively with the new National Assembly to tackle these issues, which are further manifested in the following highlights:

Waste:

The amount of waste in our system is at an intolerable proportion. The causes are numerous and they are well-known. They include poor management, fraudulent and misuse of public property, indiscipline, and neglect and general negative attitude that regards government's property as no one's property. We plan to arrest the situation with measures that will make users own and care for the properties they use, while the management of other public properties will be appropriately monitored with penalties for misuse and neglect.

Taxation:

We plan to introduce measures that will end our reputation as a society of tax dodgers and people who do not pay for the services they enjoy. The government simply cannot afford the expenditure in providing the services that the public desires without raising taxes or raising prices. The democratic side of this equation is that only those who pay their taxes are entitled to demand their right to services by the government. We thus intend to review our taxation system so as to enforce the optimal collection of revenue and to ensure that services are made available and are paid for by those who enjoy them.

Housing:

We will give considerable attention to every Nigerian and particularly for workers. It has already been agreed that the National Housing Fund should be reformed to involve the Nigerian Labour Congress (NLC) in its management.

Cost of Government:

The cost of running government at all the various levels gulps a disproportionate amount of our revenue. It is clear that the structure of government will have to be thoroughly re-examined in order to get a reasonable balance between overheads and recurrent expenditure, and capital spending. We intend to undertake such a critical review. For instance, we will undertake to monetise benefits and prerequisites to government officials, and public servants. We intend to introduce contributory pension scheme. Differentials in salary scales will be rationalised and consistently monitored.

In line with other policies developed on this matter, members of the National Assembly, like all public officers, will have their fringe benefits monetised and paid as when due. Let me draw your attention to the fact that for the financial procedures of the National Assembly, the Clerk of the National Assembly is the chief accounting officer, in the same manner that the Principal Secretary to the president is the chief accounting officer to State House. Any attempt by elected officials to interfere in this responsibility and duty would contravene the procedures and regulations as contained in Financial Rules, which must be strictly adhered to.

Discipline:

This is an issue that has continued to recur in most observations about the way our society functions. Lack of discipline is a major factor behind many of our social problems, such as our attitude toward work, inefficiency, and low productivity in our economic life and social organizations. Indiscipline has even got a popular reference called the Nigerian Way of Life or the Nigerian Factor which, everyone knows, means how to get by without regard for order, or behaving unreasonably and not abiding by the norms, rules and regulations. We owe it to ourselves to clean up this image of Nigeria and Nigerians.

Service Delivery:

Public officers are the shopping floor for government business. Regrettably, Nigerians have for too long been feeling short-changed by the quality of public service delivery by which decisions are not made without outside influence and files do not move without being pushed with inducements. Our public offices have for too long been showcases for the combined evils of inefficiency and corruption, whilst being impediments to effective implementation of government policies. Nigerians deserve better. And we will ensure they get what is better! We will undertake a comprehensive review and reform of the Civil Service and necessary measures will be taken to ensure that the Civil Service performs better and more efficiently and effectively, and Nigeria is better served.

Distinguished and honourable members of the National Assembly, the most urgent priority is the economy!

To begin with, we will leave no stone unturned to fight against criminals who have continued to bleed the Nigerian economy. We will induce and encourage legitimate investors and participants in our economy, but will wage war against those who systematically destroy our economy. We have already embarked on a war against unpatriotic Nigerians who engage in advance fee fraud. There will be no hiding place for these criminal individuals who tarnish the image of Nigeria.

While we preoccupy ourselves with the economy and its derivative progress, we must also continue the struggle for international justice and equity in this globalised world in matters of trade, debts and investments. They have direct impact on our economy.

Nigeria will work, in this connection, with all countries in situations similar to ours, which means all of the African countries and the rest of the Third World. We must all familiarise ourselves thoroughly with the dynamics of the world economy and the cutting edge of the development economics.

Inter-African cooperation, particularly the New Economic Partnership for Africa's Development (NEPAD) remain both our strategic fulcrum as well as our article of faith in Africa's future.

If we work hard on the economy, we shall, by the grace of God, make it. We have the basic resources. We can increase our acquisition of know-how. And we have the freedom to decide for ourselves. We cannot ask for more.

Distinguished Senators and Honourable Members of the House of Representatives, four years ago when Nigerians used their votes to re-establish democracy, they did so with the highest hope that democracy will usher in peace and prosperity. Let us thank God that the hope is still alive as manifested in the enthusiasm in the last elections. The expectation may even be higher, now that allowance has been made for the lessons of the past four years, that the National Assembly and the executive, working together, should deliver dividends of democracy. Distinguished and honourable legislators, we face the challenge of making a success of our nation state. Let us now gather the will, let us muster the courage, and let us join hands and consolidate the momentum to march confidently into a future that we can all be proud of, and in which we would all be happy to live in. We have a duty to shape that future with what God has richly endowed us as a country. And, if we rise fully to our call to duty and service, the bright future will be here sooner than later. Let us begin by inviting Nigerians to join us in saluting that glorious future today! I thank you.

NOTES

1. Several sources were consulted for these biographical notes. For additional details, see the following: Mike Okoye, ed., *Towards A Better Nigeria* (Ikeja, Nigeria: Times Books Limited, n.d.), 23–24; Patrick Avwenagbiku, *Olusegun Obasanjo and His Footprints* (Abuja, Nigeria: Metro Publishers, 2000); and "General Abubakar Keeps His Word, Obasanjo Takes Over: Nigeria Has High Hopes in Stable Democracy," (Abuja, Nigeria: Publications of the Federal Ministry of Information & Culture, 1999).

2. Olusegun Obasanjo, "'A New Dawn,'" Inaugural Broadcast to the Nation on May 29, 1999," *A New Dawn: Selected Speeches by Olusegun Obasanjo, President of the Federal Republic of Nigeria* (New York: Consulate-General of Nigeria, n.d.), 26–34. See also *West Africa Review 1:1* (1999) at www.icaap.org; and www.nigeria-world.com Accessed March 23, 2009.

3. Olusegun Obasanjo, "National Re-Awakening", First Inaugural Address to the Joint Session of the National Assembly, June 4, 1999. *A New Dawn: Selected Speeches by Olusegun Obasanjo, President of the Federal Republic of Nigeria, n.d.)*, 35–43.

4. Olusegun Obasanjo, "We Will Heal Nigeria" His Excellency, President Oluse-gun Obasanjo's Second Inaugural Address (Abuja, Nigeria: Federal Ministery of Information and Communications Document, 2003). See also *Great and Historical Speeches and Documents,* at www.Dawodu.com Accessed March 22, 2009. And, President Obasanjo's Inaugural Speech, *West Africa* (June 9–15, 2003), 9–10 (This version is truncated and incomplete).

5. Olusegun Obasanjo, "Fast Forward into the Future," Inaugural Address to the Joint Session of the New National Assembly on June 5, 2003. www.nigeriavillag-esquare1.com/obj.htm Accessed December 7, 2004.

Chapter Fourteen

Umaru Musa Yar'Adua

BIOGRAPHICAL NOTES ON
PRESIDENT UMARU MUSA YAR'ADUA

Umaru Musa Yar'Adua was born in Katsina on August 16, 1951 to Fulani parents. His father was a minister in Nigeria's First Republic. Both he and his father share the royal title of *mutawalli* (meaning the custodian of the treasury) of the Emirate of Katsina. Umaru Musa Yar'Adua started his primary education at Rafukka Primary School in 1958, and later transferred to Dutsinma Boarding College in 1962. He attended Government College, Keffi, 1965–1969. In 1971 he received the higher school certificate from Barewa College.

Umaru Musa Yar'Adua was educated at the Ahmadu Bello University, Zaria, from 1972 to 1975, where he obtained a combined BS degree in education and chemistry. In 1978, he returned to Ahmadu Bello University for his MS degree in analytical chemistry.

He taught at Holy Child College in Lagos, 1975–1976; and at the College of Arts, Science and Technology in Zaria (later renamed Ahmadu Bello University), Kaduna State, 1976–1979. He started work as lecturer in the College of Art and Science, from 1979 till 1983 when he resumed active business. Yar'Adua has many business interests in finance, printing, manufacturing, farming, and investment and property development. He remains a director of many corporate ventures in Nigeria.

[1] During the Second Republic, 1979–1983, he was a member of the radical and leftist-minded People's Redemption Party, even though his father was then the national vice chairman of the conservative National Party of Nigeria. In the years of Babangida's unending Transition Programme, Yar'Adua became a founding member of the Peoples Front, a political association with his elder brother, retired Major General (now late) Shehu Musa Yar'Adua, as the leader.

Umaru Musa Yar'Adua. 4th Democratic President of Nigeria and Commander-in-Chief of the Nigerian Armed Forces, May 29, 2007 to present. Born: August 16, 1951 in Katsina, Katsina State, Nigeria. Source: Courtesy of the federal ministry of information, Abuja, Nigeria, 2007.

The People's Front merged with the Social Democratic Party. He was the party's Katsina State secretary, as well as a member of the party's National Caucus.

In 1988, Umaru Yar'Adua was a member of the Constituent Assembly.

In his first attempt at the governor's mansion in 1991, he lost to a formidable opponent, Saidu Barda of the National Republican Convention. In 2001 he ran again and won. He was re-elected in 2003. Yar'Adua is known for his integrity, honesty, and transparency. He is widely respected in Nigeria as the first governor to publicly declare his assets. In 2007 when several of his fellow governors were charged by the anticorruption commission, EFCC, Yar'Adua was found to have a spotless record with no corruption of any sort.

The attention of the world turned on Katsina State in 2000, while he was the governor, when Ms. Amina Lawal was sentenced to death by stoning by Katsina's Sharia Court in the town of Bakori for committing adultery. The sentencing was later overturned.

President Olusegun Obasanjo supported Yar'Adua's nomination and candidacy during the December 16–17, 2006 presidential convention by the ruling Peoples Democratic Party for the April 2007 election. Yar'Adua won the nomination and the subsequent presidential elections, with Goodluck Jonathan, the governor of Bayelsa State, as his vice presidential candidate.

Yar'Adua is married to Ms. Turai Umaru Yar'Adua since 1975, and they are blessed with seven children and two more children from his former second wife, Hauwa Umar Radda of five years, 1992–1997.

When Nigeria took a fourth turn into democracy's alley in 2007, Yar'Adua became the fourth civilian elected president of Nigeria. His election was lauded by the global audience for it was the first time that Nigerians could effectively conduct and transition from a democratically elected civilian government to yet another civilian elected government. In hindsight, the years 1999–2007 have been remarkable for the democratic experimentation in Nigeria. Yar'Adua's first inaugural address on May 29, 2007, was historical and memorable for several reasons to many Nigerians. For one, it pointed to a maturing nation. Two, it was a re-affirmation of their belief in democracy and the people's wish for a system of governance they could point to as their own, representative of who and what they are. Three, Yar'Adua's inauguration was the end of repeated military interruptions of the democratic transitions and thus presented the fourth democratic attempt to perpetuate constitutional authority over dictatorial authority. And above all, the 2007 presidential election and inauguration signalled and symbolized the changing of the baton of leadership, from older to a younger generation of Nigerians, who were mostly born on the eve of Nigerian independence.[1]

THE FULL TEXT OF THE INAUGURAL SPEECH OF HIS EXCELLENCY, PRESIDENT UMARU MUSA YAR'ADUA DELIVERED ON MAY 29, 2007 AS THE FOURTH CIVILIAN PRESIDENT OF NIGERIA SINCE INDEPENDENCE

His Excellency Vice President Goodluck Jonathan, President of the Senate, the Speaker House of Representatives, my Lord Chief Justice of Nigeria, President Olusegun Obasanjo, distinguished Presidents and Heads of Governments who have graciously honoured us with their presence today, leaders of our nation, guests from far and near, Fellow citizens.[2]

This is a historic day for our nation, for it marks an important milestone in our march towards a maturing democracy. For the first time since we cast off the shackles of colonialism almost a half-century ago, we have at last managed an orderly transition from one elected government to another. We acknowledge that our elections had some shortcomings. Thankfully, we have well-established legal avenues of redress, and I urge anyone aggrieved to pursue them. I also believe that our experiences represent an opportunity to learn from our mistakes.

Accordingly, I will set up a panel to examine the entire electoral process with a view to ensuring that we raise the quality and standard of our general elections, and thereby deepen our democracy.

This occasion is historic also because it marks another kind of transitional generational shift when the children of independence assume the adult responsibility of running the country at the heart of Africa. My fellow citizens, I am humbled and honoured that you have elected me and Vice President Jonathan to represent that generation in the task of building a just and humane nation, where its people have a fair chance to attain their fullest potential. Luckily we are not starting from scratch. We are fortunate to have been led in the past eight years by one of our nation's greatest patriots, President Obasanjo. On behalf of all our people, I salute you, Mr. President, for your vision, your courage and your boundless energy in creating the roadmap toward that united and economically thriving Nigeria that we seek. Many of us may find it hard to believe now, but before you assumed the presidency eight years ago, the national conversation was about whether Nigeria deserved to remain one country at all. Today we are talking about Nigeria's potential, to become one of the 20 largest economies in the world by the year 2020. That is a measure of how far we have come. And we thank you. The administration of President Obasanjo has laid the foundation upon which we can build our future prosperity.

Over the past eight years Nigerians have reached a national consensus in at least four areas: to deepen democracy and the rule of law; build an economy driven primarily by the private sector, not government; display zero tolerance for corruption in all its forms, and, finally, restructure and staff our government to ensure efficiency and good governance. I commit myself to these tasks. Our goal now is to build on the greatest accomplishments of the past few years. Relying on the 7–point agenda that formed the basis of our compact with voters during the recent campaigns, we will concentrate on rebuilding our physical infrastructure and human capital in order to take our country forward. We will focus on accelerating economic and other reforms in a way that makes a concrete and visible difference to ordinary people. Our economy already has been set on the path of growth. Now we must continue to do the necessary work to create more jobs, lower interest rates, reduce inflation, and maintain a stable exchange rate. All this will increase our chances for rapid growth and development.

Central to this is rebuilding our basic infrastructure. We already have comprehensive plans for mass transportation, especially railroad development. We will make these plans a reality. Equally important, we must devote our best efforts to overcoming the energy challenge. Over the next four years we will see dramatic improvements in power generation, transmission and distribution. These plans will mean little if we do not respect the rule of law. Our government is determined to strengthen the capacity of law enforcement agencies, especially the police. The state must fulfill its constitutional responsibility of protecting life and property.

The crisis in the Niger Delta commands our urgent attention. Ending it is a matter of strategic importance to our country. I will use every resource available to me, with your help, to address this crisis in a spirit of fairness, justice, and cooperation. We have a good starting point because our predecessor already launched a master plan that can serve as a basis for a comprehensive examination of all the issues. We will involve all stakeholders in working out a solution. As part of this effort, we will move quickly to ensure security of life and property, and to make investments safe. In the meantime, I appeal to all aggrieved communities, groups and individuals to immediately suspend all violent activities and respect the law. Let us allow the impending dialogue to take place in a conducive atmosphere. We are all in this together, and we will find a way to achieve peace and justice.

As we work to resolve the challenges of the Niger Delta, so must we also tackle poverty throughout the country. By fighting poverty, we fight disease. We will make advances in public health, to control the scourge of HIV/AIDS, malaria, and other diseases that hold back our population and limit our progress. We are determined to intensify the war against corruption, more so because corruption is itself central to the spread of poverty. Its corrosive effect is all too visible in all aspects of our national life. This is an area where we have made significant progress in recent years, and we will maintain the momentum. We also are committed to rebuilding our human capital, if we are to support a modern economy. We must revive education in order to create more equality, and citizens who can function more productively in today's world.

To our larger African family, you have our commitment to the goal of African integration. We will continue to collaborate with fellow African states to reduce conflict and free our people from the leg chains of poverty. To all our friends in the international community, we pledge our continuing fidelity to the goals of progress in Africa and peace in the world. Fellow citizens, I ask you all to march with me into the age of restoration. Let us work together to restore our time-honoured value of honesty, decency, generosity, modesty, selflessness, transparency, and accountability. These fundamental values determine societies that succeed or fail. We must choose to succeed.

I will set a worthy personal example as your President. No matter what obstacles confront us, I will set a worthy personal example as your President. I have confidence and faith in our ability to overcome them.

After all, we are Nigerians!

We are a resourceful and enterprising people, and we have it within us to make our country a better place. To that end I offer myself as a servant-leader. I will be a listener and doer, and serve with humility.

To fulfil our ambitions, all our leaders at all levels whether a local government councillor or state governor, senator or cabinet minister must change our style and our attitude. We must act at all times with humility, courage, and forthrightness.

I ask you, fellow citizens, to join me in rebuilding our Nigerian family, one that defines the success of one by the happiness of many. I ask you to set aside negative attitudes, and concentrate all our energies on getting to our common destination. All hands must be on deck.

Let us join together to ease the pains of today while working for the gains of tomorrow.

Let us set aside cynicism, and strive for the good society that we know is within our reach.

Let us discard the habit of low expectations of ourselves as well as of our leaders.

Let us stop justifying every shortcoming with that unacceptable phrase, "the Nigerian Factor," as if to be a Nigerian is to settle for less.

Let us recapture the mood of optimism that defined us at the dawn of independence, that legendary can-do spirit that marked our Nigerianness.

Let us join together, now, to build a society worthy of our children.

We have the talent. We have the intelligence. We have the ability.

The challenge is great. The goal is clear. The time is now.

I thank you, and God bless you.

NOTES

1. Umaru Musa Yar'Adua. "Biodata".yaradua2007.com Yar'adua 2007. http://www.yaradua2007.com/index.php?option=com_content&task=view(id=14&Itemid=26. Accessed March 6, 2009; also Umaru Yar'Adua, wikipedia, file://G:/Umaru_Yar'Adua.htm.

2. Umaru Shehu Yar'Adua, "The Challenge Is Great; The Goal Is Clear," The First Inaugural Address of His Excellency, President Umaru Shehu Yar'Adua, President and Commander in Chief of the Federal Republic of Nigerian (Embassy of Nigeria, Information Department, Washington, D.C. 2007). See also, www.dawodu.com Accessed March 22, 2009.

Epilogue

Communication and the Construction of Nigeria's National Purpose

Nigeria is a young nation of fifty years. It becomes necessary that it does not remain a fool at fifty, when one remembers the aphorism that a fool at forty is a fool forever. But countries are not humans; countries are made by, and of humans. Countries are works in progress, and it takes time, effort, commitment and dedication to a shared purpose for countries to ever become what they really want for themselves. In fact, many countries never really attain their dreams; but they continuously pursue those dreams. Moreover, no country ever attains perfection. All nations are always in the state of becoming, with a consistent and renewed commitment to moving forward, toward being all that is possible. Therefore, I am not writing off this fifty-year-old human creation. Not yet! Like all human creations, Nigeria is riddled with imperfections. Its language, signs, words, symbols, codes, and artifacts are suffused with imperfections that only humans can create, disseminate, and mitigate by design or by accident of time, history, migration, politics, and/or social engineering. Nevertheless, there has to be the will to tweak, turn, twist, and tinker to make these symbolic creations move forward. Imperfectability calls forth more language, more signs, more codes, and more symbols. It becomes an unending act and interaction with and in symbols with the intent to reach perfection.

This epilogue may read as a lamentation. However, my friends have warned me against stepping in the same waters where Nigerian military rhetors (what an oxymoron!) have swum—the seas of blaming the elected politicians and colonialism and foreigners for the country's woes. I have decided on reaffirmation and affirmation and identification and thus transcendence. It is my belief in the capacity of Nigerians to transcend their ethnic, religious, racial, cultural, and linguistic pluralities, extremisms, and rigidities that gives me the hope in the sustainability of Nigeria. All organisms have their share of

165

struggles. The bigger they are, the larger and more complex these struggles, and the more intense their sense of limitations, self-doubts, and insecurities.

The severity of Nigeria's problems is exacerbated by the country's fear of failures, and the desire to prove wrong the colonialists, who thought Nigerians were incapable of mastering the western ways of governance, and that Nigerians lacked the self-discipline to succeed and do well without the assistance of their former masters. This Nigerians' perfection mentality swells the edification complex whereby Nigerians constantly refer to themselves as the "giant of Africa," the "largest and most populous black country in the world," and so on. Here, let me borrow from Wole Soyinka, the only Nigerian Nobel Laureate in literature, who admonished Africans that the tiger does not have to declare its tigritude. Simply explained, this aphorism means that Nigeria does not have to only speak of its exceptionalism; it must do exceptionally and act its essence or substance. It is in this performance dimension of Nigerianness that the cries for a savior and effective leadership that can deliver have been most deafening.

My conception of Nigeria's survivability is nonetheless founded on what I have come to describe as individualist collectivism. That is, that the individual only becomes all that he or she can within the group. The group energizes, supports, goads, encourages, gives pointers and yet, the same group looks away, so the individual can have his or her space. No parent wants to be around his or her children twenty-four hours and seven days a week after the children have become adults. Nigerian peoples of the one hundred ethnic groupings were adults at the time they were put together to found Nigeria. They all deserve and have earned their adultness and do not need the men in mufti or khakhi, or politicians to tell them what to do to be humans. Before Nigeria, they were humans. Therefore, the system of government that is needed to ward off perennial incursions by the soldiers and the elected official is that which would allow every ethnic group to be all that they want to be within a democratically functioning system of respectability and dialoguing. A Nigerian leader who creates and encourages public rhetorical places where Nigerians engage one another and share their common histories, experiences, and aspirations is that leader who celebrates Nigerian pluralism and its democratic experimentation toward an emergence and solidarity among its diverse populations.

Language and communication are indispensable to the evolution of all human societies. Only humans have the reflexive capacities and the ability of symbolic displacement. It is only humans with the intellectual and cognitive ability, say capacity, to imagine, store, process, comprehend, and recall, and hopefully, learn from what happened in the past, and thereby project into the future. In short, only humans have the sense of past, present and the future in a continuum. For Nigerians, this means that they have to learn from their pasts and make the present better, or demonstrate a commitment to improve on the past so the future can be better. Only a fool continues to do the same thing repeatedly, even when that repetitiveness yields no—or minimal—dividends.

The military, for example, has paraded the corridors of Nigerian politics as a corrective force, and still nothing has worked to move Nigeria ahead under military rule. The military has ruled Nigeria for twenty-eight of the fifty years of independence, and there has not been any noticeable change in social skills, cultural orientation, inter-ethnic socialization and integration, religious cross-fertilization of ideas, political maturation, military sophistication, infrastructural development, quality of life, productive capacity of the most mundane Nigerian industry, or an increase or improvement in scientific discoveries or educational advancements. It is about time the military and the civilians admitted that the fault is not in the system of government. The fault lies in who and what Nigerians are, who Nigerian spokespersons are, who Nigerian leaders are, and why they have not regarded and listened with Nigerians. Only Nigerians can invent Nigerians. Outsiders cannot do it because they do not know who Nigerians are, and what Nigerians want. Britain founded Nigeria for its own economic and political reasons. Nigerians have to invent and reinvent themselves as they want, need, and imagine through their own inventions in transformatory symbolication. At the same time, it must be noted that the military has remained the last institution that has managed to keep Nigeria united, even in her most trying moments.

Nigerians do not know each other. This lack of knowledge and understanding of the others who are the constitutive units in the country of 150 million individuals intensifies suspicion, distrust, fear, anger, hostility, jealousy, envy, and all other negative emotions. And because some sections of the country have come to see that they can bully and shoot their ways to power and therefore subdue and subjugate all other sections of the country, the always-winning sections of the country have come to see and use the military as the tools of intimidation, control, and manipulation of the entire nation. Thus, the military elites have deemed it less relevant and unnecessary to get to know the other Nigerians through dialogue and democratic experimentations.

Democracy is a form of governance by the people who choose their leaders via representative dialogism. Democracy cannot be forced down the people's throats from the top of the military hierarchy that does not even know what democracy is given the military orientation toward force and blind obedience to hierarchical structure. Democratic traditions evolve in trials and errors; bits by bits; and are never perfect. Democratic governance comes alive and sustains through continuous conversations and exchanges of ideas about what matters to the peoples and their ways of living as law-abiding citizens. It is in and by language, signs, symbols and codes which humans create by themselves that they are persuaded and led to act, not by logic and reason-giving of the dictatorial and blaming type, reminiscent of the rhetoric of military ascensions in Nigerian politics.

Democrats become in conversations and exchanges about ideas and thoughts; they become by deliberating on ways of doing, being, and becoming in negotiations, compromises, co-orienting, mutual reinforcements, listening, and understandings, reciprocal interactions and mutual respects of opposing views. Democrats, like all humans, disagree, but they are disciplined and mature enough to work dialogically towards agreements. If colonialism ruled Nigerians by force, it becomes anathema to the spirit and soul of Nigerian independence from Britain, that Nigerians rule Nigerians with force. The political, cultural, and social constitution of the Nigerian would be achieved only through the sharing of symbols, codes, language, words, artifacts, rituals, emblems, icons, and signs that are indigenously Nigerian, creatively and co-coordinately negotiated and shared among the constitutive units or peoples in the country.

Democracy has its cauldron of troubles with sometimes debilitating consequences. But Nigerians have to see it as a way of life. There is no life devoid of conflict. Democratic way of life with its inherent conflict is not all imported. Those imported elements in democracy must be nativized, localized, internalized, and Nigerianized through and in Nigerian signs, symbols, codes, artifacts, and icons. Make the Nigerian democracy Nigerian. The ingredients and the tools must be Nigerian. There can be no room for a split Nigerian democracy—one rich, and the other poor; one North and the other South; one Islam and the other Christian; one majority and the other minority. A Nigerian democracy has to use words to make democratic action real and felt; to convert potentials to actualities; to induce outliers to become insiders; and to make peripheralists active participants in the full and integrative Nigerian life—music, dance, songs, rhythms, foods, clothing, opera, festivals, fiesta, economies, industries, politics, and finances, housing, architecture, arts, designs, and all other ways of life and living.

In contrast with the military rule, the elected politicians have only reigned for twenty-two years, six years short of the military rulerships, which have ruled Nigeria for twenty-eight years. From the speeches in this book, both systems of governance have shown their disdain and incapacity to relate or communicate with the ordinary Nigerians. This distance breeds mistrust. The elites resort to weapons of mass control and intimidation. All sides comply by exploiting the common military neologism "esobee," that epithet from "apes obey" which the British officers in colonial days used, to command

and gain compliance from Nigerian draftees into the Second World War. Nigerians today cannot afford to be ruled as permanent political misfits who cannot choose fellow citizens whom they deem capable to direct the affairs of the people. What was independence all about if Nigerians cannot choose their leaders? Whose independence was it anyway if the citizens cannot talk and negotiate with one another about sharing the resources that belong to all of them? Moreover, when the rulers talk, do they speak the symbols of Nigerianness or the signs of otherness? What then are the signs and symbols of Nigerianness?

All Nigerians need to learn to communicate about their pasts in order to share in the present. A tradition that sanctions expressivity or references to an uncomfortable past, or one that delimits intercultural exchanges and relationships, and thereby perpetuates docility and unearned deference to illegitimate authorities, disengages as well as disenfranchises its citizens. For example, Nigerians have collectively and silently, or out of fear and "respect" for the dead, avoided conversing and talking about the Nigerian civil war—in which an estimated two million died to keep the country united. It is an abomination and a disregard for those lives lost for the sake of a united Nigeria. The Nigerian Civil War is a critical event in the constitution of Nigerianness, and must be freely talked about and referenced in presidential communications so that the atrocities of war become real and present in the negotiations for social and political harmonization, not hegemonization, of Nigerian symbols, codes, signs, artifacts; for there cannot be identification without division—and no syncretization without differentiation of the parts for their discerning and combining qualities, capacities and capabilities.

If Nigeria is to sustain and strive to overcome its struggles of growth and maturation, Nigerians have to change their ways of relating, communicating, interacting, transacting, doing, believing, and acting with and toward one another and their symbols and signs and codes. This means the Nigerian leadership must not only be strong, visionary, and communicative, but must also be able to enact and enforce new laws that in the end entrench the culture of Nigerianness. These leaders do not have to be military dictators. They need however, be compassionate, strong, intelligent, bold, courageous, wise, capable, and dynamic, and have the strength of character and integrity befitting heroes. A good leader must be a decision maker, a motivator, a good listener, insightful, imaginative, competent, and resolute in will and mind. Above all, he or she must be one of, and for, as well as one with, the peoples of Nigeria; he or she must be the one who knows what the people want and need to be Nigerians. And above all, that individual must have the tenacity as well as the communicative competence to get these things done through the use of all the available communication and constitutional channels in the interest of Nigeria. As Nigerians know, no ruler or leader can effectively discharge a people's work alone. All leaders need followers, advisers, counsellors, and the support of their citizenry for effectiveness. Herein lies the dialogic imperative to the functional leadership performance in the Nigerian plural democratic experiments.

Appendixes

COUP ANNOUNCEMENTS
1966–1990

Appendix A

The Full Text of the First Military Coup Announcement in Nigeria, Delivered by Major Chukwuemeka Kaduna Nzeogwu, over Radio Nigeria in Kaduna, on January 15, 1966, Which Signaled the Ascension of Military into Nigerian Politics

In the name of the Supreme Military Council of the Revolution of the Nigerian Armed Forces, I declare martial law over the Northern provinces of Nigeria.[1]

The Constitution is suspended and the regional governments and elected Assemblies are hereby dissolved. All political, cultural, tribal and trade union activities, together with all demonstrations and unauthorized gatherings, excluding religious worship, are banned until further notice.

The aim of the Revolutionary Council is to establish a strong, united and prosperous nation, free from corruption and internal strife. Our method of achieving this is strictly military, but we have no doubt that every Nigerian will give us maximum cooperation by assisting the regime and not disturbing the peace during the slight changes that are taking place.

I am to assure all foreigners living and working in this part of Nigeria that their rights will continue to be respected. All treaty obligations previously entered into with any foreign nation will be respected, and we hope that such nations will respect our country's territorial integrity and will avoid taking sides with enemies of the revolution and enemies of the people.

My dear countrymen, you will hear and probably see a lot being done by certain bodies charged by the Supreme Council with the duties of national integration, supreme justice, general security and property recovery. As an interim measure all permanent secretaries, corporation chairmen and senior heads of departments are allowed to make decisions until the new organs are functioning, so long as such decisions are not contrary to the aims and wishes of the Supreme Council. No Minister or Parliamentary Secretary possesses administrative or other forms of control over the ministry, even if they are not considered too dangerous to be arrested.

This is not a time for long speech-making and so let me acquaint you with the proclamations in the Extraordinary Orders of the Day which the

Supreme Council has promulgated. These will be modified as the situation improves. You are hereby warned that looting, arson, homosexuality, rape, embezzlement, bribery or corruption, obstruction of the revolution, sabotage, subversion, false alarms and assistance to foreign invaders, are all offences punishable by death sentence.

Demonstrations and unauthorized assembly, non-cooperation with revolutionary troops are punishable in a grave manner up to death.

Refusal or neglect to perform normal duties or any task that may of necessity be ordered by local military commanders in support of the change will be punishable by a sentence imposed by the local military commanders.

Spying, harmful or injurious publications and broadcasts of troop movements or actions will be punishable by any suitable sentence deemed fit by the local military commander.

Shouting of slogans, loitering and rowdy behavior will be rectified by any sentence of incarceration, or any more severe sentence deemed fit by the local military commander.

Doubtful loyalty will be penalized by imprisonment or any more severe punishment.

Illegal possession or carrying of firearms, smuggling, or trying to escape with documents, valuables, including money or other assets vital to the running of any establishment, will be punished by death sentence.

Wavering or sitting on the fence and failing to declare open loyalty with the revolution will be regarded as an act of hostility punishable by any sentence deemed suitable by the local military commander. Tearing down an order of the day or proclamation or other authorized notices will be penalized by death.

This is the end of the Extraordinary Order of the Day which you will soon begin to see displayed in public.

My dear countrymen, no citizen should have anything to fear, so long as that citizen is law-abiding and if that citizen has religiously obeyed the native laws of the country and those set down in every heart and conscience since October 1, 1960. Our enemies are the political profiteers, the swindlers, the men in high and low places that seek bribes and demand ten percent; those that seek to keep the country divided permanently so that they can remain in office as ministers or V.I.P.'s at least, the tribalists, the nepotists, those that make the country look big for nothing before international circles; those that have corrupted our society and put the Nigerian political calendar back by their words and deeds. Like good soldiers we are not promising anything miraculous or spectacular. But what we do promise every law-abiding citizen is freedom from fear and all forms of oppression, freedom from general inefficiency and freedom to live and strive in every field of human endeavour, both nationally and internationally. We promise that you will no more be ashamed to say that you are Nigerians.

I leave you with a message of good wishes and ask for your support at all times, so that our land, watered by the Niger and Benue, between the sandy wastes and gulf of Guinea, washed in salt by the mighty Atlantic, shall not detract Nigerians from gaining sway in any great aspect of international endeavour.

My dear countrymen, this is the end of this speech. I wish you all good luck and I hope you will cooperate to the fullest in this job which we have set for ourselves, of establishing a prosperous nation and achieving solidarity.

Thank you very much and good-bye for now.

NOTE

1. This speech was obtained from and authenticated through the following sources: S.K. Panter-Brick, ed., *Nigerian Politics and Military Rule: Prelude to the Civil War* (London: University of London Press, 1970); and A.H.M. Kirk-Greene, *Crisis and Conflict in Nigeria: A Documentary Source Book, 1966–1970, Vol.1* (London: Oxford University Press, 1971), 125–127.

Appendix B

The Full Text of the Coup Announcement by Colonel Joseph Nanven Garba on July 29, 1975, That Toppled General Yakubu Gowon and Led to the Ascension of Brigadier (Later General) Murtala Ramat Mohammed to Power

Fellow Countrymen and women,[1]

I, Colonel Joseph Nanven Garba, in consultation with my colleagues, do hereby declare that in view of what has been happening in our country in the past few months, the Nigerian Armed Forces decided to effect a change of the leadership on the Federal Military Government.

As from now, General Yakubu Gowon ceases to be the Head of the Federal Military Government and Commander-in-Chief of Armed Forces of Nigeria. The general public is advised to be calm and to go about their lawful duties.

However, in view of the traffic situation in Lagos area, all workers other than those on essential services like NEPA, Medical Services, Water Works, NPA, the P&T, all workers and all Tanker Drivers will observe today, 29th of July, as a work free day.

A dusk to dawn curfew is hereby imposed until further notice. Nigeria Airways operations are suspended and all Airports and Borders are closed till further notice.

Fellow countrymen, this has been a bloodless operation and we do not want anyone to lose his or her life. You are therefore warned in your own interest to be law abiding. Anyone caught disturbing the public order will be summarily dealt with.

We appeal to everyone to co-operate in the task ahead. Further announcements will be made in due course. Long live the Federal Republic of Nigeria.

NOTE

1. Colonel Garba's Coup D'etat Speech, July 29, 1975. From http://www.dawodu. com/garba1.htm (accessed July 29, 2009).

Appendix C

The Full Text of Lieutenant Colonel Bukar Sukar Dimka's Coup Announcement on February 13, 1976, That Ended the Life and the Government of General Murtala Ramat Mohammed, and Which Led to the Ascension of Brigadier (Later General) Olusegun Obasanjo to Power

Good morning fellow Nigerians,[1]

This is Lt. Col. Bukar Sukar Dimka of the Nigerian Army calling.

I bring you good tidings. Murtala Muhammed's deficiency has been detected. His government is now overthrown by the young revolutionaries. All the 19 military governors have no powers over the states they now govern. The states affairs will be run by military brigade commanders until further notice.

All senior military officers should remain calm in their respective spots. No divisional commanders will issue orders or instructions until further notice.

Any attempt to foil these plans from any quarters will be met with death.

You are warned, it is all over the 19 states.

Any acts of looting or raids will be death.

Everyone should be calm.

Please stay by your radio for further announcements.

All borders, air and seaports are closed until further notice.

Curfew is imposed from 6am to 6pm.

Thank you. We are all together.

NOTE

1. Mike Okoye, ed. *Toward A Better Nigeria* (Ikeja, Nigeria: Times Books Limited, n.d.), 199. See also, "Dimka's Coup Announcement—February 13, 1976." www .dawodu.com/dimka2.htm Accessed July 29, 2009.

The Full Text of Coup Announcement by Brigadier Sani Abacha on December 31, 1983, that Overthrew the Duly Elected Second Republic Executive Presidency of Alhaji Shehu Usman Shagari

Fellow countrymen and women,[1]

I, Brigadier Sanni Abacha, of the Nigerian Army address you this morning on behalf of the Nigerian Armed Forces.

You are all living witnesses to the great economic predicament and uncertainty, which an inept and corrupt leadership has imposed on our beloved nation for the past four years. I am referring to the harsh, intolerable conditions under which we are now living. Our economy has been hopelessly mismanaged; we have become a debtor and beggar nation. There is inadequacy of food at reasonable prices for our people who are now fed up with endless announcements of importation of foodstuff; health services are in shambles as our hospitals are reduced to mere consulting clinics without drugs, water and equipment.

Our educational system is deteriorating at alarming rate. Unemployment figures including the undergraduates have reached embarrassing and unacceptable proportions.

In some states, workers are being owed salary arrears of eight to twelve months and in others there are threats of salary cuts. Yet our leaders revel in squandermania, corruption and indiscipline, and continue to proliferate public appointments in complete disregard of our stark economic realities.

After due consultations over these deplorable conditions, I and my colleagues in the Armed Forces have in the discharge of our national role as promoters and protectors of our national interest decided to effect a change in the leadership of the government of the Federal Republic of Nigeria and form a Federal Military Government. This task has just been completed.

The Federal Military Government hereby decree the suspension of the provision of the Constitution of the Federal Republic of Nigeria 1979 relating to all elective and appointive offices and representative institutions including the office of the President, state governors, federal and state executive councils, special advisers, special assistants, the establishment of the National Assembly and the Houses of the Assembly including the formation of political parties.

Accordingly, Alhaji Shehu Usman Shagari ceases forthwith to be the President and Commander-in-Chief of the Armed Forces of Nigeria. All the incumbents of the above named offices shall, if they have not already done so, vacate their formal official residences, surrender all government property in their possession, and report to the nearest police station in their constituencies within 7 days.

The clerk of the National Assembly, the President of the Senate and Speaker of the House of Representatives shall, within two weeks, render account of all the properties of the national Assembly. All the political parties are banned; the bank account of FEDECO and all the political parties are frozen with immediate effect. All foreigners living in any part of the country are assured of their safety and will be adequately protected.

Henceforth, workers not on essential duties are advised to keep off the streets. All categories of workers on essential duties will, however, report at their places of work immediately.

With effect from today, a dusk to dawn curfew will be imposed between 7pm and 6am each day until further notice. All Airways flights have been suspended forthwith and all airports, seaports, and border posts closed. External communication has been cut; the Custom and Excise, Immigration and the Police will maintain vigilance and ensure watertight security at the borders. The area administrator or commanders will have themselves to blame if any of the wanted people escapes.

Fellow countrymen and women, the change in government has been a bloodless and painstaking operation and we do not want anyone to lose his or her life. People are warned in their own interest to be law abiding and to give the Federal Military Government maximum cooperation. Anyone caught disturbing public order will be summarily dealt with.

For avoidance of doubt, you are forewarned that we shall not hesitate to declare martial law in any area or state of the federation in which disturbances occur.

Fellow countrymen and women and comrades at arms, I will like to assure you that the Armed Forces of Nigeria is ready to lay its life for our dear nation but not for the present irresponsible leadership of the past civilian administration.

You are to await further announcements.

Good morning.

NOTE

1. http://www.dawodu.com/abacha2.htm Accessed May 9, 2004.

The Full Text of Brigadier Joshua Dogonyaro Coup Announcement on August 27, 1985 that Toppled General Muhammadu Buhari

I, Brigadier Joshua Nimyel Dogonyaro, of the Nigerian Army,1 hereby make the following declaration on behalf of my colleagues and members of the Nigerian Armed Forces. Fellow countrymen, the intervention of the military at the end of 1983 was welcomed by the nation with unprecedented enthusiasm.

Nigerians were unified in accepting the intervention and looked forward hopefully to progressive changes for the better. Almost two years later, it has become clear that the fulfillment of expectations is not forthcoming. Because this generation of Nigerians and indeed future generations have no other country but Nigeria, we could not stay passive and watch a small group of individuals misuse power to the detriment of our national aspirations and interest.

No nation can ever achieve meaningful strides in it development where there is an absence of cohesion in the hierarchy of government; where it has become clear that positive action by the policy makers is hindered because as a body it lacks a unity of purpose.

It is evident that the nation would be endangered with the risk of continuous misdirection. We are presently confronted with that danger.

In such a situation, if action can be taken to arrest further damage, it should and must be taken. This is precisely what we have done.

The Nigerian public has been made to believe that the slow pace of action of the Federal Government headed by Major-General Muhammadu Buhari was due to the enormity of the problems left by the last civilian administration.

Although it is true that a lot of the problems were left behind by the last civilian government, the real reason, however, for the very slow pace of action is due to lack of unanimity of purpose among the ruling body;

subsequently, the business of governance, has gradually been subjected to ill-motivated power play considerations. The ruling body, the Supreme Military Council, has, therefore, progressively been made redundant by the actions of a select few members charged with the day-to-day implementation of the SMC's policies and decision. The concept of collective leadership has been substituted by stubborn and ill-advised unilateral actions, thereby destroying the principles upon which the government came to power. Any effort made to advise the leadership, met with stubborn resistance and was viewed as a challenge to authority or disloyalty. Thus the scene was being set for systematic elimination of what, was termed oppositions.

All energies of the leadership were directed at this imaginary opposition rather than to effective leadership. The result of this misdirected effort is now very evident in the country as a whole.

The government has started to drift. The economy does not seem to be getting any better as we witness daily increased inflation. The nation's meager resources are once again being wasted on unproductive ventures.

Government has distanced itself from the people and the yearnings and aspirations of the people as constantly reflected in the media have been ignored.

This is because a few people have arrogated to themselves the right to make the decisions for the larger part of the ruling body.

All these events have shown that the present composition of our country's leadership cannot, therefore, justify its continued occupation of that position.

Furthermore, the initial objectives and programmes of action which were meant to have been implemented since the ascension to power of the Buhari Administration in January 1984 have been betrayed and discarded.

The present state of uncertainty and stagnation cannot be permitted to degenerate into suppression and retrogression. We feel duty bound to use the resources and the means at our disposal to restore hope in the minds of Nigerians and renew aspirations for a better future.

We are no prophets of doom for our beloved country, Nigeria. We, therefore, count on everyone's cooperation and assistance. I appeal to you, fellow countrymen, particularly my colleagues in arms to refrain from any act that will lead to unnecessary violence and blood shed among us. Rest assured that our action is in the interest of the nation and the armed forces.

In order to enable a new order to be introduced, the following bodies are dissolved forthwith pending further announcements: (a) The Supreme Military Council (b) The Federal Executive Council (c) The National Council of States.

All seaports and airports are closed, all borders remain closed. Finally a dusk to dawn curfew is hereby imposed in Lagos and all state capitals until further notice. All military commanders will ensure effective maintenance of law and order. Further announcements will be made in due course.

God bless Nigeria.

NOTE

1. Brigadier Joshua Dogonyaro, Coup Announcement, "We Are Not Prophets of Doom," In Mike Okoye, ed., *Towards A Better Nigeria, 321–322* (Ikeja, Nigeria: Times Books Limited, n.d.), 321–322. See also http://www.dawodu.com/dony1.htm accessed May 9, 2004.

Appendix F

The Full Text of the Coup Announcement by Major Gideon Orkar, on April 30, 1990, that Failed to Topple the Military Government under General Ibrahim Badamosi Babangida

Fellow Nigerian Citizens,[1]

On behalf of the patriotic and well-meaning peoples of the Middle Belt and the southern parts of this country, I, Major Gideon Orkar, wish to happily inform you of the successful ousting of the dictatorial, corrupt, drug baronish, evil man, deceitful, homo-sexuality-centered, prodigalistic, un-patriotic administration of General Ibrahim Badamosi Babangida. We have equally commenced their trials for unabated corruption, mismanagement of national economy, the murders of Dele Giwa, Major-General Mamman Vasta, with other officers as there was no attempted coup but mere intentions that were yet to materialise and other human rights violations.

The National Guard already in its formative stage is disbanded with immediate effect. Decrees number 2 and 46 are hereby abrogated. We wish to emphasise that this is not just another coup but a well conceived, planned and executed revolution for the marginalized, oppressed and enslaved peoples of the Middle Belt and the south with a view to freeing ourselves and children yet unborn from eternal slavery and colonisation by a clique of this country.

Our history is replete with numerous and uncontrollable instances of callous and insensitive dominatory repressive intrigues by those who think it is their birthright to dominate till eternity the political and economic privileges of this great country to the exclusion of the peoples of the Middle Belt and the south.

They have almost succeeded in subjugating the Middle Belt and making them voiceless and now extending same to the south.

It is our unflinching belief that this quest for domination, oppression and marginalization is against the wish of God and therefore, must be resisted with vehemence.

Anything that has a beginning must have an end. It will also suffice here to state that all Nigerians without skeleton in their cupboards need not to be afraid of this change. However, those with skeleton in their cupboards have all reasons to fear, because the times of reckoning has come.

For the avoidance of doubt, we wish to state the three primary reasons why we have decided to oust the satanic Babangida administration. The reasons are as follows:

- To stop Babangida's desire to cunningly, install himself as Nigeria's life president at all costs and by so doing, retard the progress of this country for life. In order to be able to achieve this undesirable goals of his, he has evidently started destroying those groups and sections he perceived as being able to question his desires. Examples of groups already neutralized, pitched against one another or completely destroyed are:
  - The Sokoto Caliphate by installing an unwanted Sultan to cause division within the hitherto strong Sokoto Caliphate
  - The destruction of the peoples of Plateau State, especially the Langtang people, as a balancing force in the body politics of this country.
  - The buying of the press by generous monetary favours and the usage of State Security Service, SSS, as a tool of terror.
  - The intent to cow the students by the promulgation of the draconian decree Number 47.
  - The cowing of the university teaching and non-teaching staff by an intended massive purge, using the 150 million dollars loan as the necessitating factor.
  - Deliberately withholding funds to the armed forces to make them ineffective and also crowning his diabolical scheme through the intended retrenchment of more than half of the members of the armed forces.

Other pointers that give credence to his desire to become a life president against the wishes of the people are:

- His appointment of himself as a minister of defense, his putting under his direct control the SSS, his deliberate manipulation of the transition programme, his introduction of inconceivable, unrealisitic and impossible political options, his recent fraternization with other African leaders that have installed themselves as life presidents and his dogged determination to create a secret force called the National Guard, independent of the Armed Forces and the Police which will be answerable to himself alone, both operationally and administratively.It is our strong view that this kind of dictatorial desire of Babangida is unacceptable to Nigerians of the 1980's, and, therefore, must be resisted by all.

• Another major reason for the change is the need to stop intrigues, domination and internal colonization of the Nigerian state by the so-called chosen few. This, in our view, has been and is still responsible for 90 percent of the problems of Nigerians. This indeed has been the major clog in our wheel of progress.

This clique has an unabated penchant for domination and unrivalled fostering of mediocrity and outright detest for accountability, all put together have been our undoing as a nation.

This will ever remain our threat if not checked immediately. It is strongly believed that without the intrigues perpetrated by this cliques and misrule, Nigeria will have in all ways achieved developmental virtues comparable to those in Korea, Taiwan, Brazil, India, and even Japan.

Evidence, therefore, this cancerous dominance has as a factor constituted by a major and unpardonable clog in the wheel of progress of the Nigerian State. It is suffice to mention a few distasteful intrigues engineered by this group of Nigerians in recent past. These are:

• The shabby and dishonourable treatment meted on the longest serving Nigerian general in the person of General Domkat Bali, who in actual fact had given credibility to the Babangida administration.
• The wholesale hijacking of Babangida's administration by the all powerful clique.
• The disgraceful and explicable removal of Commodore Ebitu Ukiwe, Professor Tam David-West, Mr. Aret Adams and so on from office.
• The now-pervasive and on-going retrenchment of Middle Belt and southerners from public offices and their instant replacement by the favoured class and their stooges.
• The deliberate disruption of the educational culture and retarding its place to suit the favoured class to the detriment of other educational minded parts of this country.
• The deliberate impoverishment of the peoples from the Middle Belt and the south, making them working ghosts and feeding on the formulae of 0–1–1–or 0–0–0 while the aristocratic class and their stooges are living in absolute affluence on a daily basis without working for it.
• Other countless examples of the exploitative, oppressive, dirty games of intrigues of its class, where people and stooges that can best be described by the fact that even though they contribute very little economically to the well being of Nigeria, they have over the years served and presided over the supposedly national wealth derived in the main from the Middle Belt and

the southern part of this country, while the people from these parts of the country have been completely deprived from benefiting from the resources given to them by God.
- The third reason for the change is the need to lay a strong egalitarian foundation for the real democratic take off of the Nigerian state or states as the circumstances may dictate.

In light of all the above and in recognition of the negativeness of the aforementioned aristocratic factor, the overall progress of the Nigerian state a temporary decision to excise the following states namely, Sokoto, Borno, Katsina, Kano, and Bauchi states from the Federal Republic of Nigeria comes into effect immediately until the following conditions are met.

The conditions to be met to necessitate the re-absorption of the aforementioned states are as following:

- To install the rightful heir to the Sultanate, Alhaji Maccido, who is the people's choice.
- To send a delegation led by the real and recognized Sultan Alhaji Maccido to the Federal Government to vouch that the feudalistic and aristocratic quest for domination and operation will be a thing of the past and will never be practised in any part of the Nigerian state.

By the same token, all citizens of the five states already mentioned are temporarily suspended from all public and private offices in Middle Belt and southern parts of this country until the mentioned conditions above are met.

They are also required to move back to their various states within one week from today. They will, however, be allowed to return and join the Federal Republic of Nigeria when the stipulated conditions are met.

In the same vein, all citizens of the Middle Belt and the south are required to come back to their various states pending when the so-called all-in-all Nigerians meet the conditions that will ensure a united Nigeria. A word is enough for the wise.

This exercise will not be complete without purging corrupt public officials and recovering their ill-gotten wealth, since the days of the oil boom till date. Even in these hard times, when Nigerians are dying from hunger, trekking many miles to work for lack of transportation, a few other Nigerians with complete impunity are living in unbelievable affluence both inside and outside the country.

We are extremely determined to recover all ill-gotten wealth back to the public treasury for the use of the masses of our people. You are all advised to remain calm as there is no cause for alarm. We are fully in control of the situation as directed by God. All airports, seaports and borders are closed forthwith.

The former Armed Forces Ruling Council is now disbanded and replaced with National Ruling Council to be chaired by the head of state with other members being a civilian vice-head of state, service chiefs, inspector-general of police, one representative each from NLC, NUJ, NBA, and NANS.

A curfew is hereby imposed from 8 P.M. to 6 A.M. until further notice. All members of the Armed Forces and the police forces are hereby confined to their respective barracks.

All unlawful and criminal acts by those attempting to cause chaos will be ruthlessly crushed. Be warned as we are prepared at all costs to defend the new order.

All radio stations are hereby advised to hook on permanently to the national network programme until further notice.

Long live all true patriots of this great country of ours.

May God and Allah through his bountiful mercies bless us all.

NOTE

1. Major Gideon Orkar, "April 1999 Coup D'etat Speech." From http://www .dawodu.com/orkar.htm, accessed July 29, 2009.

Bibliography

GOVERNMENT DOCUMENTS

Abacha, General Sani. Maiden Broadcast to the Nation as Military Head of State on November 18, 1993. Abuja, Nigeria: Federal Ministry of Information and Communications, November 18, 1993.

Abubakar, General Abdulsalami. Maiden Broadcast by the New Head of State, Commander-in-Chief of the Armed Forces of Nigeria, June 9, 1998. Washington, DC: The Nigerian Embassy, Information Department Document.

Azikiwe, Nnamdi. Respect for Human Dignity: Inaugural Address by His Excellency, Dr. Nnamdi Azikiwe, Governor-General and Commander in Chief of the Federation of Nigeria on November 16, 1960. Lagos, Nigeria: Federal Ministry of Information, 1960.

Babangida, Ibrahim. "Towards New Goals, New Directions." Maiden Speech by His Excellency, General Ibrahim Babangida, Head of the Federal Military Government and Commander in Chief of the Armed Forces on August 27, 1985. Lagos: Federal Ministry of Information, Domestic Publicity Division, Ikoyi, 1985.

The Constitution of the National Council of Nigeria and the Cameroons. Lagos: Ife-Olu Printing Works, 1945.

"General Abubakar Keeps His Word, Obasanjo Takes Over: Nigeria Has High Hopes in Stable Democracy." Abuja, Nigeria: Publications of the Federal Ministry of Information & Culture, 1999.

News From Nigeria: A Publication of the Nigerian Consulate-General. New York and San Francisco, October 4 and 26. (1975): 1 and 4.

Nigerian Newsletter: A Publication of the Embassy of the Federal Republic of Nigeria, Information Division (Cairo: Egypt, 1966).

The Problem of Nigerian Unity. Appendix 1. Enugu, Nigeria: Eastern Nigeria Ministry of Information, n.d.

Shonekan, Chief Ernest Adegunle. "State of the Nation" Address. Ministry of Foreign Affairs, Abuja, Nigeria, August 31, 1993.

A Time For Action: Collected Speeches of His Excellency General Murtalla Mu-hammed. Lagos: Federal Ministry of Information, 1975.

Yar'Adua,Umaru Shehu. "The Challenge Is Great; The Goal Is Clear." The First In-augural Address of His Excellency, President Umaru Shehu Yar'Adua, President and Commander in Chief of the Federal Republic of Nigeria. Embassy of Nigeria, Information Department, Washington, D.C., 2007.

NEWSPAPERS AND MAGAZINES

Babangida, Ibrahim Badamosi. "Deeper Commitment," *West Africa.* (September 2, 1985).

———. "Our Mission." *Africa.* 169. (September, 1985).

The British Broadcasting Corporation: Summary of World Broadcasts Section 4: The Middle East, Africa and Latin America. October 4, 1983. 5–12.

Buhari, Muhammadu. "Buhari's New Year Broadcast." *West Africa.* (January 9, 1984).

"Buhari's Ascension Speech." *Foreign Broadcast Information Service Daily Report, Middle East and Africa* 5:001. (January 3, 1984).

Kirk-Green, A.H. M. "On Swearing—An Account of Some Judicial Oaths in North-ern Nigeria." *Africa.* 57 (1955): 43–53.

The New Nigerian. October 3, 1983. 3 and 29.

SCHOLARLY JOURNAL ARTICLES

Bitzer, Lloyd F. "The Rhetorical Situation." *Philosophy and Rhetoric* 1:1. (January 1968): 1–10.

Chase, J. Richard. "The Classical Conception of Epideictic." *Quarterly Journal of Speech.* 47 (1961): 293–300.

Hart, Roderick P. "The Rhetoric of the True Believer." *Speech Monographs.* 38:4. (November 1971): 249–261.

Hauser, Gerard A. "Aristotle on Epideictic: The Formation of Public Morality." *Rhetoric Society Quarterly.* 29:1 (1999): 5–23.

McGee, Michael Calvin. "A Link between Rhetoric and Ideology." *Quarterly Journal of Speech.* 66 (1980): 1–16.

Scanlan, Ross. "The Nazi Party Speaker System, I." *Speech Monographs.* 16 (August 1949): 82–97.

———. "The Nazi Party Speaker System, II." *Speech Monographs.* 17 (June 1950): 134–148.

BOOKS

Achebe, Chinua. *Things Falls Apart.* London/New York: Heinemann Educational Books, Inc., 1958.

Ade-Ajayi, Jacob F. *Milestones in Nigerian History*. Ibadan: University of Ibadan Press, 1962.

Afigbo, Adiele E. "Nigeria and the Myth of Modern Democracy." In Toyin Falola, ed., *Nigerian History, Practices and Affairs: The Collected Essays of Adiele Afigbo*. Trenton, NJ: Africa World Press, 2005. 531–557.

Anderson, Benedict. *Imagined Communities: Reflections on the Origin and Spread of Nationalism*, Revised Edition. London: Verso Press, 1983.

Austin, J. L. *How to Do Things With Words, Second Edition*. Cambridge, MA: Harvard University Press, n.d.

Avwenagbiku, Patrick. *Olusegun Obasanjo and His Footprints*. Abuja, Nigeria: Metro Publishers, 2000.

Awolowo, Obafemi. *Awo: The Autobiography of Chief Obafemi Awolowo*. Cambridge:Cambridge University Press, 1960.

———. *Path to Nigerian Freedom*. London: Faber & Faber, 1947.

———. The People's Republic. Ibadan, Nigeria: Oxford University Press, 1968.

Ayandele, E.A. *A Visionary of the African Church, Mojola Agbe, 1860–1917*. Nairobi: East African Publishing House, 1971.

Ayandele, Emmanuel A. *The Missionary Impact on Modern Nigeria, 1842–1914*. Harlow: Longman, 1966.

Ayida, Allison A. The *Rise and Fall of Nigeria: The History and Philosophy of an Experiment in African Nation-Building*. Lagos & London: Malthouse Press Limited, 1990.

Azikiwe, Nnamdi. *The Development of Political Parties in Nigeria*. London: Office of the Commissioner in the United Kingdom for the Eastern Region of Nigeria, 1957.

———. *My Odyssey: An Autobiography*. London: G. Hurst, 1970.

———. *Political Blueprint for Nigeria*. Lagos: African Book Company, 1945.

Bello, Amadu. *Ahmadu Bello: My Life*. London: Cambridge University Press, 1962.

Bloch, Maurice, ed. *Political Language and Oratory in Traditional Society*. New York: Academic Press, 1975.

Burke, Kenneth. *Rhetoric of Motives*. Berkeley and Los Angeles, CA: The University of California Press, 1969.

Campbell, Karlyn Kohrs, and Kathleen Hall Jamieson. *Deeds Done in Words: Presidential Rhetoric and the Genres of Governance*. Chicago, IL: The University of Chicago Press, 1990.

Carter, Gwendolyn M.and Patrick O'Meara, eds., *African Independence: The First Twenty-Five Years*. Bloomington: Indiana University Press, 1985.

Cassirer, Ernst. *The Myth of the State*. New Haven, CT: Yale University Press, 1946.

Chase, M., and C. Shaw, eds. *The Imagined Past: History and Nostalgia*. New York: Manchester University Press, 1989.

Cheyfitz, Eric. *The Poetics of Imperialism: Translation and Colonialism from "The Tempest" to "Tarzan," Revised Edition*. Philadelphia, PA: The University of Pennsylvania Press, 1997.

Clark, Trevor. *A Right Honourable Gentleman, Abubakar from the Black Rock: A Narrative Chronicle of the Life and Times of Nigeria's Alhaji Sir Abubakar Tafawa Balewa*. London: Edward Arnold, 1991.

Cmiel, Kenneth. *Democratic Eloquence: The Fight over Popular Speech in Nineteenth Century America*. New York: William Morrow & Company, 1990.

Coleman, James S. *Nigeria Background to Nationalism*. Berkeley, CA: University of California Press, 1958.

Corcoran, Paul E. *Political Language and Rhetoric*. Austin, TX: The University of Texas Press, 1979.

Crowder, Michael. *The Story of Nigeria*. London: Faber & Faber, 1966.

Davidson, Basil. *Africa in History: Themes and Outlines, Revised and Expanded Edition*. London: Phoenix Press, 2001.

Diamond, Larry, Anthony Kirk-Greene, and Oyeleye Oyediran, eds. *Transition Without End: Nigerian Politics and Civil Society Under Babangida*. Boulder, CO: Lynne Riener Publishers, 1997.

Dimka, Bukar Sukar, (Lt. Col.). "Dimka's Coup Announcement-February 13, 1976." www.dawodu.com/dimka2.htm accessed July 29, 2009.

Dogonyaro, Joshua Nimyel (Brigadier). "Coup Announcement by Brigadier Dogonyaro—August 27, 1985." From http://www.dawodu.com/dony1.htm. accessed July 29, 2009.

Dryzek, John. *Discursive Democracy*. Cambridge: Cambridge University Press, 1990.

Elaigwu, J. Isawa. *Gowon: The Bibliography of a Soldier-Statesman*. Ibadan, Nigeria: West Book Publishers, Ltd., 1985.

Epelle, Sam., ed. *Tafawa Balewa: Nigeria Speaks-Speeches of Alhaji Sir Abubakar Tafawa Balewa Made Between 1957–1964*. London: Longman Press Ltd., 1964.

Falola, Toyin, et al., eds., *History of Nigeria, 3: Nigeria in the Twentieth Century*. Ikeja: Longman, 1981.

Falola, Toyin, and Julius Ihonvbere, eds. *The Rise and Fall of Nigeria's Second Republic, 1979–1984*. London: Zed Books, 1985.

Fields, Wayne. *Union of Words: A History of Presidential Eloquence*. New York: The Free Press, 1996.

Fisher, Walter R. Human. *Communication as Narration: Toward a Philosophy of Reason, Value, and Action*. Columbia, SC: University of South Carolina Press, 1987.

Garba, Joseph N. (Col.). "Colonel Garba's Coup D'etat Speech, July 29, 1975." http://www.dawodu.com/garba1.htm. Accessed July 29, 2009.

Gay, Peter. *The Cultivation of Hatred, Vol. 3 of the Bourgeois Experience, Victoria to Freud*. New York: W.W. Norton & Company, Inc., 1993.

Great and Historical Speeches and Documents. www.Dawodu.com. Accessed March 22, 2009.

Hoffer, Eric. *The True Believer: Thoughts on the Nature of Mass Movements*. New York: HarperCollins, Inc., 1989.

Isichei, Elizabeth. *A History of Nigeria*. New York: Longman, 1983.

Iweriebor, Ehiedu E.G. "Nationalism and the Struggle for Freedom, 1880–1960." In Adebayo Oyebade, ed. *The Foundations of Nigeria: Essays in Honor of Toyin Falola*. Trenton, NJ: Africa World Press, n.d. 79–105.

———. *Radical Politics in Nigeria, 1945–1950: The Significance of Zikist Movement*. Zaria: Ahmadu Bello University Press, 1966.

———. "Radicalism and the National Liberation Struggles, 1930–1950." In Adebayo Oyebade, ed. *The Foundations of Nigeria: Essays in Honor of Toyin Falola*. Trenton, NJ: Africa World Press, Inc., 2003. 7–125.

Jamieson, Kathleen Hall. *Eloquence in an Electronic Age: The Transformation of Political Speechmaking.* New York: Oxford University Press, 1988.

Kennedy, George A. *Aristotle on Rhetoric: A Theory of Civic Discourse.* New York: Oxford University Press, 1991.

Kirk-Greene, A.H.M. *Crisis and Conflict in Nigeria: A Documentary Sourcebook, 1966–1970, Vol.1.* London: Oxford University Press, 1971.

———. *Lugard and the Amalgamation of Nigeria: A Documentary Record.* London: Frank Cass, 1968.

Lynch, Hollis R. *Black Spokesman: Selected Published Writings of Edward Wilmot Blyden.* New York: Humanities Press, 1971.

———. *Edward Blyden: Pan Negro Patriot, 1832–1912.* London: Oxford University Press, 1967.

McKeon, Richard. "Symbols, Myths, and Arguments." In Mark Backman, ed., *Rhetoric: Essays in Invention and Discovery.* Woodridge, CT: OxBow Press, 1987. 66–94.

Nicolson, I. F. *The Administration of Nigeria 1900–1960: Men, Methods, and Myth.* Oxford: Clarendon Press, 1969.

Obasanjo, Olusegun. "'A New Dawn,' Inaugural Broadcast to the Nation on May 29, 1999," in *A New Dawn: Selected Speeches by Olusegun Obasanjo, President of the Federal Republic of Nigeria.* New York: Consulate-General of Nigeria, n.d. 26–34.

———. "Fast Forward into the Future." Inaugural Address to the Joint Session of the New National Assembly, June 5. 2003. From www.nigeriavillagesquare1.com/obj .htm. Accessed December 7, 2004.

Obotetukudo, Solomon W. *Presidential Thematics and Communicative Practices in a Plural Nigerian Democracy.* New York: The Edwin Mellen Press, 2010 forth-coming.

———. "The Rhetorical Constitution of Nigeria: An Examination of the Inaugural and Ascension Speeches of Nigeria's Elected and Military Heads of State, 1960–1985." Ph.D. Dissertation, University of Southern California, Los Angeles, 1992.

———. "Straightforward Ambiguity and Communication in Traditional Societies: Kenneth Burke and Soren Kierkegaard to the Rescue," Paper Presented at the 83rd Speech/ National Communication Association, Chicago, Illinois, November 19–23, 1997.

———. "That We May Be What We Always Wanted: The Communication of Nostalgia in Nigeria's Search for Permanent Democratic Experiences." 2010 Forthcoming.

Ogbalu, F.Chidozie, ed. *Dr. Zik of Africa: Biography and Speeches.* Onitsha, Nigeria: African Literature Bureau, 1955.

Ojiako, O. *13Years of Military Rule.* Lagos, Nigeria: Daily Times of Nigeria, 1979.

Ojigbo, A. Okion. *Shehu Shagari: The Biography of Nigeria's First Executive President.* Lagos, Nigeria: Tokion Publishing, 1992.

Okonjo, I.M. *British Administration in Nigeria, 1900–1950: A Nigerian View.* New York: NOK Publishers, n.d.

Okoye, Mike, ed. *Toward A Better Nigeria: A Selection of Notable Speeches by Nigerian Leaders, 1957–1989.* Ikeja, Nigeria: The Times Books Ltd., n.d.

Oliver, Robert T. *The Influence of Rhetoric in the Shaping of Great Britain: From the Roman Invasion to the Early Nineteenth Century.* Newark, DE: University of Delaware Press, 1986.

———. *Leadership in Asia: Persuasive Communication in the Making of a Nation, 1850–1950.* Newark, DE: University of Delaware Press, 1989.

———. *Public Speaking in the Re-Shaping of Great Britain.* Newark, DE: University of Delaware Press, 1987.

Olusanya, G.O. *The Second World War and Politics in Nigeria, 1939–1953.* Ibadan: Evans Brothers Publishers, 1973.

Omoruyi, Omo. *Tale of June 12, 1993: The Betrayal of the Democratic Rights of Nigerians.* London: Press Alliance Network, 1999.

Onwuke, Chika B. "Constitutional Development, 1914–1960: British Legacy or Local Exigency?" In Adebayo Oyebade, ed. *The Foundations of Nigeria.* Trenton, NJ: Africa World Press, Inc., 2003.153–180.

Orkar, Gideon (Major). "April 1999 Coup D'etat Speech." http://www.dawodu.com/orkar.htm. Accessed July 29, 2009.

Otite, Onigu, ed. *Themes in African Social and Political Thought.* Enugu: Fourth Dimension Publishers, 1978.

Oyebade, Adebayo, ed. *The Foundations of Nigeria: Essays in Honor of Toyin Falola.* Trenton, NJ: Africa World Press, Inc., 2003.

———. *The Transformation of Nigeria: Essays in Honor of Toyin Falola.* New Jersey: Africa World Press, 2002.

Paden, John N. Ahmadu *Bello: Sardauna of Sokoto-Values and Leadership in Nigeria.* London, England: Hodder and Stoughton Educational Ltd., 1986.

Paine, Robert, ed. *Politically Speaking: Cross-Cultural Studies of Rhetoric.* Philadelphia, PA: Institute for the Study of Human Issues, 1981.

Panter-Brick, S.K., ed. *Nigerian Politics and Military Rule: Prelude to the Civil War.* London: University of London Press, 1970.

Roberts, W. Rhys, trans. *Aristotle: Rhetoric.* Introduction by Edward P.J. Corbett. New York: Modern Library, 1984.

Schwarz, Frederick A.D. *Nigeria: The Tribes, The Nation or the Race: The Politics of Independence.* Cambridge, MA: M.I.T. Press, 1965.

Shagari, Shehu. *Beckoned to Serve: An Autobiography of Shehu Shagari.* Ibadan, Nigeria: Heinemann Educational Books, 2001.

Shonekan, Ernest A. http://en.wikipedia.org/wiki/Ernest_Shonekan accessed March 12, 2008.

Sklar, Richard. *Nigerian Political Parties: Power in an Emergent African Nation.* Princeton: Princeton University Press, 1963.

———. "The Colonial Imprint on African Political Thought." In Gwendolyn M. Carter and Patrick O'Meara, eds. *African Independence: The First Twenty-Five Years.* Bloomington: Indiana University Press, 1985. 1–30.

Spencer, Benjamin T. *The Quest for Nationality.* Syracuse: Syracuse University Press, 1957.

Tamuno, Tekena N. *The Evolution of the Nigerian State: The Southern Phase, 1898–1914.* New York: Humanities Press, 1972.

Tijjani, Aminu, and David Williams, eds. *Shehu Shagari: My Visions of Nigeria.* London: Frank Cass & Co., Ltd.,1981.

Uko, Ndaeyo. *Romancing the Guns: The Press as Promoters of Military Rule.* Trenton, NJ: Africa World Press, Inc., 2003.

Umoden, Gabriel E. *The Babangida Years: The First Authoritative Biography of Nigeria's Most Visionary Leader.* Lagos, Nigeria: Gabumo Publishing Co., 1992.

Whitaker, Jr., C.S. *The Politics of Tradition: Continuity and Change in Northern Nigeria, 1946–1966.* Princeton, NJ: Princeton University Press, 1970.

Williams, David. *Presidential Power in Nigeria: The Life of Shehu Shagari.* London: Frank Cass & Co., Ltd., 1982.

"Yakubu Gowon." *The Columbia Encyclopedia, Sixth Edition, 2008.* http://www.encyclopedia.com/doc/leI.Gowon-Ya.html. Accessed January 9, 2009.

Yar'Adua,Umaru. file://G/Umaru_Yar'Adua.htm. Accessed March 6, 2009.

Yar'Adua, Umaru Musa."Biodata".yaradua2007.com Yar'adua 2007. http://www.yaradua2007.com/index.php?option=com_content&task=view(id=14&Itemid=26. Accessed March 6, 2009.

About the Author

Solomon Williams Obotetukudo holds a PhD in communication from the University of Southern California Annenberg School for Communications and Journalism. He was previously a multimedia communications consultant and speechwriter in Nigeria and the United States before returning to the academy. He is currently an assistant professor of mass media arts, journalism and communication studies at Clarion University of Pennsylvania, where he has taught Public Speaking, Language and Symbols in Human Communication, Nonverbal Communication, Freedom of Speech in American Culture, and Business and Professional Communication, among many other courses. His research and scholarly interests include political communication, presidential leadership rhetoric, philosophy of language, public address, rhetorical studies, international development communication, and democratic communications. His forthcoming book is *Presidential Thematics and Communicative Practices in a Plural Nigerian Democracy,* to be published by The Edwin Mellen Press of New York, in 2010.

www.ingramcontent.com/pod-product-compliance
Lightning Source LLC
Chambersburg PA
CBHW030645110726
47901CB00002B/574